MW01609673

Catherine De Medici

... THAT IT WAS THE

THE WORKS

OF

ALEXANDRE DUMAS

CATHERINE DE MEDICI
OR: THE QUEEN MOTHER
(PART II., MARGUERITE DE VALOIS)

NEW YORK

THE CENTURY CO.

1909

THE PENNSYLVANIA STATE UNIVERSITY
COMMONWEALTH CAMPUS LIBRARIES
SCRANTON

Copyright, 1900 and 1901
By Thomas Y. Crowell & Company

CONTENTS.

Medici.

PART II.

CHAPTER XXXII.

FRATERNITY.

In saving the life of Charles, Henry had done more than save the life of a man, — he had prevented three kingdoms from changing sovereigns.

Had Charles IX. been killed, the Duc d'Anjou would have become King of France, and the Duc d'Alençon in all probability would have been King of Poland. As to Navarre, as Monsieur le Duc d'Anjou was the lover of Madame de Condé, its crown would probably have paid to the husband the complacency of his wife. Now in all this no good would have come to Henry. He would have changed masters, that would have been all. Instead of Charles IX. who tolerated him, he would have seen the Duc d'Anjou on the throne of France, and being of one heart and mind with his mother Catharine, the latter had sworn that he should die, and he would not have failed to keep his oath. All these thoughts entered his mind when the wild boar sprang at Charles IX., and we know that the result of his rapid thinking was that his own life was attached to that of Charles IX.

Charles IX. had been saved by an act of devotion, the motive of which the King could not fathom. But Marguerite had understood, and she had admired that strange courage of Henry which, like flashes of lightning, shone only in a storm.

Unfortunately it was not all to have escaped the kingdom of the Duc d'Anjou. Henry had to make himself king. He had to dispute Navarre with the Duc d'Alençon and with the Prince of Condé; above all he had to leave the court where one walked only between two precipices, and go away protected by a son of France.

As he returned from Bondy Henry pondered deeply on the

situation. On arriving at the Louvre his plan was formed. Without removing his riding-boots, just as he was, covered with dust and blood, he betook himself to the apartments of the Duc d'Alençon, whom he found striding up and down in great agitation.

On perceiving him the prince gave a start of surprise.

"Yes," said Henry, taking him by both hands; "yes, I understand, my good brother, you are angry because I was the first to call the King's attention to the fact that your ball struck the leg of his horse instead of the boar, as you intended it should. But what can you expect? I could not prevent an exclamation of surprise. Besides, the King would have noticed it, would he not?"

"No doubt, no doubt," murmured D'Alençon. "And yet I can think of it only as an evil intention on your part to denounce me as you did, and which, as you yourself saw, had no result except to make my brother Charles suspect me, and to make hard feeling between us."

"We will return to this in a few moments. As to my good or evil intentions regarding you, I have come to you on purpose that you may judge them."

"Very good!" said D'Alençon with his customary reserve. "Speak, Henry, I am listening."

"When I have spoken, François, you will readily see what my intentions are, for the confidence I am going to place in you does away with all reserve and prudence. And when I have told you, you will be able to ruin me by a single word!"

"What is it?" said François, beginning to be anxious.

"And yet," continued Henry, "I have hesitated a long time to speak to you of the thing which brings me here, especially after the way in which you turned a deaf ear to-day."

"Really," said François, growing pale, "I do not know what you mean, Henry."

"Brother, your interests are too dear to me not to tell you that the Huguenots have made advances to me."

"Advances!" said D'Alençon. "What advances?"

"One of them, Monsieur de Mouy of Saint Phal, the son of the brave De Mouy, assassinated by Maurevel, you know " —

"Yes."

"Well, he came at the risk of his life to show me that I was in captivity."

"Ah! indeed! and what did you say to him?"

" Brother, you know that I love Charles dearly. He has saved my life, and the queen mother has been like a real mother to me. So I refused all the offers he made me."

" What were these offers ? "

" The Huguenots want to reconstruct the throne of Navarre, and as in reality this throne belongs to me by inheritance, they offered it to me."

" Yes ; and Monsieur de Mouy, instead of the consent he expected to ask for, has received your relinquishment ? "

" My formal relinquishment— even in writing. But since," continued Henry.

" You have repented, brother ? " interrupted D'Alençon.

" No, I merely thought I noticed that Monsieur de Mouy had become discontented with me, and was paying his visits elsewhere."

" Where ? " asked François quickly.

" I do not know. At the Prince of Condé's perhaps."

" Yes, that might be," said the duke.

" Besides," went on Henry, " I have positive knowledge as to the leader he has chosen."

François grew pale.

" But," continued Henry, " the Huguenots are divided among themselves, and De Mouy, brave and loyal as he is, represents only one-half of the party. Now this other half, which is not to be scorned, has not given up the hope of having Henry of Navarre on the throne, who having hesitated at first may have reflected since."

" You think this ? "

" Oh, every day I receive proofs of it. The troops which joined us at the hunt, did you notice of what men it was composed ? "

" Yes, of converted gentlemen."

" Did you recognize the leader of the troop who signed to me ? "

" Yes, it was the Vicomte de Turenne."

" Did you know what they wanted of me ? "

" Yes, they proposed to you to escape."

" Then," said Henry to François, who was growing restless, " there is evidently a second party which wants something else besides what Monsieur de Mouy wants."

" A second party ? "

" Yes, and a very powerful one, I tell you, so that in order to succeed it is necessary to unite the two — Turenne and **De** Mouy. The conspiracy progresses, the troops are ready, the signal alone is waited for. Now in this supreme situation, which demands prompt solution on my part, I have come to two decisions between which I am wavering. I have come to submit these decisions to you as to a friend."

" Say rather as to a brother."

" Yes, as to a brother," went on Henry.

" Speak, then, I am listening."

" In the first place I ought to explain to you the condition of my mind, my dear François. No desire, no ambition, no ability. I am an honest country gentleman, poor, sensual, and timid. The career of conspirator offers me indignities poorly compensated for even by the certain prospect of a crown."

"Ah, brother," said François, "you do wrong. Sad indeed is the position of a prince whose fortune is limited by the boundary of the paternal estate or by a man in a career for honors! I do not believe, therefore, in what you tell me."

" And yet what I tell you is so true, brother, that if I thought I had a true friend, I would resign in his favor the power which this party wishes to give me; but," he added with a sigh, " I have none."

" Perhaps you have. You probably are mistaken."

" No, *ventre saint gris !* " said Henry, " except yourself, brother, I see no one who is attached to me; so that rather than let fail an attempt which might bring to light some unworthy man, I truly prefer to inform my brother the King of what is taking place. I will mention no names, I will designate neither country nor date, but I will foretell the catastrophe."

" Great God ! " exclaimed D'Alençon unable to repress his terror, " what do you mean ? What! you, you, the sole hope of the party since the death of the admiral; you, a converted Huguenot, a poor convert, or at least such you were thought to be, you would raise the knife against your brothers ! Henry, Henry, by doing this, do you know that you would be delivering to a second Saint Bartholomew all the Calvinists in the kingdom ? Do you know that Catharine is waiting for just such a chance to exterminate all who have survived ? "

And the duke trembling, his face spotted with red and white blotches, pressed Henry's hand to beg him to give up this idea which would ruin him.

"What!" said Henry, with an expression of perfect good-humor, "do you think there would be so much trouble, François? With the King's word, however, it seems to me that I should avoid it."

"The word of King Charles IX., Henry! Did not the admiral have it? Did not Téligny have it? Did not you yourself have it? Oh, Henry, I tell you if you do this, you will ruin us all. Not only them, but all who have had direct or indirect relations with them."

Henry seemed to ponder an instant.

"If I were an important prince at court," said he, "I should act differently. In your place, for instance, in your place, François, a son of France, and probable heir to the crown " —

François shook his head ironically.

"In my place," said he, "what would you do?"

"In your place, brother," replied Henry, "I should place myself at the head of the movement and direct it. My name and my credit should answer to my conscience for the life of the rebellious, and I should derive some benefit first for myself, then for the King, perhaps, from an enterprise which otherwise might do the greatest injury to France."

D'Alençon listened to these words with a joy which caused every muscle of his face to expand.

"Do you think," said he, "that this method is practicable and that it would save us all the disasters you foresee?"

"I think so," said Henry. "The Huguenots love you. Your bearing is modest, your position both high and interesting, and the kindness you have always shown to those of the faith will incline them to serve you."

"But," said D'Alençon, "there is a division in the party. Will those who want you want me?"

"I will undertake to bring them together by two means."

"What means?"

"First, by the confidence the leaders have in me; then by the fear that your highness, knowing their names " —

"But who will tell me these names?"

"I, *ventre saint gris!*"

"You will do that?"

"Listen, François; as I told you, you are the only one I love at court," said Henry. "This, no doubt, is because you are persecuted like myself; and then my wife, too, loves you with an affection which is unequalled " —

François flushed with pleasure.

"Believe me, brother," continued Henry; "take this thing in hand, reign in Navarre; and provided you keep a place at your table for me, and a fine forest in which to hunt, I shall consider myself fortunate."

"Reign in Navarre!" said the duke; "but if"—

"If the Duc d'Anjou is chosen King of Poland; is that it? I will finish your thought for you."

François looked at Henry with something like terror.

"Well, listen, François," continued Henry, "since nothing escapes you. This is how I reason: If the Duc d'Anjou is chosen King of Poland, and our brother Charles, God keep him! should happen to die, it is but two hundred leagues from Pau to Paris, while it is four hundred from Paris to Cracovie. So you would be here to receive the inheritance by the time the King of Poland learned it was vacant. Then, if you are satisfied with me, you could give me the kingdom of Navarre, which would thenceforth be merely one of the jewels in your crown. In that way I would accept it. The worst that could happen to you would be that you would remain king there and bring up a race of kings by living with me and my family, while here, what are you? a poor persecuted prince, a poor third son of a king, the slave of two elder brothers, and one whom a whim may send to the Bastille."

"Yes, yes," said François; "I know that very well, so well that I do not see why you should give up this plan you propose to me. Is there no throb there?"

And the Duc d'Alençon put his hand on his brother's heart.

"There are," said Henry, smiling, "burdens too heavy for some hands; therefore I shall not try to raise this one; fear of fatigue is greater than the desire of possession."

"So, Henry, you really renounce it?"

"I said so to De Mouy and I repeat it to you."

"But in such cases, my dear brother," said D'Alençon, "one does not say, one proves."

Henry breathed like a pugilist who feels his enemy's back bending.

"I will prove it this evening," said he. "At nine o'clock we shall have the names of the leaders and the plan of the undertaking. I have already sent my renunciation to De Mouy."

François took Henry's hand and pressed it effusively between his own.

At that moment Catharine entered the Duc d'Alençon's rooms, unannounced, as was her habit.

"Together!" said she, smiling; "two good brothers, truly!"

"I trust so, madame," said Henry, with great coolness, while the Duc d'Alençon turned white from distress.

Henry stepped back to leave Catharine free to speak with her son.

The queen mother drew a magnificent jewel from her bag.

"This clasp comes from Florence," said she. "I will give it to you for the belt of your sword."

Then in a low tone:

"If to-night you hear any noise in your good brother Henry's room, do not stir."

François pressed his mother's hand, and said:

"Will you allow me to show Henry the beautiful gift you have just given me?"

"You may do more. Give it to him in your name and in mine, for I have ordered a second one just like it."

"You hear, Henry," said François, "my good mother brings me this jewel and doubles its value by allowing me to give it to you."

Henry went into ecstasies over the beauty of the clasp, and was enthusiastic in his thanks. When his delight had grown calmer:

"My son," said Catharine, "I feel somewhat indisposed and I am going to bed; your brother Charles is greatly wearied from his fall and is going to do the same. So we shall not have supper together this evening, but each will be served in his own room. Oh, Henry, I forgot to congratulate you on your bravery and quickness. You saved your king and your brother, and you shall be rewarded for it."

"I am already rewarded, madame," replied Henry, bowing.

"By the feeling that you have done your duty?" replied Catharine. "That is not enough, and Charles and I will do something to pay the debt we owe you."

"Everything that comes to me from you and my good brother will be welcome, madame."

Then he bowed and withdrew.

"Ah! brother François!" thought Henry as he left, "I am sure now of not leaving alone, and the conspiracy which had a body has found a head and a heart. Only let us look out for ourselves. Catharine gives me a present, Catharine promises me a reward. There is some deviltry beneath it all. I must confer this evening with Marguerite."

CHAPTER XXXIII.

THE GRATITUDE OF KING CHARLES IX.

MAUREVEL had spent a part of the day in the King's armory; but when it was time for the hunters to return from the chase Catharine sent him into her oratory with the guards who had joined him.

Charles IX., informed by his nurse on his arrival that a man had spent part of the day in his room, was at first very angry that a stranger had been admitted into his apartments. But his nurse described the man, saying that he was the same one she herself had been ordered to admit one evening, and the King realized that it was Maurevel. Then remembering the order his mother had wrung from him that morning, he understood everything.

"Oh, ho!" murmured Charles, "the same day on which he has saved my life. The time is badly chosen."

He started to go to his mother, but one thought deterred him.

"By Heaven! If I mention this to her it will result in a never-ending discussion. Better for us to act by ourselves.

"Nurse," said he, "lock every door, and say to Queen Elizabeth [1] that I am suffering somewhat from the fall I have had, and that I shall sleep alone to-night."

The nurse obeyed, and as it was not yet time for the execution of his plan, Charles sat himself down to compose poetry. It was this occupation which made the time pass most quickly for the King. Nine o'clock struck before he thought it was more than seven. He counted the strokes of the clock one by one, and at the last he rose.

"The devil!" said he, "it is just time." Taking his hat and cloak, he left his room by a secret door he had had made in

---

[1] Charles IX. had married Elizabeth of Austria, daughter of Maximilian.

the wall, of the existence of which even Catharine herself was ignorant.

Charles went directly to Henry's apartments. On leaving the Duc d'Alençon, the latter had gone to his rooom to change his clothes and had left again at once.

" He probably has decided to take supper with Margot," said the King. " He was very pleasant with her to-day, at least so it seemed to me."

He went to the queen's apartments. Marguerite had brought back with her the Duchesse de Nevers, Coconnas, and La Mole, and was having a supper of preserves and pastry with them.

Charles knocked at the hall door, which was opened by Gillonne. But at sight of the King she was so frightened that she scarcely had sufficient presence of mind to courtesy, and instead of running to inform her mistress of the august visit she was to have, she let Charles enter without other warning than the cry that had escaped her. The King crossed the antechamber, and guided by the bursts of laughter advanced towards the dining-room.

" Poor Henriot ! " said he, "he is enjoying himself without a thought of evil."

" It is I," said he, raising the portière and showing a smiling face.

Marguerite gave a terrible cry. Smiling as he was, his face appeared to her like the face of Medusa. Seated opposite the door, she had recognized him at once. The two men turned their backs to the King.

" Your Majesty ! " cried the queen, rising in terror.

The three other guests felt their heads begin to swim; Coconnas alone retained his self-possession. He rose also, but with such tactful clumsiness that in doing so he upset the table, and with it the glass, plate, and candles. Instantly there was complete darkness and the silence of death.

" Run," said Coconnas to La Mole; " quick ! quick ! "

La Mole did not wait to be told twice. Springing to the side of the wall, he began groping with his hands for the sleeping-room, that he might hide in the cabinet that opened out of it and which he knew so well. But as he stepped across the threshold he ran against a man who had just entered by the secret corridor.

" What does all this mean ? " asked Charles, in the darkness, in a tone which was beginning to betray a formidable accent of impatience. "Am I such a mar-joy that the sight of me causes all this confusion? Come, Henriot! Henriot! where are you? Answer me."

"We are saved!" murmured Marguerite, seizing a hand which she took for that of La Mole. "The King thinks my husband is one of our guests."

"And I shall let him think so, madame, you may be sure," said Henry, answering the queen in the same tone.

"Great God!" cried Marguerite, hastily dropping the hand she held, which was that of the King of Navarre.

"Silence!" said Henry.

"In the name of a thousand devils! why are you whispering in this way?" cried Charles. "Henry, answer me; where are you?"

"Here, sire," said the King of Navarre.

"The devil!" said Coconnas, who was holding the Duchesse de Nevers in a corner, "the plot thickens."

"In that case we are doubly lost," said Henriette.

Coconnas, brave to the point of rashness, had reflected that the candles would have to be lighted sooner or later, and thinking the sooner the better, he dropped the hand of Madame de Nevers, picked up a taper from the midst of the débris, and going to a brazier blew on a piece of coal, with which he at once made a light. The chamber was again illuminated. Charles IX. glanced around inquiringly.

Henry was by the side of his wife, the Duchesse de Nevers was alone in a corner, while Coconnas stood in the centre of the room, candle-stick in hand, lighting up the whole scene.

"Excuse me, brother," said Marguerite, "we were not expecting you."

"So, as you may have perceived, your Majesty filled us with strange terror," said Henriette.

"For my part," said Henry, who had surmised everything, "I think the fear was so real that in rising I overturned the table."

Coconnas glanced at the King of Navarre as much as to say:

"Good! Here is a man who understands at once."

"What a frightful hubbub!" repeated Charles IX. "Your supper is ruined, Henriot; come with me and you shall finish it elsewhere; I will carry you off this evening."

"What, sire!" said Henry, "your Majesty will do me the honor?"

" Yes, my Majesty will do you the honor of taking you away from the Louvre. Lend him to me, Margot, I will bring him back to you to-morrow morning."

" Ah, brother," said Marguerite, "you do not need my permission for that ; you are master."

" Sire," said Henry, " I will get another cloak from my room, and will return immediately."

" You do not need it, Henriot ; the cloak you have is all right."

" But, sire," began the Béarnais.

" In the name of a thousand devils, I tell you not to go to your rooms ! Do you not hear what I say ? Come along !"

" Yes, yes, go !" said Marguerite, suddenly pressing her husband's arm ; for a singular look from Charles had convinced her that something unusual was going on.

" Here I am, sire," said Henry.

Charles looked at Coconnas, who was still carrying out his office of torch-bearer by lighting the other candles.

" Who is this gentleman ?" asked the King of Henry, eyeing the Piedmontese from head to foot. " Is he Monsieur de la Mole ?"

" Who has told him of La Mole ?" asked Marguerite in a low tone.

"No, sire," replied Henry, " Monsieur de la Mole is not here, I regret to say. Otherwise I should have the honor of presenting him to your Majesty at the same time as Monsieur de Coconnas, his friend. They are perfectly inseparable, and both are in the suite of Monsieur d'Alençon."

" Ah ! ah ! our famous marksman !" said Charles. " Good !" Then frowning :

" Is not this Monsieur de la Mole a Huguenot ?" he asked.

" He is converted, sire, and I will answer for him as for my-self."

" When you answer for any one, Henriot, after what you did to-day, I have no further right to doubt him. But I should have liked to see this Monsieur de la Mole. However, I can meet him another time."

Giving a last glance about the room, Charles embraced Marguerite, took hold of the arm of the King of Navarre, and led him off.

At the gate of the Louvre Henry wanted to speak to some one.

"Come, come! pass out quickly, Henriot," said Charles. "When I tell you that the air of the Louvre is not good for you this evening, the devil! you must believe me!"

"*Ventre saint gris!*" murmured Henry; "and what will De Mouy do all alone in my room? I trust the air which is not good for me may be no worse for him!"

"Ah!" exclaimed the King, when Henry and he had crossed the drawbridge, "does it suit you, Henry, to have the gentlemen of Monsieur d'Alençon courting your wife?"

"How so, sire?"

"Truly, is not this Monsieur de Coconnas making eyes at Margot?"

"Who told you that?"

"Well," said the King, "I heard it."

"A mere joke, sire; Monsieur de Coconnas does make eyes at some one, but it is at Madame de Nevers."

"Ah, bah."

"I can answer to your Majesty for what I tell you."

Charles burst into laughter.

"Well," said he, "let the Duc de Guise come to me again with his gossip, and I will gently pull his mustache by telling him of the exploits of his sister-in-law. But after all," said the King, thinking better of it, "I do not know whether it was Monsieur de Coconnas or Monsieur de la Mole he referred to."

"Neither the one more than the other, sire, and I can answer to you for the feelings of my wife."

"Good, Henriot, good!" said the King. "I like you better now than the way you were before. On my honor, you are such a good fellow that I shall end by being unable to get along without you."

As he spoke the King gave a peculiar whistle, whereupon four gentlemen who were waiting for him at the end of the Rue de Beauvais joined him. The whole party set out towards the middle of the city.

Ten o'clock struck.

"Well!" said Marguerite, after the King and Henry had left, "shall we go back to table?"

"Mercy, no!" cried the duchess, "I have been too badly frightened. Long live the little house in the Rue Cloche Percée! No one can enter that without regularly besieging it, and our good men have the right to use their swords there.

But what are you looking for under the furniture and in the closets, Monsieur de Coconnas ? "

" I am trying to find my friend La Mole," said the Piedmontese.

" Look in my room, monsieur," said Marguerite, " there is a certain closet " —

" Very well," said Coconnas, " I will go there."

He entered the room.

" Well ! " said a voice from the darkness; " where are we ? "

" Oh ! by Heaven ! we have reached the dessert."

" And the King of Navarre ? "

" He has seen nothing. He is a perfect husband, and I wish my wife had one like him. But I fear she never will, even if she marries again."

" And King Charles ? "

" Ah ! the King. That is another thing. He has taken off the husband."

" Really ? "

" It is as I tell you. Furthermore, he honored me by looking askance at me when he discovered that I belonged to Monsieur d'Alençon, and cross when he found out that I was your friend."

" You think, then, that he has heard me spoken of ? "

" I fear that he has heard nothing very good of you. But that is not the point. I believe these ladies have a pilgrimage to make to the Rue de Roi de Sicile, and that we are to take them there."

" Why, that is impossible ! You know that very well."

" How impossible ? "

" We are on duty at his royal highness's."

" By Heavens, that is so; I always forget that we are ranked, and that from the gentlemen we once were we have had the honor to pass into valets."

Thereupon the two friends went and told the queen and the duchess the necessity of their being present at least when Monsieur le Duc retired.

" Very well," said Madame de Nevers, " we will go by ourselves."

" Might we know where you are going ? " asked Coconnas.

" Oh ! you are too curious ! " said the duchess. " *Quære et invenies.*"

The young men bowed and went at once to Monsieur
d'Alençon.

The duke seemed to be waiting for them in his cabinet.

" Ah! ah! " said he, " you are very late, gentlemen."

" It is scarcely ten o'clock, monseigneur," said Coconnas.

The duke drew out his watch.

"That is true," said he. " And yet every one has gone to
sleep in the Louvre."

" Yes, monsieur, but we are here at your orders. Must we
admit into the chamber of your highness the gentlemen who
are with the King until he retires ? "

" On the contrary, go into the small reception-room and dismiss every one."

The young men obeyed, carried out the order, which surprised no one, because of the well-known character of the
duke, and returned to him.

" Monseigneur," said Coconnas, " your highness will probably either go to bed or work, will you not ? "

" No, gentlemen ; you may have leave of absence until to-
morrow."

" Well, well," whispered Coconnas into La Mole's ear, " the
court is going to stay up all night, apparently. It will be
devilishly pleasant. Let us have our share of it."

And both young men descended the stairs four steps at a
time, took their cloaks and their night swords, and hastily left
the Louvre after the two ladies, whom they overtook at the
corner of the Rue du Coq Saint Honoré.

Meanwhile the Duc d'Alençon, with open eyes and ears,
locked himself in his room to await the unexpected events
he had been promised.

CHAPTER XXXIV.

MAN PROPOSES BUT GOD DISPOSES.

As the duke had said to the young men, the most profound
silence reigned in the Louvre.

Marguerite and Madame de Nevers had departed for the
Rue Tizon. Coconnas and La Mole had followed them. The
King and Henry were knocking about the city. The Duc
d'Alençon was in his room vaguely and anxiously waiting for

the events which the queen mother had predicted. Catharine had gone to bed, and Madame de Sauve, seated by her, was reading some Italian stories which greatly amused the good queen. Catharine had not been in such good humor for a long time. Having done justice to a collation with her ladies in waiting, having consulted her physician and arranged the daily accounts of her household, she had ordered prayers for the success of a certain enterprise, which she said was of great importance to the happiness of her children. Under certain circumstances it was Catharine's habit — a habit, for that matter, wholly Florentine — to have prayers and masses read the object of which was known only to God and herself.

Finally she had seen Réné, and had chosen several novelties from among her rich collection of perfumed bags.

"Let me know," said Catharine, " if my daughter the Queen of Navarre is in her rooms ; and if she is there, beg her to come to me."

The page to whom this order was given withdrew, and an instant later he returned, accompanied by Gillonne.

" Well ! " said the queen mother, " I asked for the mistress, not the servant."

"Madame," said Gillonne, " I thought I ought to come myself and tell your majesty that the Queen of Navarre has gone out with her friend the Duchesse de Nevers " —

" Gone out at this hour ! " exclaimed Catharine, frowning ; " where can she have gone ? "

" To a lecture on chemistry," replied Gillonne, "which is to be held in the Hôtel de Guise, in the pavilion occupied by Madame de Nevers."

" When will she return ? " asked the queen mother.

"The lecture will last until late into the night," replied Gillonne, " so that probably her majesty will stay with her friend until to-morrow morning."

" The Queen of Navarre is happy," murmured Catharine ; " she has friends and she is queen ; she wears a crown, is called your majesty, yet has no subjects. She is happy indeed."

After this remark, which made her listeners smile inwardly :

"Well," murmured Catharine, " since she has gone out — for she has gone, you say ? "

"Half an hour ago, madame."

" Everything is for the best ; you may go."

Gillonne bowed and left.

"Go on with your reading, Charlotte," said the queen.

Madame de Sauve continued. At the end of ten minutes Catharine interrupted the story.

"Ah, by the way," said she, "have the guards dismissed from the corridor."

This was the signal for which Maurevel was waiting. The order of the queen mother was carried out, and Madame de Sauve went on with her story. She had read for about a quarter of an hour without any interruption, when a prolonged and terrible scream reached the royal chamber and made the hair of those present stand on end.

The scream was followed by the sound of a pistol-shot.

"What is it?" said Catharine; "why do you stop reading, Carlotta?"

"Madame," said the young woman, turning pale, "did you not hear?"

"What?" asked Catharine.

"That cry."

"And that pistol-shot?" added the captain of the guards.

"A cry, a pistol-shot?" asked Catharine; "I heard nothing. Besides, is a shout or a pistol-shot such a very unusual thing at the Louvre? Read, read, Carlotta."

"But listen, madame," said the latter, while Monsieur de Nancey stood up, his hand on his sword, but not daring to leave without permission from the queen, "listen, I hear steps, curses."

"Shall I go and find out about it, madame?" said De Nancey.

"Not at all, monsieur, stay where you are," said Catharine, raising herself on one hand to give more emphasis to her order. "Who, then, would protect me in case of an alarm? It is only some drunken Swiss fighting."

The calmness of the queen, contrasted with the terror on the faces of all present, was so remarkable that, timid as she was, Madame de Sauve fixed a questioning glance on the queen.

"Why, madame, I should think they were killing some one."

"Whom do you think they are killing?"

"The King of Navarre, madame; the noise comes from the direction of his apartments."

"The fool!" murmured the queen, whose lips in spite of her self-control were beginning to move strangely, for she was muttering a prayer; "the fool sees her King of Navarre everywhere."

"My God! my God!" cried Madame de Sauve, falling back in her chair.

"It is over, it is over," said Catharine. "Captain," she continued, turning to Monsieur de Nancey, "I hope if there is any scandal in the palace you will have the guilty ones severely punished to-morrow. Go on with your reading, Carlotta." And Catharine sank back on her pillow with a calmness that greatly resembled weakness, for those present noticed great drops of perspiration rolling down her face.

Madame de Sauve obeyed this formal order, but her eyes and her voice were mere machines. Her thoughts wandered to other things which represented a terrible danger hanging over a loved head. Finally, after struggling on for several minutes, she became so oppressed between her feelings and etiquette that her words became unintelligible, the book fell from her hands, and she fainted.

Suddenly a louder noise was heard; a quick, heavy step fell on the corridor, two pistol-shots shook the windows; and Catharine, astonished at the interminable struggle, rose in terror, erect, pale, with dilating eyes. As the captain of the guard was about to hurry out, she stopped him, saying:

"Let every one remain here. I myself will go and see what is the matter."

This is what was taking place, or rather what had taken place. That morning De Mouy had received the key of Henry's room from the hands of Orthon. In this key, which was piped, he had noticed a roll of paper. He drew it out with a pin. It was the password of the Louvre for that night.

Besides, Orthon had verbally transmitted to him the words of Henry, asking De Mouy to come to the king at ten o'clock in the Louvre.

At half-past nine De Mouy put on a suit of armor, the strength of which he had already more than once had occasion to test; over this he buttoned a silk doublet, fastened on his sword, put his pistols in his belt, and over everything threw the red cloak of La Mole.

We have seen how, before going back to his rooms, Henry had thought best to pay a visit to Marguerite, and how he arrived by the secret stairway just in time to run against La Mole in Marguerite's sleeping-room, and to appear in the dining-room before the King. It was at that very moment when, thanks to the password sent by Henry, and above all to the famous red cloak, that De Mouy passed under the gate of the Louvre.

The young man went directly to the apartments of the King of Navarre, imitating as well as he could, as was his habit, the gait of La Mole. He found Orthon waiting for him in the antechamber.

"Sire de Mouy," said the mountaineer, "the king has gone out, but he told me to admit you, and to tell you to wait for him. If he should be late in returning, he wants you, you know, to lie down on his bed."

De Mouy entered without asking for further explanation, for what Orthon had just told him was only the repetition of what he had already heard that morning. In order to pass away the time he took a pen and ink and, approaching a fine map of France which hung on the wall, he set to work to count and determine the stopping-places between Paris and Pau. But this was only the work of a quarter of an hour, and then De Mouy did not know what to do.

He made two or three rounds of the room, rubbed his eyes, yawned, sat down, got up, and sat down again. Finally, taking advantage of Henry's invitation, and the familiarity which existed between princes and their gentlemen, he placed his pistols and the lamp on a table, stretched himself out on the great bed with the sombre hangings which furnished the rear of the room, laid his sword by his side, and, sure of not being surprised since a servant was in the adjoining room, he fell into a pleasant sleep, the noise of which soon made the vast canopy ring with its echoes. De Mouy snored like a regular old soldier, and in this he could have vied with the King of Navarre himself.

It was then that six men, their swords in their hands and their knives at their belts, glided silently into the corridor which communicated by a small door with the apartments of Catharine and by a large one with those of Henry.

One of the six men walked ahead of the others. Besides his bare sword and his dagger, which was as strong as a hunting-knife, he carried his faithful pistols fastened to his belt by silver hooks.

This man was Maurevel. Having reached Henry's door, he stopped.

"Are you perfectly sure that the sentinels are not in the

corridor ? " he asked of the one who apparently commanded
the little band.

" Not a single one is at his post," replied the lieutenant.

" Very good," said Maurevel. " Now there is nothing
further except to find out one thing — that is, if the man we are
looking for is in his room."

" But," said the lieutenant, arresting the hand which Maurevel had laid on the handle of the door, " but, captain, these
apartments are those of the King of Navarre."

" Who said they were not ? " asked Maurevel.

The guards looked at one another in amazement, and the
lieutenant stepped back.

" What ! " exclaimed he, " arrest some one at this hour, in
the Louvre, and in the apartments of the King of Navarre ? "

" What should you say," said Maurevel, " were I to tell you
that the one you are about to arrest is the King of Navarre
himself ? "

" I should say, captain, that it is serious business and that
without an order signed by King Charles IX." —

" Read this," said Maurevel.

And drawing from his doublet the order which Catharine
had given him he handed it to the lieutenant.

" Very well," replied the latter after he had read it. " I have
nothing further to say."

" And you are ready ? "

" I am ready."

" And you ? " continued Maurevel, turning to the other five
sbirros.

They all saluted respectfully.

" Listen to me, then, gentlemen," said Maurevel ; " this is
my plan : two of you will remain at this door, two at the door
of the sleeping-room, and two will go with me."

" Afterwards ? " said the lieutenant.

" Pay close attention to this : we are ordered to prevent the
prisoner from calling out, shouting, or resisting. Any infrac-
tion of this order is to be punished by death."

" Well, well, he has full permission," said the lieutenant to
the man chosen by him to follow Maurevel into the king's
room.

" Full," said Maurevel.

" Poor devil of the King of Navarre ! " said one of the men.
" It was written above that he should not escape this."

" And here too," said Maurevel, taking Catharine's order from the hands of the lieutenant and returning it to his breast.

Maurevel inserted the key Catharine had given him into the lock, and leaving two men at the outer door, as had been agreed on, he entered the antechamber with the four others.

"Ah! ah!" said Maurevel, hearing the noisy breathing of the sleeper, the sound of which reached even as far as that, " it seems that we shall find what we are looking for."

Orthon, thinking it was his master returning, at once started up and found himself face to face with five armed men in the first chamber.

At sight of the sinister face of Maurevel, who was called the King's Slayer, the faithful servant sprang back, and placing himeslf before the second door:

" Who are you?" said he, " and what do you want?"

" In the King's name," replied Maurevel, " where is your master?"

" My master?"

" Yes, the King of Navarre."

" The King of Navarre is not in his room," said Orthon, barring the door more than ever, " so you cannot enter."

" Excuses, lies!" said Maurevel. " Come, stand back!"

The Béarnais people are stubborn; this one growled like one of his own mountain dogs, and far from being intimidated:

" You shall not enter," said he; " the king is out."

And he clung to the door.

Maurevel made a sign. The four men seized the stubborn servant, snatched him from the door-sill to which he was clinging, and as he started to open his mouth and cry out, Maurevel clapped a hand to his lips.

Orthon bit furiously at the assassin, who dropped his hand with a dull cry, and brought down the handle of his sword on the head of the servant. Orthon staggered and fell back, shouting, " Help! help! help!"

Then his voice died away. He had fainted.

The assassins stepped over his body, two stopped at the second door, and two entered the sleeping-room with Maurevel.

In the glow of the lamp burning on the night table they saw the bed.

The curtains were drawn.

" Oh! oh!" said the lieutenant, " he has stopped snoring, apparently."

"Be quick!" cried Maurevel.

At this, a sharp cry, resembling the roar of a lion rather than a human voice, came from behind the curtains, which were violently thrown back, and a man appeared sitting there armed with a cuirass, his head covered with a helmet which reached to his eyes. Two pistols were in his hand, and his sword lay across his knees.

No sooner did Maurevel perceive this figure and recognize De Mouy than he felt his hair rise on end; he became frightfully pale, foam sprang to his lips, and he stepped back as if he had come face to face with a ghost. Suddenly the armed figure rose and stepped forward as Maurevel drew back, so that from the position of threatener, the latter now became the one threatened, and *vice versa.*

"Ah, scoundrel!" cried De Mouy, in a dull voice, "so you have come to murder me as you murdered my father!"

The two guards who had entered the room with Maurevel alone heard these terrible words. As they were uttered a pistol was placed to Maurevel's forehead. The latter sank to his knees just as De Mouy put his hand on the trigger; the shot was fired and one of the guards who stood behind him and whom he had unmasked by this movement dropped to the floor, struck to the heart. At the same instant Maurevel fired back, but the ball glanced off De Mouy's cuirass.

Then, measuring the distance, De Mouy sprang forward and with the edge of his broadsword split open the head of the second guard, and turning towards Maurevel crossed swords with him.

The struggle was brief but terrible. At the fourth pass Maurevel felt the cold steel in his throat. He uttered a stifled cry and fell backwards, upsetting the lamp, which went out in the fall.

At once De Mouy, strong and agile as one of Homer's heroes, took advantage of the darkness and sprang, with head lowered, into the antechamber, knocked down one guard, pushed aside the other, and shot like an arrow between those at the outer door. He escaped two pistol-shots, the balls of which grazed the wall of the corridor, and from that moment was safe, for one loaded pistol still was left him, besides the sword which had dealt such terrible blows.

For an instant he hesitated, undecided whether to go to Monsieur d'Alençon's, the door of whose room he thought had just opened, or to try and escape from the Louvre. He determined on the latter course, continued on his way, slow at first, jumped ten steps at a time, and reaching the gate uttered the two passwords and rushed on, shouting out:

"Go upstairs; there is murder going on by order of the King."

Taking advantage of the amazement produced on the sentinel by his words and the sound of the pistol-shots, he ran on and disappeared in the Rue du Coq without having received a scratch.

It was at this moment that Catharine stopped the captain of the guards, saying:

"Stay here; I myself will go and see what is the matter."

"But, madame," replied the captain, "the danger your majesty runs compels me to follow you."

"Stay here, monsieur," said Catharine, in a still more imperious tone, "stay here. There is a more powerful protection around kings than the human sword."

The captain remained where he was.

Taking a lamp, Catharine slipped her bare feet into a pair of velvet slippers, left her room, and reaching the corridor, still full of smoke, advanced as impassible and as cold as a shadow towards the apartments of the King of Navarre.

Silence reigned supreme.

Catharine reached the door, crossed the threshold, and first saw Orthon, who had fainted in the antechamber.

"Ah! ah!" said she, "here is the servant; further on we shall probably find the master." She entered the second door.

Then her foot ran against a corpse; she lowered her lamp; it was the guard who had had his head split open. He was quite dead.

A few feet further on the lieutenant, who had been struck by a bullet, was drawing his last breath.

Finally, before the bed lay a man whose face was as pale as death and who was bleeding from a double wound in his throat. He was clinching his hands convulsively in his efforts to rise.

It was Maurevel.

Catharine shuddered. She saw the empty bed, she looked around the room seeking in vain for the body she hoped to find among the three corpses.

Maurevel recognized Catharine. His eyes were horribly dilated and he made a despairing gesture towards her.

"Well," said she in a whisper, "where is he? what has happened? Unfortunate man! have you let him escape?"

Maurevel strove to speak, but an unintelligible sound came from his throat, a bloody foam covered his lips, and he shook his head in sign of inability and pain.

"Speak!" cried Catharine, "speak! if only one word!"

Maurevel pointed to his wound, again made several inarticulate gasps, which ended in a hoarse rattle, and fainted.

Catharine looked around her. She was surrounded by the bodies of dead and dying; blood flowed in every direction, and the silence of death hovered over everything.

Once again she spoke to Maurevel, but failed to rouse him; he was not only silent but motionless; a paper was in his doublet. It was the order of arrest signed by the King. Catharine seized it and hid it in her breast. Just then she heard a light step behind her, and turning, she saw the Duc d'Alençon at the door. In spite of himself he had been drawn thither by the noise, and the sight before him fascinated him.

"You here?" said she.

"Yes, madame. For God's sake what has happened?"

"Go back to your room, François; you will know soon enough."

D'Alençon was not as ignorant of the affair as Catharine supposed.

At the sound of the first steps in the corridor he had listened. Seeing some men enter the apartments of the King of Navarre, and by connecting this with some words Catharine had uttered, he had guessed what was about to take place, and was rejoiced at having so dangerous an enemy destroyed by a hand stronger than his own. Before long the noises of pistol-shots and the rapid steps of a man running had attracted his attention, and he had seen disappearing in the light space caused by the opening of the door leading to the stairway the red cloak too well known not to be recognized.

"De Mouy!" he cried, "De Mouy in the apartments of the King of Navarre! Why, that is impossible! Can it be Monsieur de la Mole?"

He grew alarmed. Remembering that the young man had been recommended to him by Marguerite herself, and wishing to make sure that it was he whom he had just seen, he ascended hurriedly to the chamber of the two young men. It was vacant. But in a corner he found the famous red cloak hanging against the wall. His suspicions were confirmed. It was not La Mole, but De Mouy. Pale and trembling lest the Huguenot should be discovered, and would betray the secrets of the conspiracy, he rushed to the gate of the Louvre. There he was told that the red cloak had escaped safe and sound, shouting out as he passed that some one was being murdered in the Louvre by order of the King.

"He is mistaken," murmured D'Alençon; "it is by order of the queen mother."

Returning to the scene of combat, he found Catharine wandering like a hyena among the dead.

At the order from his mother the young man returned to his rooms, affecting calmness and obedience, in spite of the tumultuous thoughts which were passing through his mind.

In despair at the failure of this new attempt' Catharine called the captain of the guards, had the bodies removed, gave orders that Maurevel, who was only wounded, be carried to his home, and told them not to waken the King.

"Oh!" she murmured, as she returned to her rooms, her head sunk on her bosom, "he has again escaped. The hand of God is over this man. He will reign! he will reign!"

Entering her room, she passed her hand across her brow, and assumed an ordinary smile.

"What was the matter, madame?" asked every one except Madame de Sauve, who was too frightened to ask any questions.

"Nothing," replied Catharine; "a noise, that was all."

"Oh!" cried Madame de Sauve, suddenly pointing to the floor, "your majesty says there is nothing the matter, and every one of your majesty's steps leaves a trace of blood on the carpet!"

CHAPTER XXXV.

A NIGHT OF KINGS.

CHARLES IX. walked along with Henry leaning on his arm, followed by his four gentlemen and preceded by two torch-bearers.

"When I leave the Louvre," said the poor King, "I feel a pleasure similar to that which comes to me when I enter a beautiful forest. I breathe, I live, I am free."

Henry smiled.

"In that case," said he, "your Majesty would be in your element among the mountains of the Béarn."

"Yes, and I understand that you want to go back to them; but if you are very anxious to do so, Henriot," added Charles, laughing, "my advice is to be careful, for my mother Catharine loves you so dearly that it is absolutely impossible for her to get along without you."

"What does your Majesty plan to do this evening?" asked Henry, changing this dangerous conversation.

"I want to have you meet some one, Henriot, and you shall give me your opinion."

"I am at your Majesty's orders."

"To the right! to the right! We will take the Rue des Barres."

The two kings, followed by their escort, had passed the Rue de la Savonnerie, when in front of the Hôtel de Condé they saw two men, wrapped in large cloaks, coming out of a secret door which one of them noiselessly closed behind him.

"Oh! oh!" said the King to Henry, who as usual had seen everything, but had not spoken, "this deserves attention."

"Why do you say that, sire?" asked the King of Navarre.

"It is not on your account, Henriot. You are sure of your wife," added Charles with a smile; "but your cousin De Condé is not sure of his, or if so, he is making a mistake, the devil!"

"But how do you know, sire, that it is Madame de Condé whom these gentlemen have been visiting?"

"Instinct tells me. The fact that the men stood in the doorway without moving until they saw us; then the cut of the shorter one's cloak — by Heaven! that would be strange!"

"What?"

"Nothing. An idea I had, that is all; let us go on."

He walked up to the two men, who, seeing him, started to walk away.

"Hello, gentlemen!" cried the King; "stop!"

"Are you speaking to us?" asked a voice which made Charles and his companion tremble.

"Well, Henriot," said Charles, "do you recognize the voice now?"

"Sire," said Henry, "if your brother the Duc d'Anjou was not at La Rochelle, I would swear it was he speaking."

"Well," said Charles, "he is not at La Rochelle, that is all."

"But who is with him?"

"Do you not recognize his companion?"

"No, sire."

"Yet his figure is unmistakable. Wait, you shall see who he is — hello, there! I tell you," cried the King, "do you not hear, by Heaven?"

"Are you the watch, that you order us to stop?" said the taller of the two men, freeing his arm from the folds of his cloak.

"Pretend that we are the watch," said the King, "and stop when we tell you to do so."

Leaning over to Henry's ear, he added:

"Now you will see the volcano send forth its fire."

"There are eight of you," said the taller of the two men, this time showing not only his arm but his face, "but were you a hundred, pass on!"

"Ah! ah! the Duc de Guise!" said Henry.

"Ah! our cousin from Lorraine," said the King; "at last you will meet! How fortunate!"

"The King!" cried the duke.

At these words the other man covered himself with his cloak and stood motionless, having first uncovered out of respect.

"Sire," said the Duc de Guise, "I have just been paying a visit to my sister-in-law, Madame de Condé."

"Yes — and you brought one of your gentlemen with you? Which one?"

"Sire," replied the duke, "your Majesty does not know him."

"We will meet him, however," said the King.

Walking up to the other figure, he signed to one of the lackeys to bring a torch.

"Pardon me, brother!" said the Duc d'Anjou, opening his cloak and bowing with poorly disguised anger.

"Ah! ah! Henry, is it you? But no, it is not possible, I am mistaken — my brother of Anjou would not have gone to see any one else before first calling on me. He knows that for royal princes, returning to the capital, Paris has but one entrance, the gate of the Louvre."

"Pardon me, sire," said the Duc d'Anjou; "I beg your Majesty to excuse my thoughtlessness."

" Ah, yes !" replied the King, mockingly ; " and what were you doing, brother, at the Hôtel de Condé ? "

" Why," said the King of Navarre in his sly way, " what your Majesty intimated just now."

And leaning over to the King he ended his sentence in a burst of laughter.

" What is it ? " asked the Duc de Guise, haughtily ; for like every one else at court, he had a way of treating the poor King of Navarre very rudely, " why should I not go and see my sister-in-law. Does not Monsieur le Duc d'Alençon visit his ? "

Henry flushed slightly.

" What sister-in-law ? " asked Charles. " I know none except Queen Elizabeth."

" Pardon, sire ! it was your sister I should have said — Madame Marguerite, whom we saw pass in her litter as we came by here half an hour ago. She was accompanied by two courtiers who rode on either side of her."

" Indeed !" said Charles. " What do you say to that, Henry ? "

" That the Queen of Navarre is perfectly free to go where she pleases, but I doubt if she has left the Louvre."

" Well, I am sure she did," said the Duc de Guise.

" And I too," said the Duc d'Anjou, " from the fact that the litter stopped in the Rue Cloche Percée."

" Your sister-in-law, not this one," said Henry, pointing to the Hôtel de Condé, " but that one," turning in the direction of the Hôtel de Guise, " must also be of the party, for we left them together, and, as you know, they are inseparable."

" I do not know what your majesty means," replied the Duc de Guise.

" On the contrary," said the king, " nothing is simpler. That is why a courtier was riding at either side of the litter."

" Well !" said the duke, " if there is any scandal concerning my sisters-in-law, let us beg the King to withhold justice."

" Well, by Heaven," said Henry, " let us leave Madame de Condé and Madame de Nevers ; the King is not anxious about his sister — and I have confidence in my wife."

" No, no," said Charles, " I want to make sure of it ; but let us attend to the matter ourselves. The litter stopped in the Rue Cloche Percée, you say, cousin ? "

" Yes, sire."

" Do you know the house ? "

" Yes, sire."

" Well, let us go to it. And if in order to find out who is in it, it is necessary to burn it down, we will burn it."

It was with this end in view, which was rather discouraging for the tranquillity of those concerned, that the four chief lords of the Christian world set out to the Rue Saint Antoine.

They reached the Rue Cloche Percée. Charles, who wished to work privately, dismissed the gentlemen of his suite, saying that they might have the rest of the night to themselves, but for them to be at the Bastille with two horses at six o'clock in the morning.

There were only three houses in the Rue Cloche Percée. The search was much less difficult as two of the buildings were perfectly willing to open their doors. One of the houses faced the Rue Saint Antoine and the other the Rue du Roi de Sicile.

As to the third house, that was a different matter. It was the one which was guarded by the German janitor, and this janitor was not easily managed. That night Paris seemed destined to offer memorable examples of conjugal fidelity. In vain did Monsieur de Guise threaten in his purest Saxon ; in vain did Henry of Anjou offer a purse filled with gold ; in vain Charles went so far as to say that he was lieutenant of the watch ; the brave German paid attention neither to the statement, the offer, nor the threats. Seeing that they insisted, and in a way that was becoming importunate, he slipped the nose of a gun under the iron bars, a move which brought forth bursts of laughter from three of the four visitors. Henry of Navarre stood apart, as if the affair had no interest for him. But as the weapon could not be turned between the bars, it was scarcely dangerous for any except a blind man, who might stand directly in front of it.

Seeing that the porter was neither to be intimidated, bribed, nor persuaded, the Duc de Guise pretended to leave with his companions ; but the retreat did not last long. At the corner of the Rue Saint Antoine the duke found what he sought. This was a rock similar in size to those which three thousand years before had been moved by Ajax, son of Telamon, and Diomed. The duke raised it to his shoulder and came back, signing to his companions to follow. Just then the janitor, who had seen those he took for malefactors depart, closed the door. But he had not time to draw the bolts before the Duc de Guise took advantage of the moment, and hurled his veritable living catapult against the door. The lock broke, carrying away a portion of the wall to which it had been fastened. The door sprang open, knocking down the German, who, in falling, gave a terrible cry. This cry awakened the garrison, which otherwise would have run great risk of being surprised.

At that moment La Mole and Marguerite were translating an idyl of Theocritus, and Coconnas, pretending that he too was a Greek, was drinking some strong wine from Syracuse with Henriette. The scientific and bacchanalian conversation was violently interrupted.

La Mole and Coconnas at once extinguished the candles, and opening the windows, sprang out on the balcony. Then perceiving four men in the darkness, they set to work to hurl at them everything they had at hand, in the meantime making a frightful noise with blows from the flat of their swords, which, however, struck nothing but the wall. Charles, the most infuriated of the besiegers, received a sharp blow on the shoulder, the Duc d'Anjou a bowl full of orange and lemon marmalade, and the Duc de Guise a leg of venison. Henry received nothing. He was downstairs questioning the porter, whom Monsieur de Guise had strapped to the door, and who continued to answer by his eternal " *Ich verstehe nicht.*" The women encouraged the besieged by handing them projectiles, which succeeded one another like hailstones.

"The devil!" exclaimed Charles IX., as a table struck his head, driving his hat over his eyes, "if they don't open the door pretty soon I will have them all hanged."

"My brother!" whispered Marguerite to La Mole.

"The King!" cried the latter to Henriette.

"The King! the King!" repeated Henriette to Coconnas, who was dragging a chest to the window, and who was trying to exterminate the Duc de Guise. Without knowing who the latter was he was having a private struggle with him.

"The King, I tell you," repeated Henriette.

Coconnas let go of the chest and looked up in amazement.

"The King?" said he.

"Yes, the King."

"Then let us hide."

"Yes. La Mole and Marguerite have already fled. Come!"

"Where?"

"Come, I tell you."

And seizing him by the hand, Henriette pushed Coconnas through the secret door which connected with the adjoining house, and all four, having locked this door behind them, escaped into the Rue Tizon.

"Oh! oh!" said Charles, "I think that the garrison has surrendered."

They waited a few minutes. No sound reached the besiegers.

"They are preparing some ruse," said the Duc de Guise.

"It is more likely that they have recognized my brother's voice and have fled," said the Duc d'Anjou.

"They would have to pass by here," said Charles.

"Yes," said the Duc d'Anjou, "unless the house has two exits."

"Cousin," said the King, "take up your stone again and hurl it against the other door as you did at this."

The duke thought it unnecessary to resort to such means, and as he had noticed that the second door was not as solid as the first he broke it down by a simple kick.

"The torches! the torches!" cried the King.

The lackeys approached. The torches were out, but the men had everything necessary for relighting them. This was done. Charles IX. took one and handed the other to the Duc d'Anjou.

The Duc de Guise entered first, sword in hand.

Henry brought up the rear.

They reached the first floor.

In the dining-room the table was set or rather upset, for it was the supper which had furnished the projectiles. The candlesticks were overturned, the furniture topsy-turvy, and everything which was not silver plate lay in fragments.

They entered the reception-room, but found no more clue there than in the other room as to the identity of the revellers. Some Greek and Latin books and several musical instruments were all they saw.

The sleeping-room was more silent still. A night lamp burned in an alabaster globe suspended from the ceiling; but it was evident that the room had not been occupied.

"There is a second door," said the King.

"Very likely," said the Duc d'Anjou.

"But where is it?" asked the Duc de Guise.

They looked everywhere, but could not find it.

" Where is the janitor ? " asked the King.

"I bound him to the gate," said the Duc de Guise.

" Ask him, cousin."

" He will not answer."

" Bah! we will have a dry fire built around his legs," said the King, laughing, "then he will speak."

Henry glanced hurriedly out of the window.

" He is not there," said he.

" Who untied him ? " asked the Duc de Guise, quickly.

" The devil ! " exclaimed the King, " and we know nothing as yet."

" Well ! " said Henry, " you see very clearly, sire, that there is nothing to prove that my wife and Monsieur de Guise's sister-in-law have been in this house."

" That is so," said Charles. " The Scriptures tell us that there are three things which leave no trace — the bird in the air, the fish in the sea, and the woman — no, I am wrong, the man, in "—

" So," interrupted Henry, " what we had better do is " —

" Yes," said Charles, " what we had better do is for me to look after my bruise, for you, D'Anjou, to wipe off your orange marmalade, and for you, De Guise, to get rid of the grease." Thereupon they left without even troubling to close the door. Reaching the Rue Saint Antoine :

" Where are you bound for, gentlemen ? " asked the King of the Duc d'Anjou and the Duc de Guise.

" Sire, we are going to the house of Nantouillet, who is expecting my Lorraine cousin and myself to supper. Will your Majesty come with us ? "

" No, thanks, we are going in a different direction. Will you take one of my torch-bearers ? "

" Thank you, no, sire," said the Duc d'Anjou, hastily.

" Good ; he is afraid I will spy on him," whispered Charles to the King of Navarre.

Then taking the latter by the arm :

" Come, Henriot," said he, " I will take you to supper to-night."

" Are we not going back to the Louvre ? " asked Henry.

" No, I tell you, you stupid ! Come with me, since I tell you to come. Come ! "

And he dragged Henry down the Rue Geoffroy Lasnier.

CHAPTER XXXVI.

THE ANAGRAM.

THE Rue Garnier sur l'Eau runs into the Rue Geoffroy Lasnier, and the Rue des Barres lies at right angles to the former.

On the right, a short distance down the Rue de la Mortellerie, stands a small house in the centre of a garden surrounded by a high wall, which has but one entrance. Charles drew a key from his pocket and inserted it into the lock. The gate was unbolted and immediately opened. Telling Henry and the lackey bearing the torch to enter, the King closed and locked the gate behind him.

Light came from one small window which Charles smilingly pointed out to Henry.

" Sire, I do not understand," said the latter.

" But you will, Henriot."

The King of Navarre looked at Charles in amazement. His voice and his face had assumed an expression of gentleness so different from usual that Henry scarcely recognized him.

" Henriot," said the King, " I told you that when I left the Louvre I came out of hell. When I enter here I am in paradise."

" Sire," said Henry, " I am happy that your Majesty has thought me worthy of taking this trip to Heaven with you."

" The road thither is a narrow one," said the King, turning to a small stairway, " but nothing can be compared to it."

" Who is the angel who guards the entrance to your Eden, sire ? "

" You shall see," replied Charles IX.

Signing to Henry to follow him noiselessly, he opened first one door, then another, and finally paused on a threshold.

" Look ! " said he.

Henry approached and gazed on one of the most beautiful pictures he had ever seen.

A young woman of eighteen or nineteen lay sleeping, her head resting on the foot of a little bed in which a child was asleep. The woman held its little feet close to her lips, while her long hair fell over her shoulders like a flood of gold. It

MARIE UTTERED A CRY AND FELL ON HER KNEES

was like one of Albane's pictures of the Virgin and the Child Jesus.

"Oh, sire," said the King of Navarre, "who is this lovely creature ? "

"The angel of my paradise, Henriot, the only one who loves me."

Henry smiled.

"Yes," said Charles, "for she loved me before she knew I was King."

"And since she has known it ? "

"Well, since she has known it," said Charles, with a smile which showed that royalty sometimes weighed heavily on him, "since she has known it she loves me still; so you may judge."

The King approached the woman softly and pressed a kiss as light as that which a bee gives to a lily on her rosy cheek.

Yet, light as it was, she awakened at once.

"Charles!" she murmured, opening her eyes.

"You see," said the King, "she calls me Charles. The queen says ' sire ' ! "

"Oh!" cried the young woman, "you are not alone, my King."

"No, my sweet Marie, I wanted to bring you another king, happier than myself because he has no crown; more unhappy than I because he has no Marie Touchet. God makes compensation for everything."

"Sire, is it the King of Navarre ? " asked Marie.

"Yes, my child; come here, Henriot." The King of Navarre drew near; Charles took him by the hand.

"See this hand, Marie," said he, "it is the hand of a good brother and a loyal friend. Were it not for this hand "—

"Well, sire ? "

"Well, had it not been for this hand to-day, Marie, our child would have no father."

Marie uttered a cry, fell on her knees, and seizing Henry's hand covered it with kisses.

"Very good, Marie, very good," said Charles.

"What have you done to thank him, sire ? "

"I have done for him what he did for me."

Henry looked at Charles in astonishment.

"Some day you will know what I mean, Henriot; meanwhile

come here and see." He approached the bed, on which the
child still slept.

"Ah!" said he, "if this little fellow were in the Louvre
instead of here in this little house in the Rue des Barres, many
things would be changed for the present as well as for the
future perhaps."[1]

"Sire," said Marie, "if your Majesty is willing, I prefer
him to stay here; he sleeps better."

"Let us not disturb his slumber, then," said the King; "it
is so sweet to sleep when one does not dream!"

"Well, sire," said Marie, pointing to a door opening out of
the room.

"Yes, you are right, Marie," said Charles IX., "let us have
supper."

"My well-beloved Charles," said Marie, "you will ask the
king your brother to excuse me, will you not?"

"Why?"

"For having dismissed our servants, sire," continued Marie,
turning to the King of Navarre; "you must know that Charles
wants to be served by me alone."

"*Ventre saint gris!*" said Henry, "I should think so!"

Both men entered the dining-room. The mother, anxious
and careful, laid a warm blanket over the little Charles, who,
thanks to the sound sleep of childhood, so envied by his
father, had not wakened.

Marie rejoined them.

"There are only two covers!" said the King.

"Permit me," said Marie, "to serve your majesties."

"Now," said Charles, "this is where you cause me trouble,
Henriot"

"How so, sire?"

"Did you not hear?"

"Forgive me, Charles, forgive me."

"Yes, I will forgive you. But sit here, near me, between
us."

"I will obey," said Marie.

She brought a plate, sat down between the two kings, and
served them.

"Is it not good, Henriot," said Charles, "to have one place

---

[1] Had this natural child, no other than the famous Duc d'Angoulême, who died in
1650, been legitimate, he would have supplanted Henry III., Henry IV., Louis XIII., and
Louis XIV. What would he have given in place of them? The imagination gropes
hopelessly about among the shadows of such a question.

in the world in which one can eat and drink without needing any one to taste the meats and wines beforehand ? "

" Sire," said Henry, smiling, and by the smile replying to the constant fear in his own mind, " believe me, I appreciate your happiness more than any one."

" And tell her, Henriot, that in order for us to live happily, she must not mingle in politics. Above all, she must not become acquainted with my mother."

" Queen Catharine loves your Majesty so passionately that she would be jealous of any other love," replied Henry, finding by a subterfuge the means of avoiding the dangerous confidence of the King.

" Marie," said the latter, " I have brought you one of the finest and the wittiest men I know. At court, you see, and this is saying a great deal, he puts every one in the shade. I alone have clearly understood, not his heart, perhaps, but his mind."

" Sire," said Henry, " I am sorry that in exaggerating the one as you do, you mistrust the other."

" I exaggerate nothing, Henriot," said the King; " besides, you will be known some day."

Then turning to the young woman :

" He makes delightful anagrams. Ask him to make one of your name. I will answer that he will do it."

" Oh, what could you expect to find in the name of a poor girl like me ? what gentle thought could there be in the letters with which chance spelled Marie Touchet ? "

" Oh ! the anagram from this name, sire," said Henry, " is so easy that there is no great merit in finding it."

" Ah ! ah ! it is already found," said Charles. " You see — Marie."

Henry drew his tablets from the pocket of his doublet, tore out a paper, and below the name *Marie Touchet* wrote *Je charme tout.* Then he handed the paper to the young woman.

" Truly," she cried, " it is impossible ! "

" What has he found ? " asked Charles.

" Sire, I dare not repeat it."

" Sire," said Henry, " in the name Marie Touchet there is, letter for letter, by changing the ' i ' into a ' j,' as is often done, *Je charme tout.*" (I charm all.)

" Yes," exclaimed Charles, " letter for letter. I want this to be your motto, Marie, do you hear ? Never was one better deserved. Thanks, Henriot. Marie, I will give it to you written in diamonds."

The supper over, two o'clock struck from Nôtre-Dame.

"Now," said Charles, "in return for this compliment, Marie, you will give the king an armchair, in which he can sleep until daybreak; but let it be some distance from us, because he snores frightfully. Then if you waken before I do, you will rouse me, for at six o'clock we have to be at the Bastille. Good-night, Henriot. Make yourself as comfortable as possible. But," he added, approaching the King of Navarre and laying his hand on his shoulder, "for your life, Henry, — do you hear? for your life, — do not leave here without me, especially to return to the Louvre."

Henry had suspected too many things in what still remained unexplained to him to disobey such advice. Charles IX. entered his room, and Henry, the sturdy mountaineer, settled himself in an armchair, in which he soon justified the precaution taken by his brother-in-law in keeping at a distance.

At dawn he was awakened by Charles. As he had not undressed, it did not take him long to finish his toilet. The King was more happy and smiling than he ever was at the Louvre. The hours spent by him in that little house in the Rue des Barres were his hours of sunshine.

Both men went out through the sleeping-room. The young woman was still in bed. The child was asleep in its cradle. Both were smiling.

Charles looked at them for a moment with infinite tenderness.

Then turning to the King of Navarre:

"Henriot," said he, "if you ever hear what I did for you last night, or if misfortune come to me, remember this child asleep in its cradle."

Then kissing both mother and child on the forehead, without giving Henry time to question him:

"Good-by, my angels," said he, and went out.

Henry followed, deep in thought. The horses were waiting for them at the Bastille, held by the gentlemen to whom Charles IX. had given the order.

Charles signed to Henry to mount, sprang into his own saddle, and riding through the garden of the Arbalite, followed the outside highways.

"Where are we going?" asked Henry.

"We are going to see if the Duc d'Anjou returned for Madame de Condé alone," replied Charles, "and if there is as much ambition as love in his heart, which I greatly doubt."

Henry did not understand the answer, but followed Charles in silence.

They reached the Marais, and as from the shadow of the palisades they could see all which at that time was called the Faubourg Saint Laurent, Charles pointed out to Henry through the grayish mist of the morning some men wrapped in great cloaks and wearing fur caps. They were on horseback, and rode ahead of a wagon which was heavily laden. As they drew near they became outlined more clearly, and one could see another man in a long brown cloak, his face hidden by a French hat, riding and talking with them.

"Ah! ah!" said Charles, smiling, "I thought so."

"Well, sire," said Henry, "if I am not mistaken, that rider in the brown cloak is the Duc d'Anjou."

"Yes," said Charles IX. "Turn out a little, Henriot, I do not want him to see us."

"But," asked Henry, "who are the men in gray cloaks with fur caps?"

"Those men," said Charles, "are Polish ambassadors, and in that wagon is a crown. And now," said he, urging his horse to a gallop, and turning into the road of the Porte du Temple, "come, Henriot, I have seen all that I wanted to see."

CHAPTER XXXVII.

THE RETURN TO THE LOUVRE.

When Catharine thought that everything was over in the King of Navarre's rooms, when the dead guards had been removed, when Maurevel had been carried to her apartments, and the carpet had been cleaned, she dismissed her women, for it was almost midnight, and strove to sleep. But the shock had been too violent, and the disappointment too keen.

That detested Henry, constantly escaping her snares, which were usually fatal, seemed protected by some invincible power which Catharine persisted in calling chance, although in her heart of hearts a voice told her that its true name was destiny.

The thought that the report of the new attempt in spreading throughout the Louvre and beyond the Louvre would give a greater confidence than ever in the future to Henry and the Huguenots exasperated her, and at that moment had chance, against which she was so unfortunately struggling, delivered her enemy into her hands, surely with the little Florentine dagger she wore at her belt she could have thwarted that destiny so favorable to the King of Navarre.

The hours of the night, hours so long for one waiting and watching struck one after another without Catharine's being able to close her eyes. A whole world of new plans unrolled in her visionary mind during those nocturnal hours. Finally at daybreak she rose, dressed herself, and went to the apartments of Charles IX.

The guards, who were accustomed to see her go to the King at all hours of the day and night, let her pass. She crossed the antechamber, therefore, and reached the armory. But there she found the nurse of Charles, who was awake.

" My son ? " said the queen.

" Madame, he gave orders that no one was to be admitted to his room before eight o'clock."

" This order was not for me, nurse."

" It was for every one, madame."

Catharine smiled.

" Yes, I know very well," said the nurse, " that no one has any right to oppose your majesty; I therefore beg you to listen to the prayer of a poor woman and to refrain from entering."

" Nurse, I must speak to my son."

" Madame, I will not open the door except on a formal order from your majesty."

" Open, nurse," said Catharine, " I order you to open ! "

At this voice, more respected and much more feared in the Louvre than that of Charles himself, the nurse handed the key to Catharine, but the queen had no need of it. She drew from her pocket her own key of the room, and under its heavy pressure the door yielded.

The room was vacant, Charles's bed was untouched, and his greyhound Acteon, asleep on the bear-skin that covered the step of the bed, rose and came forward to lick the ivory hands of Catharine.

" Ah ! " said the queen, frowning, " he is out ! I will wait for him."

She seated herself, pensive and gloomy, at the window which overlooked the court of the Louvre, and from which the chief entrance was visible.

For two hours she sat there, as motionless and pale as a marble statue, when at length she perceived a troop of horsemen returning to the Louvre, at whose head she recognized Charles and Henry of Navarre.

Then she understood all. Instead of arguing with her in regard to the arrest of his brother-in-law, Charles had taken him away and so had saved him.

"Blind, blind, blind!" she murmured. Then she waited. An instant later footsteps were heard in the adjoining room, which was the armory.

"But, sire," Henry was saying, "now that we have returned to the Louvre, tell me why you took me away and what is the service you have rendered me."

"No, no, Henriot," replied Charles, laughing, "some day, perhaps, you will find out; but for the present it must remain a mystery. Know only that for the time being you have in all probability brought about a fierce quarrel between my mother and me."

As he uttered these words, Charles raised the curtain and found himself face to face with Catharine.

Behind him and above his shoulder rose the pale, anxious countenance of the Béarnais.

"Ah! you here, madame?" said Charles IX., frowning.

"Yes, my son," said Catharine, "I want to speak to you."

"To me?"

"To you alone."

"Well, well," said Charles, turning to his brother-in-law, "since there is no escape, the sooner the better."

"I will leave you, sire," said Henry.

"Yes, yes, leave us," replied Charles; "and as you are a Catholic, Henriot, go and hear a mass for me while I stay for the sermon."

Henry bowed and withdrew.

Charles IX. went directly to the point.

"Well, madame," said he, trying to make a joke of the affair. "By Heaven! you are waiting to scold me, are you not? I wickedly upset your little plan. Well, the devil! I could not let the man who had just saved my life be arrested and taken to the Bastille. Nor did I want to quarrel with my mother. I am a good son. Moreover," he added in a low tone, "the Lord punishes children who quarrel with their mothers. Witness my brother François II. Forgive me, therefore, frankly, and confess that the joke was a good one."

"Sire," said Catharine, "your Majesty is mistaken; it is not a joke."

"Yes, yes! and you will end by looking at it in that way, or the devil take me!"

"Sire, by your blunder you have baffled a project which would have led to an important discovery."

"Bah! a project. Are you embarrassed because of a baffled project, mother? You can make twenty others, and in those, — well, I promise I will second you."

"Now that you will second me it is too late, for he is warned and will be on his guard."

"Well," said the King, "let us come to the point. What have you against Henriot?"

"The fact that he conspires."

"Yes, I know that this is your constant accusation; but does not every one conspire more or less in this charming royal household called the Louvre?"

"But he conspires more than any one, and he is much more dangerous than one imagines."

"A regular Lorenzino!" said Charles.

"Listen," said Catharine, becoming gloomy at mention of this name, which reminded her of one of the bloodiest catastrophies in the history of Florence. "Listen; there is a way of proving to me that I am wrong."

"What way, mother?"

"Ask Henry who was in his room last night."

"In his room last night?"

"Yes; and if he tells you" —

"Well?"

"Well, I shall be ready to admit that I have been mistaken."

"But in case it was a woman, we cannot ask."

"A woman?"

"Yes."

"A woman who killed two of your guards and perhaps mortally wounded Monsieur de Maurevel!"

"Oh! oh!" said the King, "this is serious. Was there any bloodshed?"

"Three men were stretched on the floor."

" And the one who reduced them to this state ? "

"Escaped safe and sound."

" By Gog and Magog ! " exclaimed Charles, " he was a brave fellow, and you are right, mother, I must know him."

"Well, I tell you in advance that you will not know him, at least not through Henry."

" But through you, mother ? The man did not escape without leaving some trace, without your noticing some part of his clothing."

"Nothing was noticed except the very elegant red cloak which he wore."

" Ah ! ah ! a red cloak ! " cried Charles. " I know only one at court remarkable enough to attract attention."

"Exactly," said Catharine.

" Well ? " demanded Charles.

" Well," said Catharine, " wait for me in your rooms, my son, and I will go and see if my orders have been carried out."

Catharine left, and Charles, alone, began walking up and down distractedly, whistling a hunting-song, one hand in his doublet, the other hanging down, which his dog licked every time he paused.

As to Henry he had left his brother-in-law greatly disturbed, and instead of going along the main corridor he had taken the small private stairway, to which we have already referred more than once, and which led to the second story. Scarcely had he ascended four steps before he perceived a figure at the first landing. He stopped, raising his hand to his dagger. But he soon saw it was a woman, who took hold of his hand and said in a charming voice which he well knew:

"Thank God, sire, you are safe and sound. I was so afraid for you, but no doubt God heard my prayer."

" What has happened ? " said Henry.

" You will know when you reach your rooms. You need not worry over Orthon. I have seen to him."

The young woman descended the stairs hastily, making Henry believe that she had met him by chance.

"That is strange," said Henry to himself. " What is the matter ? What has happened to Orthon ? "

Unfortunately, the question was not heard by Madame de Sauve, for the latter had already disappeared.

Suddenly at the top of the stairs Henry perceived another figure, but this time it was that of a man.

" Hush ! " said the man.

" Ah ! is it you, François ? "

" Do not call me by my name."

" What has happened ? "

" Return to your rooms and you will see, then slip into the corridor, look carefully around to make sure that no one is spying on you, and come to my apartments.   The door will be ajar."

He, too, disappeared down the stairs, like the phantoms in a theatre who glide through a trap door.

" *Ventre saint gris !* " murmured the Béarnais, " the puzzle continues ; but since the answer is in my rooms, let us go thither and find it."

However, it was not without emotion that Henry went on his way.   He had the sensitiveness and the superstition of youth.   Everything was clearly reflected on his mind, the surface of which was as smooth as a mirror, and what he had just heard foretold trouble.

He reached the door of his rooms and listened.   Not a sound.   Besides, since Charlotte had said to return to his apartments, it was evident that there was nothing for him to fear by doing so.   He glanced hurriedly around the first room — it was vacant.   Nothing showed that anything had occurred.

" Orthon is not here," said he.

He passed on to the next room.   There everything was explained.

In spite of the water which had been thrown on in bucketsful, great red spots covered the floor.   A piece of furniture was broken, the bed curtains had been slashed by the sword, a Venetian mirror had been shattered by a bullet ; and a bloody hand which had left its terrible imprint on the wall showed that this silent chamber had been the scene of a frightful struggle.   Henry embraced all these details at a glance, and passing his hand across his forehead, now damp with perspiration, murmured :

" Ah, I know now the service the King has rendered me. They came here to assassinate me — and — ah ! De Mouy ! what have they done to De Mouy ?   The wretches !   They may have killed him ! "

And as anxious to learn the news as the Duc d'Alençon was to tell it, Henry threw a last mournful glance on the surrounding objects, hurried from the room, reached the corridor, made sure that it was vacant, and pushing open the half-closed door, which he carefully shut behind him, he hurried to the Duc d'Alençon's.

The duke was waiting for him in the first room. Laying his finger on his lips, he hastily took Henry's hand and drew him into a small round tower which was completely isolated, and which consequently was out of range of spies.

" Ah, brother," said he, " what a horrible night ! "

" What happened ? " asked Henry.

" They tried to arrest you."

" Me ? "

" Yes, you."

" For what reason ? "

" I do not know. Where were you ? "

" The King took me into the city with him last night."

" Then he knew about it," said D'Alençon. " But since you were not in your rooms, who was ? "

" Was some one there ? " asked Henry as if he were ignorant of the fact.

" Yes, a man. When I had heard the noise, I ran to help you; but it was too late."

" Was the man arrested ? " asked Henry, anxiously.

" No, he escaped, after he had wounded Maurevel dangerously and killed two guards."

" Ah ! brave De Mouy ! " cried Henry.

" It was De Mouy, then ? " said D'Alençon, quickly.

Henry saw that he had made a mistake.

" I presume so," said he, " for I had an appointment with him to discuss your escape, and to tell him that I had yielded all my rights to the throne of Navarre to you."

" If that is known," said D'Alençon, growing pale, " we are lost."

" Yes, for Maurevel will speak."

" Maurevel received a sword-thrust in his throat, and I found out from the surgeon who dressed the wound that it would be a week before he would utter a single word."

" A week ! That is more than enough for De Mouy to escape."

" For that matter," said D'Alençon, " it might have been some one besides Monsieur de Mouy."

" You think so ? " said Henry.

"Yes, the man disappeared very quickly, and nothing but his red cloak was seen."

"And a red cloak," said Henry, "is more apt to be worn by a courtier than by a soldier. I should never suspect De Mouy in a red cloak."

"No, if any one were suspected," said D'Alençon, "it would be more apt to be " —

He stopped.

"It would be more likely to be Monsieur de la Mole," said Henry.

"Certainly, since I myself, who saw the man running away, thought so for an instant."

"You thought so? Why, it must have been Monsieur de la Mole, then."

"Does he know anything?" asked D'Alençon.

"Absolutely nothing; at least, nothing of importance."

"Brother," said the duke; "I really think now that it was he."

"The devil!" said Henry; "if it was, that will trouble the queen greatly, for she is interested in him."

"Interested, you say?" said D'Alençon in amazement.

"Yes. Do you not remember, François, that it was your sister who recommended him to you?"

"Yes," said the duke, in a dull voice; "so I tried to be agreeable to him. The proof of this is that, fearing his red cloak might compromise him, I went up to his rooms and took the cloak away."

"Oh! oh!" exclaimed Henry, "that was doubly prudent. And now I would not bet, but I would swear, that it was he."

"Even in court?" asked François.

"Faith, yes," replied Henry. "He probably came to bring me some message from Marguerite."

"If I were sure of being upheld by your testimony," said D'Alençon, "I would almost accuse him."

"If you were to accuse him," replied Henry, "you understand, brother, that I would not contradict you."

"But the queen?" said D'Alençon.

"Ah, yes, the queen."

"We must know what she would do."

"I will undertake to find out."

"Plague it, brother! she will do wrong to lie to us, for this affair will make a glorious reputation of bravery for the young man, and which cannot have cost him dear either, for he probably bought it on credit. Furthermore, it is true that he is well able to pay back both interest and capital."

" Well, what can you expect ? " said Henry ; " in this base world one has nothing for nothing ! "

And bowing and smiling to D'Alençon, he cautiously thrust his head into the corridor, and making sure that no one had been listening, he hurried rapidly away, and disappeared down the private stairway which led to the apartments of Marguerite.

As far as she was concerned, the Queen of Navarre was no less anxious than her husband. The night's expedition sent against her and the Duchesse de Nevers by the King, the Duc d'Anjou, the Duc de Guise, and Henry, whom she had recognized, troubled her greatly. In all probability there was nothing which could compromise her. The janitor unfastened from the gate by La Mole and Coconnas had promised to be silent. But four lords like those with whom two simple gentlemen, such as La Mole and Coconnas, had coped, would not have gone out of their way by chance, or without having had some reason for thus inconveniencing themselves. Marguerite had returned at daybreak, having passed the rest of the night with the Duchesse de Nevers. She had retired at once, but had been unable to sleep, and had started at the slightest sound.

In the midst of this anxiety she heard some one knocking at the secret door, and being informed that the visitor was Gillonne, she gave orders to have her admitted.

Henry waited at the outer door. Nothing in his appearance showed the wounded husband. His usual smile lay on his delicate lips, and not a muscle of his face betrayed the terrible anxiety through which he had just passed. He seemed to glance inquiringly at Marguerite to discover if she would allow him to talk with her alone. Marguerite understood her husband's look, and signed to Gillonne to withdraw.

" Madame," said Henry, " I know how deeply you are attached to your friends, and I fear I bring you bad news."

" What is it, monsieur ? " asked Marguerite.

" One of your dearest servants is at present greatly compromised."

" Which one ? "

" The dear Count de la Mole."

" Monsieur le Comte de la Mole compromised !   And why ? "

" Because of the affair of last night."

In spite of her self-control Marguerite could not keep from blushing.

But she made an effort over herself.

" What affair ? " she asked.

" What," said Henry, " did you not hear all the noise which was made in the Louvre ? "

" No, monsieur."

" I congratulate you, madame," said Henry, with charming simplicity.   " This proves that you are a sound sleeper."

" But what happened ? "

" It seems that our good mother gave an order to Monsieur de Maurevel and six of his men to arrest me."

" You, monsieur, you ? "

" Yes, me."

" For what reason ? "

" Ah, who can tell the reasons of a mind as subtle as that of your mother ?   I suspect the reasons, but I do not know them positively."

" And you were not in your rooms ? "

" No ; I happened not to be.   You have guessed rightly, madame, I was not.   Last evening the King asked me to go out with him.   But, although I was not in my rooms, some one else was."

" Who ? "

" It seems that it was the Count de la Mole."

" The Count de la Mole ! " exclaimed Marguerite, astonished.

" By Heavens ! what a lively little fellow this man from the provinces is ! " continued Henry.   " Do you know that he wounded Maurevel and killed two guards ? "

" Wounded Monsieur de Maurevel and killed two guards ! — impossible ! "

" What !   You doubt his courage, madame ? "

" No, but I say that Monsieur de la Mole could not have been in your rooms."

" Why not ? "

" Why, because — because " — said Marguerite, embarrassed, " because he was elsewhere."

" Ah !   If he can prove an alibi," said Henry, " that is different ; he will tell where he was, and the matter will be settled."

"Where was he?" said Marguerite, quickly.

"In all probability the day will not pass without his being arrested and questioned. But unfortunately as there are proofs " —

"Proofs! what proofs?"

"The man who made this desperate defence wore a red cloak."

"But Monsieur de la Mole is not the only one who has a red cloak — I know another man who has one."

"No doubt, and I too know one. But this is what will happen: if it was not Monsieur de la Mole who was in my rooms, it must have been the other man who wears a red cloak, like La Mole. Now, do you know who this other man is?"

"Heavens!"

"There lies the danger. You, as well as myself, madame, have seen it. Your emotion proves this. Let us now talk like two people who are discussing the most desirable thing in the world — a throne; a most precious gift — life. De Mouy arrested, we are ruined."

"Yes, I understand that."

"While Monsieur de la Mole compromises no one; at least you would not suppose him capable of inventing a story such as, for instance, that he was with some ladies — whom I know?"

"Monsieur," said Marguerite, "if you fear only that, you may be easy. He will not say it."

"What!" said Henry, "would he remain silent if death were to be the price of his silence?"

"He would remain silent, monsieur."

"You are sure of this?"

"I am sure."

"Then everything is for the best," said Henry, rising.

"You are going, monsieur?" asked Marguerite, quickly.

"Oh, my God, yes. This is all I had to say to you."

"And you are going" —

"To try and get out of the trouble we have been put to by this devil of a man in the red cloak."

"Oh, my God! my God! the poor young man!" cried Marguerite, pitifully, wringing her hands.

"Really," said Henry, as he went out, "this dear Monsieur de la Mole is a faithful servant."

CHAPTER XXXVIII.

THE GIRDLE OF THE QUEEN MOTHER.

CHARLES entered his room, smiling and joking. But after a conversation of ten minutes with his mother, one would have said that the latter had given him her pallor and anger in exchange for the light-heartedness of her son.

" Monsieur de la Mole," said Charles, " Monsieur de la Mole ! Henry and the Duc d'Alençon must be sent for. Henry, because this young man was a Huguenot; the Duc d'Alençon, because he is in his service."

" Send for them if you wish, my son, but you will learn nothing. Henry and François, I fear, are much more closely bound together than one would suppose from appearances. To question them is to suspect them. I think it would be better to wait for the slow but sure proof of time. If you give the guilty ones time to breathe again, my son, if you let them think they have escaped your vigilance, they will become bold and triumphant, and will give you a better opportunity to punish them. Then we shall know everything."

Charles walked up and down, undecided, gnawing his anger, as a horse gnaws his bit, and pressing his clinched hand to his heart, which was consumed by his one idea.

" No, no," said he, at length; " I will not wait. You do not know what it is to wait, beset with suspicions as I am. Besides, every day these courtiers become more insolent. Even last night did not two of them dare to cope with us ? If Monsieur de la Mole is innocent, very good; but I should not be sorry to know where Monsieur de la Mole was last night, while they were attacking my guards in the Louvre, and me in the Rue Cloche Percée. So let the Duc d'Alençon be sent for, and afterwards Henry. I will question them separately. You may remain, mother."

Catharine sat down. For a determined spirit such as hers was, every incident turned by her powerful hand would lead her to her goal, although it might seem to be leading away from it. From every blow there would result noise and a spark. The noise would guide, the spark give light.

The Duc d'Alençon entered. His previous conversation

with Henry had prepared him for this interview; therefore he
was quite calm.

His replies were very exact.   Warned by his mother to remain
in his own rooms, he was completely ignorant of the events of
the night.   But as his apartments opened upon the same corridor as did those of the King of Navarre, he had at first
thought he heard a sound like that of a door being broken in,
then curses, then pistol-shots.   Thereupon he had ventured to
push his door partly open, and had seen a man in a red cloak
running away.

Charles and his mother exchanged glances.

" In a red cloak ? " said the King.

" In a red cloak," replied D'Alençon.

" And did you have any suspicions regarding this red
cloak ? "

D'Alençon rallied all his strength that he might lie as
naturally as possible.

" At first sight," said he, " I must confess to your Majesty that
I thought I recognized the red cloak of one of my gentlemen."

" What is the name of this gentleman ? "

" Monsieur de la Mole."

" Why was not Monsieur de la Mole with you as his duty
required him to be ? "

" I had given him leave of absence," said the duke.

" That is well ; now you may go," said Charles.

The Duc d'Alençon started towards the door by which he
had entered.

" Not that way," said Charles ; " this way."

And he indicated the door opening into his nurse's room.
Charles did not want François and Henry to meet.

He did not know that they had already seen each other for
an instant, and that this instant had sufficed for the two
brothers-in-law to agree on their plans.

At a sign from Charles, Henry entered.

He did not wait for Charles to question him, however.

" Sire," said he, " your Majesty has done well to send for
me, for I was just coming to demand justice of you."

Charles frowned.

" Yes, justice," said Henry.   " I will begin by thanking your
Majesty for having taken me with you last night ; for, by doing this, I now know that you saved my life.   But what had I
done that an attempt should be made to assassinate me ? "

"Not to assassinate," said Catharine, quickly, "but to arrest you."

"Well," said Henry, "even so. What crime have I committed to merit arrest? If I am guilty I am as much so this morning as I was last evening. Tell me my offence, sire."

Embarrassed as to what reply to make, Charles looked at his mother.

"My son," said Catharine, "you receive suspicious characters."

"Very good," said Henry, "and these suspicious characters compromise me; is that it, madame?"

"Yes, Henry."

"Give me their names! Give me their names! Who are they? Let me see them!"

"Really," said Charles, "Henriot has the right to demand an explanation."

"And I do demand it!" said Henry, realizing the superiority of his position and anxious to make the most of it. "I ask it from my good brother Charles, and from my good mother Catharine. Since my marriage with Marguerite have I not been a kind husband? ask Marguerite. A good Catholic? ask my confessor. A good relative? ask those who were at the hunt yesterday."

"Yes, that is true, Henriot," said the King; "but what can you do? They claim that you conspire."

"Against whom?"

"Against me."

"Sire, if I had been conspiring against you, I had merely to let events take their course, when your horse broke his knee and could not rise, or when the furious boar turned on your Majesty."

"Well, the devil! mother, do you know that he is right?"

"But who was in your rooms last night?"

"Madame," said Henry, "in times when so few dare to answer for themselves, I should never attempt to answer for others. I left my rooms at seven o'clock in the evening, at ten o'clock my brother Charles took me away, and I spent the night with him. I could not be with your Majesty and know what was going on in my rooms at the same time."

"But," said Catharine, "it is none the less true that one of your men killed two of his Majesty's guards and wounded Monsieur de Maurevel."

"One of my men?" said Henry. "What man, madame? Name him."

"Every one accuses Monsieur de la Mole."

"Monsieur de la Mole is not in my suite, madame; Monsieur de la Mole belongs to Monsieur d'Alençon, to whom he was recommended by your daughter."

"But," said Charles, "was it Monsieur de la Mole who was in your rooms, Henriot?"

"How can you expect me to know, sire? I can say neither yes nor no. Monsieur de la Mole is an exceptional servant, thoroughly devoted to the Queen of Navarre. He often brings me messages, either from Marguerite, to whom he is grateful for having recommended him to Monsieur le Duc d'Alençon, or from Monsieur le Duc himself. I cannot say that it was not Monsieur de la Mole" —

"It was he," said Catharine. "His red cloak was recognized."

"Has Monsieur de la Mole a red cloak, then?"

"Yes."

"And the man who so cleverly disposed of two of my guards and Monsieur de Maurevel" —

"Had a red cloak?" asked Henry.

"Exactly," said Charles.

"I have nothing to say," said the Béarnais. "But in any case it seems to me that instead of summoning me here, since I was not in my rooms, it is Monsieur de la Mole, who, having been there, as you say, should be questioned. But," said Henry, "I must observe one thing to your Majesty."

"What is that?"

"This, that if I had seen an order signed by my King and had defended myself instead of obeying this order, I should be guilty and should deserve all sorts of punishment; but it was not I but some stranger whom this order in no way concerned. There was an attempt made to arrest him unjustly, he defended himself too well, perhaps, but he was in the right."

"And yet" — murmured Catharine.

"Madame," said Henry, "was the order to arrest me?"

"Yes," said Catharine, "and his Majesty himself signed it."

"Was it an order to arrest any one found in my place in case I was not there?"

"No," said Catharine.

"Well!" said Henry, "unless you prove that I was conspiring and that the man who was in my rooms was conspiring with me, this man is innocent."

Then turning to Charles IX. :

" Sire," continued Henry, " I shall not leave the Louvre. At a simple word from your Majesty I shall even be ready to enter any state prison you may be pleased to suggest. But while waiting for the proof to the contrary I have the right to call myself and I do call myself the very faithful servant, subject, and brother of your Majesty."

And with a dignity hitherto unknown in him, Henry bowed to Charles and withdrew.

" Bravo, Henriot! " said Charles, when the King of Navarre had left.

" Bravo! because he has defeated us? " said Catharine.

" Why should I not applaud ? When we fence together and he touches me do I not say ' bravo ' ? Mother, you are wrong to hate this boy as you do."

" My son," said Catharine, pressing the hand of Charles IX., " I do not hate him, I fear him."

" Well, you are wrong, mother. Henriot is my friend, and as he said, had he been conspiring against me he had only to let the wild boar alone."

" Yes," said Catharine, " so that Monsieur le Duc d'Anjou, his personal enemy, might be King of France."

" Mother, whatever Henriot's motive in saving my life, the fact is that he saved it, and, the devil! I do not want any harm to come to him. As to Monsieur de la Mole, well, I will talk about him with my brother D'Alençon, to whom he belongs."

This was Charles IX.'s way of dismissing his mother, who withdrew endeavoring to fix her suspicions. On account of his unimportance, Monsieur de la Mole did not answer to her needs.

Returning to her rooms, Catharine found Marguerite waiting for her.

" Ah! ah! " said she, " is it you, my daughter ? I sent for you last evening."

" I know it, madame, but I had gone out."

" And this morning ? "

" This morning, madame, I have come to tell your majesty that you are about to do a great wrong."

" What is that ? "

"You are going to have Monsieur le Comte de la Mole arrested."

"You are mistaken, my daughter, I am going to have no one arrested. It is the King, not I, who gives orders for arrests."

"Let us not quibble over the words, madame, when the circumstances are serious. Monsieur de la Mole is going to be arrested, is he not?"

"Very likely."

"Accused of having been found in the chamber of the King of Navarre last night, and of having killed two guards and wounded Monsieur de Maurevel?"

"Such indeed is the crime they impute to him."

"They impute it to him wrongly, madame," said Marguerite; "Monsieur de la Mole is not guilty."

"Monsieur de la Mole not guilty!" said Catharine, giving a start of joy, and thinking that what Marguerite was about to tell her would throw light on the subject.

"No," went on Marguerite, "he is not guilty, he cannot be so, for he was not in the king's room."

"Where was he, then?"

"In my room, madame."

"In your room?"

"Yes, in my room."

At this avowal from a daughter of France, Catharine felt like hurling a withering glance at Marguerite, but she merely crossed her arms on her lap.

"And," said she after a moment's silence, "if Monsieur de la Mole is arrested and questioned" —

"He will say where he was and with whom he was, mother," replied Marguerite, although she felt sure of the contrary.

"Since this is so, you are right, my daughter; Monsieur de la Mole must not be arrested."

Marguerite shivered. It seemed to her that there was something strange and terrible in the way her mother uttered these words; but she had nothing to say, for what she had come to ask for had been granted her.

"But," said Catharine, "if it was not Monsieur de la Mole who was in the king's room, it was some one else!"

Marguerite was silent.

"Do you know who it was, my daughter?" said Catharine.

"No, mother," said Marguerite, in an unsteady voice.

"Come, do not be half confidential."

"I repeat, madame, that I do not know," replied Marguerite again, growing pale in spite of herself.

"Well, well," said Catharine, carelessly, "we shall find out. Go now, my daughter. You may rest assured that your mother will watch over your honor."

Marguerite went out.

"Ah!" murmured Catharine, "they are in league. Henry and Marguerite are working together. While the wife is silent, the husband is blind. Ah, you are very clever, my children, and you think yourselves very strong. But your strength is in your union and I will break you, one after the other. Besides, the day will come when Maurevel can speak or write, utter a name, or spell six letters, and then we shall know everything. Yes, but in the meantime the guilty shall be in safe-keeping. The best thing to do would be to separate them at once."

Thereupon Catharine set out for the apartments of her son, whom she found holding a conference with D'Alençon.

"Ah! ah!" exclaimed Charles IX., frowning, "is it you, mother ?"

"Why did you not say '*again*'? The word was in your mind, Charles."

"What is in my mind belongs to me, madame," said the King, in the rough tone he sometimes used even when speaking to Catharine. "What do you want of me? Tell me quickly."

"Well, you were right, my son," said Catharine to Charles, "and you, D'Alençon, were wrong."

"In what respect, madame ?" asked both princes.

"It was not Monsieur de la Mole who was in the apartments of the King of Navarre."

"Ah! ah!" cried François, growing pale.

"Who was it, then ?" asked Charles.

"We do not know yet, but we shall know when Maurevel is able to speak. So let us drop the subject, which will soon be explained, and return to Monsieur de la Mole."

"Well, what do you want of Monsieur de la Mole, mother, since he was not in the rooms of the King of Navarre ?"

"No," said Catharine, "he was not there, but he was with —the queen."

"With the queen !" cried Charles, bursting into a nervous laugh.

"With the queen," murmured D'Alençon, turning as pale as death.

"No, no," said Charles, " De Guise told me he had met Marguerite's litter."

" Yes," said Catharine, " she has a house in town."

" In the Rue Cloche Perceé!" cried the King.

" Oh! oh! this is too much," said D'Alençon, driving his nails into his breast. "And to have had him recommended to me!"

" Ah! now that I think of it!" said the King, stopping suddenly, " it was he who defended himself against us last night, and who hurled the silver bowl at my head, the wretch!"

" Oh, yes!" repeated François, " the wretch!"

" You are right, my children," said Catharine, without appearing to understand the feelings which incited both of her sons to speak. " You are right, for a single indiscreet act of this gentleman might cause a horrible scandal, and ruin a daughter of France. One moment of madness would be enough for that."

" Or of vanity," said François.

" No doubt, no doubt," said Charles. " And yet we cannot bring the case into court unless Henriot consents to appear as plaintiff."

" My son," said Catharine, placing her hand on Charles's shoulder in such a way as to call the King's attention to what she was about to propose, " listen to what I say. A crime has been committed, and there may be scandal. But this sort of offence to royalty is not punished by judges and hangmen. If you were simple gentlemen, I should have nothing to say to you, for you are both brave, but you are princes, you cannot cross swords with mere country squires. Think how you can avenge yourselves as princes."

" The devil!" cried Charles, " you are right, mother, and I will consider it."

" I will help you, brother," cried François.

" And I," said Catharine, unfastening the black silk girdle which was wound three times about her waist, and the two tassels of which fell to her knees. " I will retire, but I leave you this to represent me."

And she threw the girdle at the feet of the two princes.

" Ah! ah!" said Charles, " I understand."

" This girdle " — said D'Alençon, picking it up.

" Is punishment and silence," said Catharine, victorious;

" but," she added, "there would be no harm in mentioning this
to Henry."

She withdrew.

" By Heaven!" said D'Alençon; " a good idea, and when
Henry knows that his wife has betrayed him — So," he
added, turning to the King, "you will adopt our mother's
suggestion?"

" In every detail," said Charles, not doubting but that he
would drive a thousand daggers into D'Alençon's heart. " This
will annoy Marguerite, but it will delight Henriot."

Then, calling one of his guards, he ordered Henry summoned, but thinking better of it:

"No, no," said he, "I will go for him myself. Do you,
D'Alençon, inform D'Anjou and De Guise."

Leaving his apartments, he ascended the private stairway to
the second floor, which led to Henry's chamber.

CHAPTER XXXIX.

PROJECTS OF REVENGE.

HENRY took advantage of the respite afforded him by his
well-sustained examination to go to Madame de Sauve's. He
found Orthon completely recovered from his fainting-fit. But
Orthon could tell him nothing, except that some men had
broken into the king's rooms, that the leader had struck him
with the handle of his sword, and that the blow had stunned
him. No one had troubled about Orthon. Catharine had seen
that he had fainted and had believed him to be dead.

As he had come to himself between the departure of the
queen mother and the arrival of the captain of the guards
charged with clearing up the room, he had taken refuge in
Madame de Sauve's apartments.

Henry begged Charlotte to keep the young man until news
came from De Mouy, who would not fail to write him from his
hiding-place. Then he would send Orthon to carry his answer
to De Mouy, and instead of one devoted man he could count
on two. This decided on, he returned to his rooms and
began further to consider matters, walking up and down the
while. Suddenly the door opened and the King appeared.

"Your Majesty!" cried Henry, rising to meet him.

"In person. Really, Henriot, you are a good fellow, and I love you more and more."

"Sire," said Henry, "your Majesty overwhelms me."

"You have but one fault, Henriot."

"What is that? The one for which your Majesty has already reproached me several times?" said Henry. "My preferring to hunt animals rather than birds?"

"No, no, I am not referring to that, Henriot, I mean something else."

"If your Majesty will explain," said Henry, who saw from the smile on Charles's lips that the King was in a good humor, "I will try and correct it."

"It is this, that having such good eyes, you see no better than you do."

"Bah!" said Henry, "can I be short-sighted, then, sire, without knowing it?"

"Worse than that, Henry, worse than that, you are blind."

"Ah, indeed," said the Béarnais, "but is it not when I shut my eyes that this happens?"

"Well, yes!" said Charles, "you are perfectly capable of that. At all events, I am going to open your eyes."

"God said, 'Let there be light,' and there was light. Your Majesty is the representative of God on earth. Therefore you can do here what God does in heaven. Proceed; I am all attention."

"When De Guise said last night that your wife had just passed escorted by a gallant you would not believe it."

"Sire," said Henry, "how could I believe that the sister of your Majesty could commit an act of such imprudence?"

"When he told you that your wife had gone to the Rue Cloche Percée, you would not believe that either!"

"How was I to suppose, sire, that a daughter of France would thus publicly risk her reputation?"

"When we besieged the house in the Rue Cloche Percée, and when I had a silver bowl hurled at my shoulder, D'Anjou some orange marmalade on his head, and De Guise a haunch of venison in the face, you saw two women and two men, did you not?"

"I saw nothing, sire. Does not your Majesty remember that I was questioning the janitor?"

"Yes, but, by Heaven, I saw" —

"Ah, if your Majesty saw anything, that is a different thing."

"I saw two men and two women. Well, I know now beyond a doubt that one of the women was Margot, and that one of the men was Monsieur de la Mole."

"Well," said Henry, "if Monsieur de la Mole was in the Rue Cloche Percée, he was not here."

"No," said Charles, "he was not here. But never mind who was here; we shall know this as soon as that imbecile of a Maurevel is able to speak or write. The point is that Margot is deceiving you."

"Bah!" said Henry; "do not believe such nonsense."

"When I tell you that you are more than near-sighted, that you are blind, the devil! will you believe me just once, stupid? I tell you that Margot is deceiving you, and that this evening we are going to strangle her lover."

Henry gave a start of surprise, and looked at his brother-in-law in amazement.

"Confess, Henry, that at heart you are not sorry. Margot will cry out like a thousand Niobes; but, faith! so much the worse. I do not want you to be made a fool of. If Condé is deceived by the Duc d'Anjou, I will wink; Condé is my enemy. But you are my brother; more than this, you are my friend."

"But, sire"—

"And I do not want you to be annoyed, and made a fool of. You have been a quintain long enough for all these popinjays who come from the provinces to gather our crumbs, and court our women. Let them come, or rather let them come again. By Heaven! you have been deceived, Henriot, — that might happen to any one, — but I swear, you shall have shining satisfaction, and to-morrow they shall say: In the name of a thousand devils! it seems that King Charles loves his brother Henriot, for last night he had Monsieur de la Mole's tongue pulled out in a most amusing manner."

"Is this really decided on, sire?" asked Henry.

"Decided on, determined on, arranged. The coxcomb will have no time to plead his cause. The expedition will consist of myself, D'Anjou, D'Alençon, and De Guise — a king, two sons of France, and a sovereign prince, without counting you."

"How without counting me?"

"Why, you are to be one of us."

" I ! "

" Yes, you ! you shall stab the fellow in a royal manner, while the rest of us strangle him."

" Sire," said Henry, " your kindness overpowers me ; but how do you know " —

" Why, the devil ! it seems that the fellow boasts of it. He goes sometimes to your wife's apartments in the Louvre, sometimes to the Rue Cloche Percée. They compose verses together. I should like to see the stanzas that fop writes. Pastorales they are. They discuss Bion and Moschus, and read first Daphne and then Corydon. Ah! take a good dagger with you ! "

" Sire," said Henry, " upon reflection " —

" What ? "

" Your Majesty will see that I cannot join such an expedition. It seems to me it would be inconvenient to be there in person. I am too much interested in the affair to take any calm part in it. Your Majesty will avenge the honor of your sister on a coxcomb who boasts of having calumniated my wife; nothing is simpler, and Marguerite, whom I hold to be innocent, sire, is in no way dishonored. But were I of the party, it would be a different thing. My co-operation would convert an act of justice into an act of revenge. It would no longer be an execution, but an assassination. My wife would no longer be calumniated, but guilty."

" By Heaven, Henry, as I said just now to my mother, you speak words of wisdom. You have a devilishly quick mind."

And Charles gazed complacently at his brother-in-law, who bowed in return for the compliment.

" Nevertheless," added Charles, " you are willing to be rid of this coxcomb, are you not ? "

" Everything your Majesty does is well done," replied the King of Navarre.

" Well, well, let me do your work for you. You may be sure it shall not be the worse for it."

" I leave it to you, sire," said Henry.

" At what time does he usually go to your wife's room ? "

" About nine o'clock."

" And he leaves ? "

" Before I reach there, for 1 never see him."

" About " —

" About eleven."

" Very well. Come this evening at midnight. The deed will be done."

Charles pressed Henry's hand cordially, and renewing his vows of friendship, left the apartment, whistling his favorite hunting-song.

" *Ventre saint gris!* " said the Béarnais, watching Charles, " either I am greatly mistaken, or the queeen mother is responsible for all this deviltry. Truly, she does nothing but invent plots to make trouble between my wife and myself. Such a pleasant household ! "

And Henry began to laugh as he was in the habit of laughing when no one could see or hear him.

About seven o'clock that evening a handsome young man, who had just taken a bath, was finishing his toilet as he calmly moved about his room, humming a little air, before a mirror in one of the rooms of the Louvre. Near him another young man was sleeping, or rather lying on a bed.

The one was our friend La Mole who, unconsciously, had been the object of so much discussion all day ; the other was his companion Coconnas.

The great storm had passed over him without his having heard the rumble of the thunder or seen the lightning. He had returned at three o'clock in the morning, had stayed in bed until three in the afternoon, half asleep, half awake, building castles on that uncertain sand called the future. Then he had risen, had spent an hour at a fashionable bath, had dined at Maître La Hurière's, and returning to the Louvre had set himself to finish his toilet before making his usual call on the queen.

" And you say you have dined ? " asked Coconnas, yawning.

" Faith, yes, and I was hungry too."

" Why did you not take me with you, selfish man ? "

" Faith, you were sleeping so soundly that I did not like to waken you. But you shall sup with me instead. Be sure not to forget to ask Maître La Hurière for some of that light wine from Anjou, which arrived a few days ago."

" Is it good ? "

" I merely tell you to ask for it."

" Where are you going ? "

" Where am I going ? " said La Mole, surprised that his friend should ask him such a question; " I am going to pay my respects to the queen."

"Well," said Coconnas, "if I were going to dine in our little house in the Rue Cloche Percée, I should have what was left over from yesterday. There is a certain wine of Alicante which is most refreshing."

"It would be imprudent to go there, Annibal, my friend, after what occurred last right. Besides, did we not promise that we would not go back there alone? Hand me my cloak."

"That is so," said Coconnas, "I had forgotten. But where the devil is your cloak? Ah! here it is."

"No, you have given me the black one, and it is the red one I want. The queen likes me better in that."

"Ah, faith," said Coconnas, searching everywhere, "look for yourself, I cannot find it."

"What!" said La Mole, "you cannot find it? Why, where can it be?"

"You probably sold it."

"Why, I have six crowns left."

"Well, take mine."

"Ah, yes, — a yellow cloak with a green doublet! I should look like a popinjay!"

"Faith, you are over-particular, so wear what you please."

Having tossed everything topsy-turvy in his search, La Mole was beginning to abuse the thieves who managed to enter even the Louvre, when a page from the Duc d'Alençon appeared bringing the precious cloak in question.

"Ah!" cried La Mole, "here it is at last!"

"Is this your cloak, monsieur?" said the page. "Yes; monseigneur sent for it to decide a wager he made regarding its color."

"Oh!" said La Mole, "I asked for it only because I was going out, but if his highness desires to keep it longer" —

"No, Monsieur le Comte, he is through with it."

The page left. La Mole fastened his cloak.

"Well," he went on, "what have you decided to do?"

"I do not know."

"Shall I find you here this evening?"

"How can I tell?"

"Do you not know what you are going to do for two hours?"

"I know well enough what I shall do, but I do not know what I may be ordered to do."

"By the Duchesse de Nevers?"

"No, by the Duc d'Alençon."

"As a matter of fact," said La Mole, "I have noticed for some time that he has been friendly to you."

"Yes," said Coconnas.

"Then your fortune is made," said La Mole, laughing.

"Poof!" said Coconnas. "He is only a younger brother!"

"Oh!" said La Mole, "he is so anxious to become the elder one that perhaps Heaven will work some miracle in his favor."

"So you do not know where you will be this evening?"

"No."

"Go to the devil, then, — I mean good-by!"

"That La Mole is a terrible fellow," thought Coconnas, "always wanting me to tell him where I am going to be! as if I knew. Besides, I believe I am sleepy." And he threw himself on the bed again.

La Mole betook himself to the apartments of the queen. In the corridor he met the Duc d'Alençon.

"Ah! you here, Monsieur la Mole?" said the prince.

"Yes, my lord," replied La Mole, bowing respectfully.

"Are you going away from the Louvre?"

"No, your highness. I am on my way to pay my respects to her Majesty the Queen of Navarre."

"About what time shall you leave, Monsieur de la Mole?"

"Has monseigneur any orders for me?"

"No, not at present, but I shall want to speak to you this evening."

"About what time?"

"Between nine and ten."

"I shall do myself the honor of waiting on your highness at that time."

"Very good. I shall depend on you."

La Mole bowed and went on.

"There are times," said he, "when the duke is as pale as death. It is very strange."

He knocked at the door of the queen's apartments. Gillonne, who apparently was expecting him, led him to Marguerite.

The latter was occupied with some work which seemed to be wearying her greatly. A paper covered with notes and a volume of Isocrates lay before her. She signed to La Mole to let her finish a paragraph. Then, in a few moments, she threw down her pen and invited the young man to sit beside her. La Mole was radiant. Never had he been so handsome or so light-hearted.

"Greek!" said he, glancing at the book. "A speech of Isocrates! What are you doing with that? Ah! and Latin on this sheet of paper! *Ad Sarmatiæ legatos reginæ Margaritæ concio!* So you are going to harangue these barbarians in Latin?"

"I must," said Marguerite, "since they do not speak French."

"But how can you write the answer before you have the speech?"

"A greater coquette than I would make you believe that this was impromptu; but I cannot deceive you, my Hyacinthe: I was told the speech in advance, and I am answering it."

"Are these ambassadors about to arrive?"

"Better still, they arrived this morning."

"Does any one know it?"

"They came incognito. Their formal arrival is planned for to-morrow afternoon, I believe, and you will see," said Marguerite, with a little satisfied air not wholly free from pedantry, "that what I have done this evening is quite Ciceronian. But let us drop these important matters and speak of what has happened to you."

"To me?"

"Yes."

"What has happened to me?"

"Ah! it is in vain you pretend to be brave, you look pale."

"Then it is from having slept too much. I am humbly sorry for it."

"Come, come, let us not play the braggart; I know every-thing."

"Have the kindness to inform me, then, my pearl, for I know nothing."

"Well, answer me frankly. What did the queen mother ask you?"

"Had she something to say to me?"

"What! Have you not seen her?"

"No."

"Nor King Charles?"

"No."

"Nor the King of Navarre?"

"No."

" But you have seen the Duc d'Alençon ? "

" Yes, I met him just now in the corridor."

" What did he say to you ? "

" That he had some orders to give me between nine and ten o'clock this evening."

" Nothing else ? "

" Nothing else."

" That is strange."

" But what is strange ? Tell me."

" That nothing has been said to you."

" What has happened ? "

" All day, unfortunately, you have been hanging over an abyss."

" I ? "

" Yes, you."

" Why ? "

" Well, listen. It seems that last night De Mouy was surprised in the apartments of the King of Navarre, who was to have been arrested. De Mouy killed three men, and escaped without anything about him having been recognized except the famous red cloak."

" Well ? "

" Well, this red cloak, which once deceived me, has thrown others besides myself off the track. You have been suspected and even accused of this triple murder. This morning they wanted to arrest, judge, and perhaps convict you. Who knows ? For in order to save yourself you would not have told where you were, would you ? "

" Tell where I was ? " cried La Mole; " compromise you, my beautiful queen ? Oh! you are right. I should have died singing, to spare your sweet eyes one tear."

" Alas! " said Marguerite, " my sweet eyes would have been filled with many, many tears."

" But what caused the great storm to subside ? "

" Guess."

" How can I tell ? "

" There was only one way to prove that you were not in the king's room."

" And that was " —

" To tell where you were."

" Well ? "

" Well, I told."

"UNFORTUNATE MAN!" SHE CRIED, HOLDING OUT THE PAPER.

"Whom did you tell?"

"My mother."

"And Queen Catharine"—

"Queen Catharine knows that I love you."

"Oh, madame! after having done so much for me, you can demand anything from your servant. Ah, Marguerite, truly, what you did was noble and beautiful. My life is yours, Marguerite."

"I hope so, for I have snatched it from those who wanted to take it from me. But now you are saved."

"And by you!" cried the young man; "by my adored queen!"

At that instant a sharp noise made them start. La Mole sprang back, filled with a vague terror. Marguerite uttered a cry, and stood with her eyes riveted on the broken glass of one of the window-panes.

Through this window a stone the size of an egg had entered and lay on the floor.

La Mole saw the broken pane, and realized the cause of the noise.

. "Who dared to do this?" he cried, springing to the window.

"One moment," said Marguerite. "It seems to me that something is tied around the stone."

"Yes," said La Mole, "it looks like a piece of paper."

Marguerite went to the strange projectile and removed the thin sheet which, folded like a narrow band, encircled the middle of the stone.

The paper was attached to a cord, which came through the broken window.

Marguerite unfolded the letter and read.

"Unfortunate man!" she cried, holding out the paper to La Mole, who stood as pale and motionless as a statue of Terror.

With a heart filled with gloomy forebodings he read these words:

"*They are waiting for Monsieur de la Mole, with long swords, in the corridor leading to the apartments of Monsieur d'Alençon. Perhaps he would prefer to escape by this window and join Monsieur de Mouy at Mantes*"—

"Well!" asked La Mole, after reading it, "are these swords longer than mine?"

"No, but there may be ten against one."

" Who is the friend who has sent us this note ? " asked La Mole.

Marguerite took it from the young man's hand and looked at it attentively.

" The King of Navarre's handwriting ! " she cried. " If he warns us, the danger is great. Flee, La Mole, flee, I beg you."

" How ? " asked La Mole.

" By this window. Does not the note refer to it ? "

" Command, my queen, and I will leap from the window to obey you, if I broke my head twenty times by the fall."

" Wait, wait," said Marguerite. " It seems to me that there is a weight attached to this cord."

" Let us see," said La Mole.

Both drew up the cord, and with indescribable joy saw a ladder of hair and silk at the end of it.

" Ah ! you are saved," cried Marguerite.

" It is a miracle of heaven ! "

" No, it is a gift from the King of Navarre."

" But suppose it were a snare ? " said La Mole. " If this ladder were to break under me ? Madame, did you not acknowledge your love for me to-day ? "

Marguerite, whose joy had dissipated her grief, became ashy pale.

" You are right," said she, " that is possible."

She started to the door.

" What are you going to do ? " cried La Mole.

" To find out if they are really waiting for you in the corridor."

" Never ! never ! For their anger to fall on you ? "

" What can they do to a daughter of France ? As a woman and a royal princess I am doubly inviolable."

The queen uttered these words with so much dignity that La Mole understood she ran no risk, and that he must let her do as she wished.

Marguerite put La Mole under the protection of Gillonne, leaving to him to decide, according to circumstances, whether to run or await her return, and started down the corridor. A side hall led to the library as well as to several reception-rooms, and at the end led to the apartments of the King, the queen mother, and to the small private stairway by which one reached the apartments of the Duc d'Alençon and Henry.

Although it was scarcely nine o'clock, all the lights were extinguished, and the corridor, except for the dim glimmer which came from the side hall, was quite dark. The Queen of Navarre advanced boldly. When she had gone about a third of the distance she heard whispering which sounded mysterious and startling from an evident effort made to suppress it. It ceased almost instantly, as if by order from some superior, and silence was restored. The light, dim as it was, seemed to grow less. Marguerite walked on directly into the face of the danger if danger there was. To all appearances she was calm, although her clinched hands indicated a violent nervous tension. As she approached, the intense silence increased, while a shadow like that of a hand obscured the wavering and uncertain light.

At the point where the transverse hall crossed the main corridor a man sprang in front of the queen, uncovered a red candlestick, and cried out:

"Here he is!"

Marguerite stood face to face with her brother Charles. Behind him, a silken cord in hand, was the Duc d'Alençon. At the rear, in the darkness, stood two figures side by side, reflecting no light other than that of the drawn swords which they held in their hands. Marguerite saw everything at a glance. Making a supreme effort, she said smilingly to Charles:

"You mean, here *she* is, sire!"

Charles recoiled. The others stood motionless.

"You, Margot!" said he. "Where are you going at this hour?"

"At this hour!" said Marguerite. "Is it so late?"

"I ask where you are going?"

"To find a book of Cicero's speeches, which I think I left at our mother's."

"Without a light?"

"I supposed the corridor was lighted."

"Do you come from your own apartments?"

"Yes."

"What are you doing this evening?"

"Preparing my address for the Polish ambassadors. Is there not a council to-morrow? and does not each one have to submit his address to your Majesty?"

"Have you not some one helping you with this work?"

Marguerite summoned all her strength.

"Yes, brother," said she, "Monsieur de la Mole. He is very learned."

"So much so," said the Duc d'Alençon, "that I asked him when he had finished with you, sister, to come and help me, for I am not as clever as you are."

"And were you waiting for him?" asked Marguerite as naturally as possible.

"Yes," said D'Alençon, impatiently.

"Then," said Marguerite, "I will send him to you, brother, for we have finished my work."

"But your book?" said Charles.

"I will have Gillonne get it."

The two brothers exchanged a sign.

"Go," said Charles, "and we will continue our round."

"Your round!" said Marguerite; "whom are you looking for?"

"The little red man," said Charles. "Do you not know that there is a little red man who is said to haunt the old Louvre? My brother D'Alençon claims to have seen him, and we are looking for him."

"Good luck to you," said Marguerite, and she turned round. Glancing behind her, she saw the four figures gather close to the wall as if in conference. In an instant she had reached her own door.

"Open, Gillonne," said she, "open."

Gillonne obeyed.

Marguerite sprang into the room and found La Mole waiting for her, calm and quiet, but with drawn sword.

"Flee," said she, "flee. Do not lose a second. They are waiting for you in the corridor to kill you."

"You command me to do this?" said La Mole.

"I command it. We must part in order to see each other again."

While Marguerite had been away La Mole had made sure of the ladder at the window. He now stepped out, but before placing his foot on the first round he tenderly kissed the queen's hand.

"If the ladder is a trap and I should perish, Marguerite, remember your promise."

"It was not a promise, La Mole, but an oath. Fear nothing. Adieu!"

And La Mole, thus encouraged, let himself slip down the ladder. At the same instant there was a knock at the door.

Marguerite watched La Mole's perilous descent and did not turn away from the window until she was sure he had reached the ground in safety.

" Madame," said Gillonne, " madame ! "

" Well ? " asked Marguerite.

" The King is knocking at the door."

" Open it."

Gillonne did so.

The four princes, impatient at waiting, no doubt, stood on the threshold.

Charles entered.

Marguerite came forward, a smile on her lips.

The King cast a rapid glance around.

" Whom are you looking for, brother ? " asked Marguerite.

" Why," said Charles, " I am looking — I am looking — why, the devil ! I am looking for Monsieur de la Mole."

" Monsieur de la Mole ! "

" Yes; where is he ? "

Marguerite took her brother by the hand and led him to the window.

Just then two horsemen were seen galloping away, around the wooden tower. One of them unfastened his white satin scarf and waved it in the darkness, as a sign of adieu. The two men were La Mole and Orthon.

Marguerite pointed them out to Charles.

" Well ! " said the King, " what does this mean ? "

" It means," replied Marguerite, " that Monsieur le Duc d'Alençon may put his cord back into his pocket, and that Messieurs d'Anjou and de Guise may sheathe their swords, for Monsieur de la Mole will not pass through the corridor again to-night."

CHAPTER XL.

THE ATRIDES.

SINCE his return to Paris, Henry of Anjou had not seen his mother Catharine alone, and, as every one knows, he was her favorite son.

This visit was not merely for the sake of etiquette, nor the carrying out of a painful ceremony, but the accomplishment of a very sweet duty for this son who, if he did not love his mother, was at least sure of being tenderly loved by her.

Catharine loved this son best either because of his bravery, his beauty, — for besides the mother, there was the woman in Catharine,— or because, according to some scandalous chronicles, Henry of Anjou reminded the Florentine of a certain happy epoch of secret love.

Catharine alone knew of the return of the Duc d'Anjou to Paris. Charles IX. would have been ignorant of it had not chance led him to the Hôtel de Condé just as his brother was leaving it. Charles had not expected him until the following day, and Henry of Anjou had hoped to conceal from him the two motives which had hastened his arrival by a day, namely, his visit to the beautiful Marie of Cleves, princess of Condé, and his conference with the Polish ambassadors.

It was this last reason, of the object of which Charles was uncertain, which the Duc d'Anjou had to explain to his mother. And the reader, ignorant on this point as was Henry of Navarre, will profit by the explanation.

When the Duc d'Anjou, so long expected, entered his mother's rooms, Catharine, usually so cold and formal, and who since the departure of her favorite son had embraced with effusion no one but Coligny, who was to be assassinated the following day, opened her arms to the child of her love, and pressed him to her heart with a burst of maternal affection most surprising in a heart already long grown cold.

Then pushing him from her she gazed at him and again drew him into her arms.

"Ah, madame," said he, "since Heaven grants me the privilege of embracing my mother in private, console me, for I am the most wretched man alive."

" Oh, my God ! my beloved child," cried Catharine, " what has happened to you ? "

" Nothing which you do not know, mother. I am in love. I am loved ; but it is this very love which is the cause of my unhappiness."

" Tell me about it, my son," said Catharine.

" Well, mother, — these ambassadors, — this departure " —

" Yes," said Catharine, " the ambassadors have arrived ; the departure is near at hand."

" It need not be near at hand, mother, but my brother hastens it. He detests me. I am in his way, and he wants to rid himself of me."

Catharine smiled.

" By giving you a throne, poor, unhappy crowned head ! "

" Oh, no, mother," said Henry in agony, " I do not wish to go away. I, a son of France, brought up in the refinement of polite society, near the best of mothers, loved by one of the dearest women in the world, must I go among snows, to the ends of the earth, to die by inches among those rough people who are intoxicated from morning until night, and who gauge the capacity of their king by that of a cask, according to what he can hold ? No, mother, I do not want to go ; I should die ! "

" Come, Henry," said Catharine, pressing her son's hands, " come, is that the real reason ? "

Henry's eyes fell, as though even to his mother he did not dare to confess what was in his heart.

" Is there no other reason ? " asked Catharine ; " less romantic, but more rational, more political ? "

" Mother, it is not my fault if this thought comes to me, and takes stronger hold of me, perhaps, than it should ; but did not you yourself tell me that the horoscope of my brother Charles prophesied that he would die young ? "

" Yes," said Catharine, " but a horoscope may lie, my son. Indeed, I myself hope that all horoscopes are not true."

" But his horoscope said this, did it not ? "

" His horoscope spoke of a quarter of a century ; but it did not say whether it referred to his life or his reign."

" Well, mother, bring it about so that I can stay. My brother is almost twenty-four. In one year the question will be settled."

Catharine pondered deeply.

"Yes," said she; "it would certainly be better if it could be so arranged."

"Oh, imagine my despair, mother," cried Henry, "if I were to exchange the crown of France for that of Poland! My being tormented there with the idea that I might be reigning in the Louvre in the midst of this elegant and lettered court, near the best mother in the world, whose advice would spare me half my work and fatigue, who, accustomed to bearing, with my father, a portion of the burden of the State, would like to bear it with me too! Ah, mother, I should have been a great king!"

"There! there! dear child," said Catharine, to whom this outlook had always been a very sweet hope, "there! do not despair. Have you thought of any way of arranging the matter?"

"Oh, yes, certainly, and that is why I came back two or three days before I was expected, letting my brother Charles suppose that it was on account of Madame de Condé. Then I have been with De Lasco, the chief ambassador. I became acquainted with him, and did all I could in that first interview to make him hate me. I hope I have succeeded."

"Ah, my dear child," said Catharine, "that is wrong. You must place the interest of France above your petty dislikes."

"Mother, in case any accident happened to my brother, would it be to the interest of France for the Duc d'Alençon or the King of Navarre to reign?"

"Oh! the King of Navarre, never, never!" murmured Catharine, letting anxiety cover her face with that veil of care which spread over it every time this question arose.

"Faith," continued Henry, "my brother D'Alençon is not worth much more, and is no fonder of you."

"Well," said Catharine, "what did Lasco say?"

"Even Lasco hesitated when I urged him to seek an audience. Oh, if he could write to Poland and annul this election!"

"Folly, my son, madness! What a Diet has consecrated is sacred."

"But, mother, could not these Poles be prevailed on to accept my brother in my stead?"

"It would be difficult, if not impossible," said Catharine.

"Never mind, try, make the attempt, speak to the King, mother. Ascribe everything to my love for Madame de

Condé; say that I am mad over her, that I am losing my mind. He saw me coming out of the prince's hôtel with De Guise, who did everything for me a friend could do."

" Yes, in order to help the League. You do not see this, but I do."

" Yes, mother, yes ; but meanwhile I am making use of him. Should we not be glad when a man serves us while serving himself ? "

" And what did the King say when he met you ? "

" He apparently believed what I told him, that love alone had brought me back to Paris."

" But did he ask you what you did the rest of the night ? "

" Yes, mother ; but I had supper at Nantouillet's, where I made a frightful riot, so that the report of it might get abroad and deceive the King as to where I was."

" Then he is ignorant of your visit to Lasco ? "

" Absolutely."

" Good, so much the better. I will try to influence him in your favor, dear child. But you know no influence makes any impression on his coarse nature."

" Oh, mother, mother, what happiness if I could stay ! I would love you even more than I do now if that were possible ! "

" If you stay you will be sent to war."

" Oh, never mind ! if only I do not have to leave France."

" You will be killed."

" Mother, one does not die from blows ; one dies from grief, from meanness. But Charles will not let me remain ; he hates me."

" He is jealous of you, my beautiful conqueror, that is well known. Why are you so brave and so fortunate ? Why, at scarcely twenty years of age, have you won battles like Alexander or Cæsar ? But, in the meantime, do not let your wishes be known to any one ; pretend to be resigned, pay your court to the King. To-day there is a private council to read and discuss the speeches which are to be made at the ceremony. Act like the King of Poland, and leave the rest to me. By the way, how about your expedition of last night ? "

" It failed, mother. The gallant was warned and escaped by the window."

" Well," said Catharine, "some day I shall know who this evil genius is who upsets all my plans in this way. Meanwhile I suspect and — let him beware ! "

" So, mother " — said the Duc d'Anjou.

" Let me manage this affair."

She kissed Henry tenderly on his eyes and pushed him from the room.

Before long the princes of her household arrived at the rooms of the queen.   Charles was in a good humor, for the cleverness of his sister Margot had pleased rather than vexed him.   Moreover, he had nothing against La Mole, and he had waited for him somewhat eagerly in the corridor merely because it was a kind of hunt.

D'Alençon, on the contrary, was greatly preoccupied.   The repulsion he had always felt for La Mole had turned into hate the instant he knew that La Mole was loved by his sister.

Marguerite possessed both a dreamy mind and a quick eye. She had to remember as well as to watch.

The Polish deputies had sent a copy of the speeches which they were to make.

Marguerite, to whom no more mention had been made of the affair of the previous evening than as if it had never occurred, read the speeches, and, except Charles, every one discussed what he would answer.   Charles let Marguerite reply as she pleased.   As far as D'Alençon was concerned he was very particular as to the choice of terms; but as to the discourse of Henry of Anjou he seemed determined to attack it, and made numerous corrections.

This council, without being in any way decisive, had greatly embittered the feelings of those present.

Henry of Anjou, who had to rewrite nearly all his discourse, withdrew to begin the task.

Marguerite, who had not heard of the King of Navarre since the injury he had given to her window-pane, returned to her rooms, hoping to find him there.

D'Alençon, who had read hesitation in the eyes of his brother of Anjou, and who had surprised a meaning glance between him and his mother, retired to ponder on what he regarded as a fresh plot.   Charles was about to go to his workshop to finish a boar-spear he was making for himself when Catharine stopped him.

The King, who suspected that he was to meet some opposition to his will, paused and looked at his mother closely.

" Well," he said, " what now ? "

" A final word, sire, which we forgot, and yet it is of much importance: what day shall we decide on for the public reception?"

"Ah, that is true," said the King, seating himself again. "Well, what day would suit you?"

"I thought," replied Catharine, "from your Majesty's silence and apparent forgetfulness, that there was some deep-laid plan."

"No," said Charles; "why so, mother?"

"Because," added Catharine, very gently, "it seems to me, my son, that these Poles should not see us so eager after their crown."

"On the contrary, mother," said Charles, "it is they who are in haste. They have come from Varsovia by forced marches. Honor for honor, courtesy for courtesy."

"Your Majesty may be right in one sense; I am not curious. So your idea is that the public reception should be held soon?"

"Faith, yes, mother; is this not your idea too?"

"You know that my ideas are only such as can further your glory. I will tell you, therefore, that by this haste I fear you will be accused of profiting very quickly by this opportunity to relieve the house of France of the burdens your brother imposes on it, but which he certainly returns in glory and devotion."

"Mother," said Charles, "on his departure from France I will endow my brother so richly that no one will ever dare to think what you fear may be said."

"Well," said Catharine, "I surrender, since you have such a ready reply to each of my objections. But to receive this warlike people, who judge of the power of the states by exterior signs, you must have a considerable array of troops, and I do not think there are enough yet assembled in the Isle de France."

"Pardon me, mother. I have foreseen this event, and am prepared for it. I have recalled two battalions from Normandy and one from Guyenne; my company of archers arrived yesterday from Brittany; the light horse, scattered throughout Lorraine, will be in Paris in the course of the day; and while it is supposed that I have scarcely four regiments at my disposition, I have twenty thousand men ready to appear."

"Ah, ah!" said Catharine, surprised. "In that case only one thing is lacking, but that can be procured."

" What is that ? "

" Money. I believe that you are not furnished with an over-supply."

" On the contrary, madame, on the contrary," said Charles IX., " I have fourteen hundred thousand crowns in the Bastille; my private estates have yielded me during the last few days eight hundred thousand crowns, which I have put in my cellar in the Louvre, and in case of need Nantouillet holds three hundred thousand crowns at my disposal."

Catharine shivered. Until then she had known Charles to be violent and passionate, but never provident.

" Well," said she, " your Majesty thinks of everything. That is fine; and provided the tailors, the embroiderers, and the jewellers make haste, your Majesty will be in a position to hold this audience within six weeks."

" Six weeks ! " exclaimed Charles. " Mother, the tailors, the embroiderers, and the jewellers have been at work ever since we heard of my brother's nomination. As a matter of fact, everything could be ready to-day, but, at the latest, it will take only three or four days."

" Oh ! " murmured Catharine; " you are in greater haste than I supposed, my son."

" Honor for honor, I told you."

" Well, is it this honor done to the house of France which flatters you ? "

" Certainly."

" And is your chief desire to see a son of France on the throne of Poland ? "

" Exactly."

" Then it is the event, the fact, and not the man, which is of interest to you, and whoever reigns there " —

" No, no, mother, by Heaven ! Let us keep to the point ! The Poles have made a good choice. They are a skilful and strong people ! A military people, a nation of soldiers, they choose a captain for their ruler. That is logical, plague it ! D'Anjou is just the man for them. The hero of Jarnac and Montcontour fits them like a glove. Whom would you have me send them ? D'Alençon ? a coward ! He would give them a fine idea of the Valois ! — D'Alençon ! He would run at the first bullet that whistled by his ears, while Henry of Anjou is a fighter. Yes ! his sword always in his hand, he is ever pushing forward, on foot or horseback ! — forward ! thrust !

overpower! kill! Ah! my brother of Anjou is a man, a valiant soldier, who will lead them to battle from morning until night, from one year's end to the next. He is not a hard drinker, it is true; but he will kill in cold blood. That is all. This dear Henry will be in his element; there! quick! quick! to battle! Sound the trumpet and the drum! Long live the king! Long live the conqueror! Long live the general! He will be proclaimed *imperator* three times a year. That will be fine for the house of France, and for the honor of the Valois; he may be killed, but, by Heaven, it will be a glorious death!"

Catharine shuddered. Her eyes flashed fire.

" Say that you wish to send Henry of Anjou away from you," she cried, " say that you do not love your brother!"

" Ah! ah! ah!" cried Charles, bursting into a nervous laugh, " you have guessed, have you, that I want to send him away? You have guessed that I do not love him? And when did you reach this conclusion? Come! Love my brother! Why should I love him? Ah! ah! ah! Do you want to make me laugh?"

As he spoke, his pale cheeks grew flushed with a feverish glow.

" Does he love me? Do you love me? Has any one, except my dogs, and Marie Touchet, and my nurse, ever loved me? No! I do not love my brother, I love only myself. Do you hear? And I shall not prevent my brother from doing as I do."

" Sire," said Catharine, growing excited on her part, " since you have opened your heart to me I must open mine to you. You are acting like a weak king, like an ill-advised monarch; you are sending away your second brother, the natural support of the throne, who is in every way worthy to succeed you if any accident happened, in which case your crown would be left in jeopardy. As you said, D'Alençon is young, incapable, weak, more than weak, cowardly! And the Béarnais rises up in the background, you understand?"

" Well, the devil!" exclaimed Charles, " what does it matter to me what happens when I am dead? The Béarnais rises behind my brother, you say! By Heaven! so much the better! I said that I loved no one — I was mistaken, I love Henriot. Yes, I love this good Henriot. He has a frank manner, a warm handshake, while I see nothing but false looks around me, and touch only icy hands. He is incapable of treason towards me, I swear. Besides, I owe him amends, poor boy! His mother was poisoned by some members of my family, I am told. Moreover, I am well. But if I were to be taken ill, I would call him, I should want him to stay with me, I would take nothing except from him, and when I died I would make him King of France and of Navarre. And by Heaven! instead of laughing at my death as my brothers would do, he would weep, or at least he would pretend to weep."

Had a thunderbolt fallen at Catharine's feet she would have been less startled than at these words. She stood speechless, gazing at Charles with haggard eyes. Then at the end of a few moments:

"Henry of Navarre!" she cried, "Henry of Navarre King of France to the detriment of my children! Ah! Holy Virgin! we shall see! So this is why you wish to send away my son?"

"Your son — and what am I, then? the son of a wolf, like Romulus?" cried Charles, trembling with anger, his eyes shining as though they were on fire. "Your son, you are right; the King of France is not your son, the King of France has no brothers, the King of France has no mother, the King of France has only subjects. The King of France has no need of feelings, he has wishes. He can get on without being loved, but he shall be obeyed."

"Sire, you have misunderstood my words. I called my son the one who was going to leave me. I love him better just now because just now he is the one I am most afraid I shall lose. Is it a crime for a mother to wish that her child should not leave her?"

"And I, I tell you that he shall leave you. I tell you that he shall leave France, that he shall go to Poland, and within two days, too, and if you add one word he shall go to-morrow. Moreover, if you do not smooth your brow, if you do not take that threatening look from your eyes, I will strangle him this evening, as yesterday you yourself would have strangled your daughter's lover. Only I shall not fail, as we failed in regard to La Mole."

At the first threat Catharine's head fell; but she raised it again almost immediately.

"Ah, poor child!" said she, "your brother would kill you. But do not fear, your mother will protect you."

"Ah, you defy me!" cried Charles. "Well! by the blood of Christ, he shall die, not this evening, not soon, but this very instant. Ah, a weapon! a dagger! a knife! Ah!"

Having looked around in vain for what he wanted, Charles perceived the little dagger his mother always wore at her belt, sprang toward it, snatched it from its shagreen case encrusted with silver, and rushed from the room to strike down Henry of Anjou wherever he might meet him. But on reaching the hall, his strength, excited beyond human endurance, suddenly left him. He put out his arm, dropped the sharp weapon, which stuck point downwards into the wood, uttered a piercing cry, sank down, and rolled over on the floor.

At the same instant a quantity of blood spurted forth from his mouth and nose.

"Jesus!" said he. "They kill me! Help! help!"

Catharine, who had followed, saw him fall. For one instant she stood motionless, watching him. Then recollecting herself, not because of any maternal affection, but because of the awkwardness of the situation, she called out:

"The King is ill! Help! help!"

At the cry a crowd of servants, officers, and courtiers gathered around the young King. But ahead of them all a woman rushed out, pushed aside the others, and raised Charles, who had grown as pale as death.

"They kill me, nurse, they kill me," murmured the King, covered with perspiration and blood.

"They kill you, my Charles?" cried the good woman, glancing at the group of faces with a look which reached even Catharine. "Who kills you?"

Charles heaved a feeble sigh, and fainted.

"Ah!" said the physician, Ambroise Paré, who was summoned at once, "ah! the King is very ill!"

"Now, from necessity or compulsion," said the implacable Catharine to herself, "he will have to grant a delay."

Whereupon she left the King to join her second son, who was in the oratory, anxiously waiting to hear the result of an interview which was of such importance to him.

CHAPTER XLI.

THE HOROSCOPE.

On leaving the oratory, in which she had just informed Henry all that had occurred, Catharine found Réné in her chamber. It was the first time that the queen and the astrologer had seen each other since the visit the queen had made to his shop at the Pont Saint Michel. But the previous evening she had written him, and Réné had brought the answer to her note in person.

"Well," said the queen, "have you seen him?"

"Yes."

"How is he?"

"Somewhat better."

"Can he speak?"

"No, the sword traversed his larynx."

"I told you in that case to have him write."

"I tried. He collected all his strength, but his hand could trace only two letters. They are almost illegible. Then he fainted. The jugular vein was cut and the blood he lost has taken away all his strength."

"Have you seen the letters?"

"Here they are."

Réné drew a paper from his pocket and handed it to Catharine, who hastily unfolded it.

"An *m* and an *o*," said she. "Could it have been La Mole, and was all that acting of Marguerite done to throw me off the track?"

"Madame," said Réné, "if I dared to express my opinion in a matter about which your majesty hesitates to give yours I should say that I believe Monsieur de la Mole is too much in love to be seriously interested in politics."

"You think so?"

"Yes, and above all too much in love with the Queen of Navarre to serve the King very devotedly; for there is no real love without jealousy."

"You think that he is very much in love, then?"

"I am sure of it."

"Has he been to you?"

"Yes."

" Did he ask you for some potion or philter ? "

" No, we kept to the wax figure."

" Pierced to the heart ? "

" To the heart."

" And this figure still exists ? "

" Yes."

" Have you it ? "

" It is in my rooms."

" It would be strange," said Catharine, " if these cabalistic preparations really had the power attributed to them."

" Your majesty is a better judge of that than I."

" Is the Queen of Navarre in love with Monsieur de la Mole ? "

" She loves him enough to ruin herself for him. Yesterday she saved him from death at the risk of her honor and her life. You see, madame, and yet you still doubt."

" Doubt what ? "

" Science."

" Science also deceives me," said Catharine, looking steadily at Réné, who bore her gaze without flinching.

" About what ? "

" Oh ! you know what I mean; unless, of course, it was the scholar and not science."

" I do not know what you mean, madame," replied the Florentine.

" Réné, have your perfumes lost their odor ? "

" No, madame, not when I use them ; but it is possible that in passing through the hands of others " —

Catharine smiled and shook her head.

" Your opiate has done wonders, Réné," said she; " Madame de Sauve's lips are fresher and rosier than ever."

" It is not my opiate that is responsible for that, madame. The Baroness de Sauve, using the privilege of every pretty woman to be capricious, has said nothing more to me about this opiate, and after the suggestion from your majesty I thought it best to send her no more of it. So that all the boxes are still in my house just as you left them, with the exception of one which disappeared, I know not how or why."

" That is well, Réné," said Catharine; " perhaps later we may return to this. In the meantime, let us speak of the other matter."

" I am all attention, madame."

" What is necessary to gain an idea of the length of any one's life ? "

" In the first place to know the day of his birth, his age, and under what condition he first saw light."

" And then ? "

" To have some of his blood and a lock of his hair."

" If I bring you some of his blood and a lock of his hair, if I tell you the circumstance connected with his birth, the time, and his present age, will you tell me the probable date of his death ? "

" Yes, to within a few days."

" Very well ; I have a lock of his hair and will get some of his blood."

" Was he born during the day or night ? "

" At twenty-three minutes past five in the afternoon."

" Be at my room at five o'clock to-morrow. The experiment must be made at the hour of his birth."

" Very well," said Catharine, " *we* will be there."

Réné bowed, and withdrew without apparently noticing the " *we* will be there," which, however, contrary to her usual habit, indicated that Catharine would not go alone.

The following morning at dawn Catharine went to her son's apartments. At midnight she had sent to inquire after him, and had been told that Maître Ambroise Paré was with him, ready to bleed him if the nervous troubles continued.

Still starting up from his sleep, and still pale from loss of blood, Charles dozed on the shoulder of his faithful nurse, who leaning against the bed had not moved for three hours for fear of waking her dear child.

A slight foam appeared from time to time on the lips of the sick man, and the nurse wiped it off with a fine embroidered linen handkerchief. On the bed lay another handkerchief covered with great spots of blood.

For an instant Catharine thought she would take possession of the handkerchief ; but she feared that this blood mixed with the saliva would be weak, and would not be efficacious. She asked the nurse if the doctor had bled her son as he had said he would do. The nurse answered " Yes " and that the flow of blood had been so great that Charles had fainted twice. The queen mother, who, like all princesses in those days, had some knowledge of medicine, asked to see the blood. Nothing was easier to do, as the physician had ordered that the blood be kept in order that he might examine it. It was in a basin in an adjoining closet. Catharine went in to look at it, poured some into a small bottle which she had brought for this purpose; and then came back, hiding in her pocket her fingers, the tips of which otherwise would have betrayed her.

Just as she came back from the closet Charles opened his eyes and saw his mother. Then remembering as in a dream all his bitter thoughts:

" Ah ! is it you, madame ? " said he. " Well, say to your well loved son, to your Henry of Anjou, that it shall be to-morrow."

" My dear Charles," said Catharine, " it shall be just when you please. Be quiet now and go to sleep."

As if yielding to this advice Charles closed his eyes; and Catharine, who had spoken to him as one does to calm a sick person or a child, left the room. But when he heard the door close Charles suddenly sat up, and in a voice still weak from suffering, said:

" My chancellor! The seals! the court!—send for them all."

The nurse, with gentle insistence, laid the head of the King back on her shoulder, and in order to put him to sleep strove to rock him as she would have done a child.

" No, no, nurse, I cannot sleep any more. Call my attendants. I must work this morning."

When Charles spoke in that way he was obeyed; and even the nurse, in spite of the privileges allowed her by her foster-child, dared not disobey. She sent for those whom the King wanted, and the council was planned, not for the next day, which was out of the question, but for five days from then.

At the hour agreed on, that is, at five o'clock, the queen mother and the Duc d'Anjou repaired to the rooms of Réné, who, expecting their visit, had everything ready for the mysterious seance. In the room to the right, that is, in the chamber of sacrifices, a steel blade was heating over a glowing brazier. From its fanciful arabesques this blade was intended to represent the events of the destiny about which the oracle was to be consulted. On the altar lay the Book of Fate, and during the night, which had been very clear, Réné had studied the course and the position of the stars.

Henry of Anjou entered first. He wore a wig, a mask concealed his face, and a long cloak hid his figure. His mother followed. Had she not known beforehand that the man who had preceded her was her son she never would have recognized him. Catharine removed her mask; the Duc d'Anjou kept his on.

"Did you make any observations last night?" asked Catharine.

"Yes, madame," said Réné; "and the answer of the stars has already told me the past. The one you wish to know about, like every one born under the sign of the Cancer, has a warm heart and great pride. He is powerful. He has lived nearly a quarter of a century. He has until now had glory and wealth. Is this so, madame?"

"Possibly," said Catharine.

"Have you a lock of his hair, and some of his blood?"

"Yes."

Catharine handed to the necromancer a lock of fair hair and a small bottle filled with blood.

Réné took the flask, shook it thoroughly, so that the fibrine and water would mix, and poured a large drop of it on the glowing steel. The living liquid boiled for an instant, and then spread out into fantastic figures.

"Oh, madame," cried Réné, "I see him twisting in awful agony. Hear how he groans, how he calls for help! Do you see how everything around him becomes blood? Do you see how about his death-bed great combats are taking place? See, here are the lances; and look, there are the swords!"

"Will it be long before this happens?" asked Catharine, trembling from an indescribable emotion and laying her hand on that of Henry of Anjou, who in his eager curiosity was leaning over the brazier.

Réné approached the altar and repeated a cabalistic prayer, putting such energy and conviction into the act that the veins of his temples swelled, and caused the prophetic convulsions and nervous twinges from which the ancient priestesses suffered before their tripods, and even on their death-beds.

At length he rose and announced that everything was ready, took the flask, still three-quarters full, in one hand, and in the other the lock of hair. Then telling Catharine to open the book at random, and to read the first words she looked at, he poured the rest of the blood on the steel blade, and threw the hair into the brazier, pronouncing a cabalistic sentence composed of Hebrew words which he himself did not understand.

Instantly the Duc d'Anjou and Catharine saw a white figure appear on the sword like that of a corpse wrapped in his shroud. Another figure, which seemed that of a woman, was leaning over the first.

At the same time the hair caught fire and threw out a single flame, clear, swift, and barbed like a fiery tongue.

"One year," cried Réné, " scarcely one year, and this man shall die. A woman alone shall weep for him. But no, there at the end of the sword is another woman, with a child in her arms."

Catharine looked at her son, and, mother though she was, seemed to ask him who these two women were.

But Réné had scarcely finished speaking before the steel became white and everything gradually disappeared from its surface. Then Catharine opened the book and read the following lines in a voice which, in spite of her effort at control, she could not keep from shaking :

> "' *Ains a peri cil que l'on redoutoit,*
> *Plus tôt, trop tôt, si prudence n'étoit.*' " [1]

A deep silence reigned for some moments.

" For the one whom you know," asked Catharine, " what are the signs for this month ? "

"As favorable as ever, madame ; unless Providence interferes with his destiny he will be fortunate. And yet " —

" And yet what ? "

"One of the stars in his pleiad was covered with a black cloud while I made my observations."

"Ah!" exclaimed Catharine, "a black cloud—there is some hope, then ? "

"Of whom are you speaking, madame ? " asked the Duc d'Anjou.

Catharine drew her son away from the light of the brazier and spoke to him in a low tone.

Meanwhile Réné knelt down, and in the glow of the flame poured into his hand the last drop of blood which had remained in the bottom of the flask.

" Strange contradiction," said he, " which proves how little to be depended on is the evidence of simple science practised by ordinary men ! To any one but myself, a physician, a

---

[1] " Thus had perished one who was feared,
Sooner, too soon, would he have died, had it not been for prudence."

scholar, even for Maître Ambroise Paré, this blood would seem so pure, so healthy, so full of life and animal spirits, that it would promise long years of life; and yet all this vigor will soon disappear, all this life will be extinct within a year!"

Catharine and Henry of Anjou had turned round and were listening.

The eyes of the prince glowed through his mask.

"Ah!" continued Réné, "the present alone is known to ordinary mortals; while to us the past and the future are known."

"So," continued Catharine, "you still think he will die within the year?"

"As surely as we are three living persons who some day will rest in our coffins."

"Yet you said that the blood was pure and healthy, and that it indicated a long life."

"Yes, if things followed their natural course. But might not an accident" —

"Ah, yes, do you hear?" said Catharine to Henry, "an accident" —

"Alas!" said the latter, "all the more reason for my staying."

"Oh, think no more about that: it is not possible."

Then turning to Réné:

"Thanks," said the young man, disguising his voice, "thanks; take this purse."

"Come, *count*," said Catharine, intentionally giving her son this title to throw Réné off the track.

They left.

"Oh, mother, you see," said Henry, "an accident — and if an accident should happen, I shall not be on hand; I shall be four hundred leagues from you"—

"Four hundred leagues are accomplished in eight days, my son."

"Yes; but how do I know whether those Poles will let me come back? If I could only wait, mother!"

"Who knows?" said Catharine; "might not this accident of which Réné speaks be the one which since yesterday has laid the King on a bed of pain? Listen, return by yourself, my child. I shall go back by the private door of the monastery of the Augustines. My suite is waiting for me in this convent. Go, now, Henry, go, and keep from irritating your brother in case you see him."

CHAPTER XLII.

CONFIDENCES.

THE first thing the Duc d'Anjou heard on arriving at the Louvre was that the formal reception of the ambassadors was arranged for the fifth day from that. The tailors and the jewellers were waiting for the prince with magnificent clothes and superb jewels which the King had ordered for him.

While the duke tried them on with an anger which brought the tears to his eyes, Henry of Navarre was very gay in a magnificent collar of emeralds, a sword with a gold handle, and a precious ring which Charles had sent him that morning.

D'Alençon had just received a letter and had shut himself up in his own room to read it.

As to Coconnas, he was searching every corner of the Louvre for his friend.

In fact, as may easily be imagined, he had been somewhat surprised at not seeing La Mole return that night, and by morning had begun to feel some anxiety.

Consequently he had started out to find his friend. He began his search at the Hôtel de la Belle Étoile, went from there to the Rue Cloche Percée, from the Rue Cloche Percée to the Rue Tizon, from there to the Pont Saint Michel, and finally from the Pont Saint Michel to the Louvre. This search, so far as those who had been questioned were concerned, had been carried on in a way so original and exacting (which may easily be believed when one realizes the eccentric character of Coconnas) that it had caused some explanations between him and three courtiers. These explanations had ended, as was the fashion of the times, on the ground. In these encounters Coconnas had been as conscientious as he usually was in affairs of that kind, and had killed the first man and wounded the two others, saying:

" Poor La Mole, he knew Latin so well ! "

The last victim, who was the Baron de Boissey, said as he fell:

" Oh, for the love of Heaven, Coconnas, do vary a little and at least say that he knew Greek ! "

At last the report of the adventure in the corridor leaked out. Coconnas was heartbroken over it; for an instant he thought that all these kings and princes had killed his friend and thrown him into some dungeon.

He learned that D'Alençon had been of the party; and over-looking the majesty which surrounded a prince of the blood, he went to him and demanded an explanation as he would have done of a simple gentleman.

At first D'Alençon was inclined to thrust out of the door the impertinent fellow who came and asked for an account of his actions. But Coconnas spoke so curtly, his eyes flashed with such brightness, and the affair of the three duels in less than twenty-four hours had raised the Piedmontese so high, that D'Alençon reflected, and instead of yielding to his first inclination, he answered the gentleman with a charming smile:

"My dear Coconnas, it is true that the King was furious at receiving a silver bowl on his shoulder, that the Duc d'Anjou was vexed at being hit on the head by some orange marmalade, and the Duc de Guise humiliated at having the breath knocked out of him by a haunch of venison, and so they were all determined to kill Monsieur de la Mole. But a friend of your friend's turned aside the blow. The party therefore failed in their attempt. I give you my word as prince."

"Ah!" said Coconnas, breathing as hard as a pair of bellows. "By Heaven, monseigneur, this is good news, and I should like to know this friend to show him my gratitude."

Monsieur d'Alençon made no reply, but smiled more pleasantly than he had yet done, implying to Coconnas that this friend was none other than the prince himself.

"Well, monseigneur!" said Coconnas, "since you have gone so far as to tell me the beginning of the story, crown your kindness by finishing it. They tried to kill him, but failed, you say. Well, what happened then? I am brave and can bear the news. Have they thrown him into some dungeon? So much the better. It will make him more careful in future. He never would listen to my advice; besides, we can get him out, by Heaven! Stone does not baffle every one."

D'Alençon shook his head.

"The worst of all this, my brave Coconnas," said he, "is that your friend disappeared after the affair, and no one knows where he went."

"By Heaven!" cried the Piedmontese, again growing pale, "had he gone to hell I should at least have known where he is."

"Listen," said D'Alençon, who, although for different reasons, was as anxious as Coconnas to know La Mole's whereabouts, "I will give you the advice of a friend."

"Give it, my lord," said Coconnas, eagerly.

"Go to Queen Marguerite. She must know what has become of the friend you mourn."

"I will confess to your highness," said Coconnas, "that I had thought of going to her, but I scarcely dared. Madame Marguerite has a way of making me feel somewhat uncomfortable at times, and besides this, I feared that I might find her in tears. But since your highness assures me that La Mole is not dead and that her majesty knows where he is I will take heart and go to her."

"Do so, my friend," said François. "And when you find out where La Mole is, let me know, for really I am as anxious as you are. But remember one thing, Coconnas"—

"What?"

"Do not say you have come at my suggestion, for if you do you will learn nothing."

"Monseigneur," said Coconnas, "since your highness recommends secrecy on this point, I shall be as silent as a tench or as the queen mother."

"What a kind, good, generous prince he is!" murmured Coconnas as he set out to find the Queen of Navarre.

Marguerite was expecting Coconnas, for the report of his despair had reached her, and on hearing by what exploits his grief had showed itself she almost forgave him for his somewhat rude treatment of her friend Madame la Duchesse de Nevers, to whom he had not spoken for two or three days, owing to some misunderstanding between them. Therefore as soon as he was announced to the queen he was admitted.

Coconnas entered the room, unable to overcome the constraint which he had mentioned to D'Alençon, and which he had always felt in the presence of the queen. It was caused more by her superior intellect than by her rank. But Marguerite received him with a smile which at once put him at his ease.

"Ah, madame," said he, "give me back my friend, I beg you, or at least tell me what has become of him, for without him I cannot live. Imagine Euryalus without Nisus, Damon without Pythias, or Orestes without Pylades, and pity my grief for the sake of one of the heroes I have just mentioned, whose heart, I swear, was no more tender than mine."

Marguerite smiled, and having made Coconnas promise not to reveal the secret, she told him of La Mole's escape from the window. As to his hiding-place, insistent as were the prayers of the Piedmontese, she preserved the strictest silence. This only half satisfied Coconnas, so he resorted to diplomatic speeches of the highest order.

The result was that Marguerite saw clearly that the Duc d'Alençon was partly the cause of the courtier's great desire to know what had become of La Mole.

"Well," said the queen, "if you must know something definite about your friend, ask King Henry of Navarre. He alone has the right to speak. As to me, all I can tell you is that the friend for whom you are searching is alive, and you may believe what I say."

"I believe one thing still more, madame," replied Coconnas; "that is, that your beautiful eyes have not wept."

Thereupon, thinking that there was nothing to add to a remark which had the double advantage of expressing his thought as well as the high opinion he had of La Mole, Coconnas withdrew, pondering on a reconciliation with Madame de Nevers, not on her account, but in order that he might find out from her what he had been unable to learn from Marguerite.

Deep griefs are abnormal conditions in which the mind shakes off the yoke as soon as possible. The thought of leaving Marguerite had at first broken La Mole's heart, and it was in order to save the reputation of the queen rather than to preserve his own life that he had consented to run away.

Therefore, the following evening he returned to Paris to see Marguerite from her balcony. As if instinct told her of the young man's plan, the queen spent the whole evening at her window. The result was that the lovers met again with the indescribable delight which accompanies forbidden pleasures. More than this, the melancholy and romantic temperament of La Mole found a certain charm in the situation. But a man really in love is happy only for the time being, while he sees or is with the woman he loves. After he has left her he suffers. Anxious to see Marguerite again, La Mole set himself busily to work to bring about the event which would make it possible for him to be with her; namely, the flight of the King of Navarre.

Marguerite on her part willingly gave herself up to the hap-

piness of being loved with so pure a devotion. Often she was
angry with herself for what she regarded as a weakness. Her
strong mind despised the poverty of ordinary love, insensible
to the details which for tender souls make it the sweetest, the
most delicate, and the most desirable of all pleasures. So she
felt that the days, if not happily filled, were at least happily
ended. When, at about nine o'clock every evening, she stepped
out on her balcony in a white dressing-gown, she perceived
in the darkness of the quay a horseman whose hand was raised
first to his lips, then to his heart. Then a significant cough
reminded the lover of a cherished voice. Sometimes a note
was thrown by a little hand, and in the note was hidden some
costly jewel, precious not on account of its value, but because
it had belonged to her who threw it; and this would fall on
the pavement a few feet from the young man. Then La Mole
would swoop down on it like a kite, press it to his heart, answer
in the same voice, while Marguerite stood at her balcony until
the sound of the horse's hoofs had died away in the darkness. The steed, ridden at full speed when coming, on leaving
seemed as if made of material as lifeless as that of the famous
horse which lost Troy.

This was why the queen was not anxious as to the fate of
La Mole. But fearing that he might be watched and followed
she persistently refused all interviews except these clandestine
ones, which began immediately after La Mole's flight and continued every evening until the time set for the formal reception
of the ambassadors, a reception which by the express orders
of Ambroise Paré, as we have seen, was postponed for several
days.

The evening before this reception, at about nine o'clock, when
every one in the Louvre was engaged in preparations for the
following day, Marguerite opened her window and stepped out
upon her balcony. As she did so, without waiting for her
note, La Mole, in greater haste than usual, threw his note
which with his usual skill fell at the feet of his royal mistress.

Marguerite realized that the missive contained something
special, and retired from the balcony to read it. The note
consisted of two separate sheets.

On the first page were these words:

*"Madame, I must speak to the King of Navarre. The
matter is urgent. I will wait."*

On the second page were these words:

" My lady and my queen, arrange so that I may give you one of the kisses I now send you.   I will wait."

Marguerite had scarcely finished the second part of the letter when she heard the voice of Henry of Navarre, who with his usual caution had knocked on the outer door, and was asking Gillonne if he might enter.

The queen at once separated the letter, put one of the sheets in her robe, the other in her pocket, hurriedly closed the window, and stepped to the door.

"Enter, sire," said she.

Notwithstanding the fact that Marguerite had been careful to close the window quickly and gently, the sound had reached Henry, whose acute senses, in the midst of people he greatly mistrusted, had almost acquired the exquisite delicacy they attain in the savage.   But the King of Navarre was not one of those tyrants who forbid their wives from taking the air and watching the stars.

Henry was as gracious and smiling as ever.

"Madame," said he, "while every one is rehearsing the coming ceremonial, I thought I would come and have a little talk with you about my affairs, which you still regard as yours, do you not?"

"Certainly, monsieur," replied Marguerite; "are not our interests one and the same?"

"Yes, madame, and that is why I wanted to ask what you thought about Monsieur le Duc d'Alençon's avoiding me so for the last few days.   The day before yesterday he even went to Saint Germain.   Does it not mean either that he is planning to leave by himself, for he is watched very little, or that he is not going to leave at all?   Give me your opinion, madame, if you please.   I confess it will be a great relief to me to tell you mine."

"Your majesty is right in being anxious at my brother's silence.   I have been thinking about it all day, and my idea is that as circumstances have changed he has changed with them."

"You mean, do you not, that seeing King Charles ill and the Duc d'Anjou King of Poland he would not be averse to staying in Paris to keep watch over the crown of France?"

"Exactly."

"Be it so. I ask nothing better than for him to remain," said Henry; "only that will change our entire plan. To leave without him I shall need three times the guarantees I should have asked for had I gone with your brother, whose name and presence in the enterprise would have been my safeguard. But what surprises me is that I have not heard from Monsieur de Mouy. It is not like him to stay away so long. Have you had any news of him, madame "

"I, sire!" exclaimed Marguerite, in astonishment; "why, how could you expect "—

"Why, by Heaven, my dear, nothing would be more natural. In order to please me, you were kind enough to save the life of young La Mole, — he must have reached Nantes, — and if one can get to a place he can easily get away from it."

"Ah! this explains an enigma, the answer to which I could not make out," said Marguerite. "I had left my window open, and found, on coming back to my room, a note on my floor."

"There now," said Henry.

"A note which at first I could not understand, and to which I attached no importance whatsoever," continued Marguerite. "Perhaps I was wrong, and that it comes from that quarter."

"That is possible," said Henry; "I might even say probable. Might I see this note?"

"Certainly, sire," replied Marguerite, handing to the king the missive she had put into her pocket. The king glanced at it.

"Is it not Monsieur de la Mole's handwriting?" said he.

"I do not know," replied Marguerite. "It looks to me like a counterfeit."

"No matter, let us read it." And he read:

"*Madame, I must speak to the King of Navarre. The matter is urgent. I will wait.*"

"So!" said Henry — "you see, he says he will wait."

"Certainly I see that," said Marguerite. "But what would you expect?"

"Why! *ventre saint gris!* I expect that he is waiting!"

"That he is waiting!" cried Marguerite, looking at her husband in astonishment. "How can you say such a thing, sire? A man whom the King tried to kill — a man who is watched, threatened — waiting, you say! Would that be possible? — are the doors made for those who have been "—

"Obliged to escape by the window — you were going to say?"

"Yes, you have finished my sentence."

"Well, but if they know the way by the window, let them take it, since it is perfectly impossible for them to enter by the door. It is very simple."

"Do you think so?" said Marguerite, flushing with pleasure at the thought of again being near La Mole.

"I am sure of it."

"But how could one reach the window?" asked the queen.

"Did you not keep the rope ladder I sent you? Where is your usual foresight?"

"Yes, sire, I kept it," said Marguerite.

"In that case there will be no difficulty," said Henry.

"What does your majesty wish?"

"Why, it is very simple," said Henry. "Fasten it to your balcony and let it hang down. If it is De Mouy who is waiting and he wants to mount it, he will do so."

Without losing his gravity Henry took the candle to aid Marguerite in her search for the ladder. They did not have to look long; it was in a wardrobe in the famous closet.

"There it is," said Henry; "now, madame, if I am not asking too much, fasten it to the balcony, I beg you."

"Why should I fasten it and not you, sire?" said Marguerite.

"Because the best conspirators are the most careful. Seeing a man might perhaps frighten away our friend, you see."

Marguerite smiled and tied the ladder.

"There," said Henry, concealing himself in a corner of the room, "stand so he can see you; now drop the ladder; good! I am sure that De Mouy will climb up."

In fact, about ten minutes later a man, mad with joy, stepped over the balcony, but seeing that the queen did not come to him, he hesitated a moment. Instead of Marguerite it was Henry who stepped forward.

"Ah!" said he, graciously, "it is not De Mouy, but Monsieur de la Mole. Good evening, Monsieur de la Mole. Come in, I beg you."

La Mole paused a moment, overwhelmed. Had he still been on the ladder instead of on the balcony he might possibly have fallen backward.

"You wanted to speak to the King of Navarre on matters

of importance," said Marguerite. " I have told him so and here he is."

Henry closed the window.

" I love you," said Marguerite, hastily pressing the young man's hand.

" Well, monsieur," said Henry, placing a chair for La Mole, " what is it ? "

" This, sire," replied La Mole. " I have left Monsieur de Mouy at the city gates. He desires to know if Maurevel has spoken, and if his presence in your majesty's room is known."

" Not yet, but it will be before long ; so we must make haste."

" That is my opinion, sire, and if to-morrow evening Monsieur d'Alençon is ready to start, De Mouy will be at the Porte Saint Marcel with five hundred men. These will take you to Fontainebleau. Then you can easily reach Blois, Angoulême, and Bordeaux."

" Madame," said Henry, turning to his wife, " I can be ready by to-morrow ; can you ? "

La Mole's eyes were anxiously fixed on those of Marguerite.

" You have my promise," said the queen. " Wherever you go, I will follow. But you know Monsieur d'Alençon must leave at the same time. No half way with him ; either he serves us or he betrays us. If he hesitates we do not stir."

" Does he know anything of this plan, Monsieur de la Mole ? " asked Henry.

" He should have received a letter from Monsieur de Mouy several days ago."

" Why," said Henry, " he said nothing to me about it ! "

" Be careful, monsieur," said Marguerite, " be careful."

" I shall be on my guard, you may be sure. How can we get an answer to De Mouy ? "

" Do not worry, sire. On the right, on the left, of your majesty, visible or invisible, he will be on hand to-morrow during the reception of the ambassadors. One word in the address of the queen will suffice for him to understand whether you consent or not, whether he must leave or wait for you. If the Duc d'Alençon refuses, he asks but a fortnight to reorganize everything in your name."

" Really," said Henry, " De Mouy is invaluable. Can you insert the necessary words in your address, madame ? "

" Nothing will be easier," replied Marguerite.

"Then I will see Monsieur d'Alençon to-morrow," said Henry. "Let De Mouy be at his post ready to understand at a word."

"He will be there, sire."

"And, Monsieur de la Mole," said Henry, "take my answer to him. You probably have a horse or a servant near by?"

"Orthon is waiting for me at the quay."

"Go back to him, monsieur. Oh, no, not by the window, which is good only for an emergency. You might be seen, and as it would not be known that you had taken this risk for me, it might compromise the queen."

"How shall I leave, sire?"

"Although you may not be able to enter the Louvre by yourself, you can at least leave it with me, for I have the password. You have your cloak, I have mine; we will put them on and can pass the gate without difficulty. Besides, I shall be glad to give some special orders to Orthon. Wait here while I go and see if there is any one in the corridor."

With the most natural air possible Henry went out to investigate. La Mole was left alone with the queen.

"Ah! when shall I see you again?" said he.

"To-morrow evening, if we leave. Otherwise some evening soon in the Rue Cloche Percée."

"Monsieur de la Mole," said Henry, returning, "you can come; there is no one here."

La Mole bowed respectfully to the queen.

"Give him your hand to kiss, madame," said Henry; "Monsieur de la Mole is no ordinary servitor."

Marguerite obeyed.

"By the way," said Henry, "be sure and keep the rope ladder. It is a valuable instrument for conspirators; and when we least expect it we may need it. Come, Monsieur de la Mole."

CHAPTER XLIII.

THE AMBASSADORS.

THE following day the entire population of Paris rushed towards the Faubourg Saint Antoine, by which it had been decided that the Polish ambassadors were to enter. A line of Swiss restrained the crowd, and a regiment of horse protected the lords and the ladies of the court who rode ahead of the procession.

Soon, near the Abbey Saint Antoine, a troop of cavaliers appeared, dressed in red and yellow, with caps and furred mantles, and carrying long curved sabres like Turkish cimeters.

The officers rode at the side of the lines.

Behind this troop came a second, clothed with Oriental magnificence. They preceded the ambassadors, who, four in number, represented in a gorgeous manner the most mythological of the chivalrous kingdoms of the sixteenth century.

One of the ambassadors was the Bishop of Cracow. His costume was half ecclesiastical, half military, resplendent with gold and precious stones.

His white horse, with long mane and tail, walked with proud step and seemed to breathe out fire from his nostrils. No one would have supposed that for a month the noble animal had made fifteen leagues daily over roads which the weather had rendered almost impassable.

Beside the bishop rode the Palatine Lasco, a powerful noble, closely related to the royal family, as rich as a king and as proud.

Behind these two chief ambassadors, who were accompanied by two other palatines of high rank, came a number of Polish lords, whose horses in their harness of silk, studded with gold and precious stones, excited the applause of the people. The French horsemen, in spite of their rich apparel, were completely eclipsed by the newcomers, whom they scornfully called barbarians.

Up to the last moment Catharine had hoped the reception would be postponed on account of the King's illness. But when the day came, and she saw Charles, as pale as a corpse, put on the gorgeous royal mantle, she realized that apparently at least she must yield to his iron will, and began to believe that after all the safest plan for Henry of Anjou was to accept the magnificent exile to which he was condemned. With the exception of the few words he had uttered when he opened his eyes as his mother came out of the closet, Charles had not spoken to Catharine since the scene which had brought about the illness to which he had succumbed. Every one in the Louvre knew that there had been a dreadful altercation between mother and son, but no one knew the cause of it, and the boldest trembled before that coldness and silence, as birds tremble before the calm which precedes a storm.

Everything had been prepared in the Louvre, not as though there were to be a reception, but as if some funeral ceremony were to occur. Every one had obeyed orders in a gloomy or passive manner. It was known that Catharine had almost trembled, and consequently every one else trembled.

The large reception-hall of the palace had been prepared, and as such ceremonies were usually public, the guards and the sentinels had received orders to admit with the ambassadors as many people as the apartments and the courts would hold. As for Paris, it presented the same aspect that every large city presents under similar circumstances; that is, confusion and curiosity. But had any one looked closely at the population that day, he would have noticed, among the groups of honest bourgeois with smiling faces, a considerable number of men in long cloaks, who exchanged glances and signs when at a distance, and when they met, a few rapid words in a low tone. These men seemed greatly occupied with the procession, followed it closely, and appeared to receive their orders from an old man, whose sharp black eyes, in spite of his white beard and grayish eyebrows, showed a vigorous activity. This old man, either by his own efforts or by those of his companions, was among the first to gain admission to the Louvre, and, thanks to the kindness of the Swiss guard, succeeded in finding a place behind the ambassadors, opposite Marguerite and Henry of Navarre.

Henry, informed by La Mole that De Mouy would be present in some disguise or other, looked round on all sides. At last his eyes encountered those of the old man and held them.

A sign from De Mouy had dispelled all doubt. He was so changed that Henry himself was doubtful whether this old man with the white beard could be the intrepid Huguenot chief who five or six days before had made so desperate a defence.

A word from Henry whispered into Marguerite's ear called the attention of the queen to De Mouy. Then her beautiful eyes wandered around the great hall in search of La Mole; but in vain — La Mole was not there.

The speeches began. The first was to the King. Lasco, in the name of the Diet, asked him to consent that the crown of Poland be offered to a prince of the house of France.

Charles's reply was short and to the point. He presented his brother, the Duc d'Anjou, whose courage he praised highly to the Polish ambassadors. He spoke in French, and an interpreter translated his reply at the end of each sentence. While the interpreter was speaking, the King was seen applying a handkerchief to his lips, and each time he removed it, it was covered with blood. When Charles's reply was finished, Lasco turned to the Duc d'Anjou, bowed, and began a Latin address, in which he offered him the throne in the name of the Polish nation.

The duke replied in the same language, and in a voice he strove in vain to render firm, that he accepted with gratitude the honor which was offered to him. While he spoke, Charles remained standing, with lips compressed, and fixed on him eyes as calm and threatening as those of an eagle.

When the duke had finished, Lasco took the crown of the Jagellos from the red velvet cushion on which it rested, and while two Polish nobles placed the royal mantle on the duke, he laid the crown in Charles's hands.

Charles signed to his brother, the Duc d'Anjou knelt down before him, and with his own hand the King placed the crown on his brother's head. Then the two kings exchanged one of the most bitter kisses ever exchanged between two brothers.

At once a herald cried :

"Alexander Edward Henry of France, Duc d'Anjou, is crowned King of Poland. Long live the King of Poland!"

The entire assembly repeated the cry: "Long live the King of Poland!" Then Lasco turned to Marguerite. The discourse of the beautiful queen had been reserved for the last. Now, as it was a compliment accorded her in order to display her brilliant talents, as they were called, every one paid great attention to the reply, which was in Latin, and which, as we have said, Marguerite had composed herself. Lasco's address was more of a eulogy than an address. He had yielded, Sarmatian that he was, to the admiration which the beautiful queen of Navarre inspired in every one. He had borrowed his language from Ovid; his style was that of Ronsard. He said that having left Varsovia in the middle of a very dark night, neither he nor his companions would have been able to find their way, had they not, like the Magi, been guided by two stars which became more and more brilliant as they drew nearer to France, and which now they recognized as the two beautiful eyes of the Queen of Navarre. Finally, passing from the Gospel to the Koran, from Syria to Arabia, from Nazareth to Mecca, he concluded by saying that he was quite prepared to do what the ardent votaries of the prophet did. When they were fortunate enough to see his tomb, they put out their eyes, feeling that after they had looked at such a sight, nothing in the world was worth being admired.

This address was loudly applauded by those who understood Latin because they were of the same opinion as the orator, and by those who did not understand it because they wished to appear as though they did.

Marguerite made a gracious courtesy to the gallant Sarmatian; then fixing her eyes on De Mouy, began her reply in these words:

"*Quod nunc hac in aulâ insperati adestis exultaremus, ego et conjux, nisi ideo immineret calamitas, scilicet non solum fratris sed etiam amici orbitas.*"[1]

These words had a double meaning, and, while intended for De Mouy, were apparently addressed to Henry of Anjou. The latter, therefore, bowed in token of gratitude.

Charles did not remember having read this sentence in the address which had been submitted to him some days before; but he attached no importance to Marguerite's words, which he knew were merely conventional. Besides, he understood Latin very imperfectly.

Marguerite continued:

"*Adeo dolemur a te dividi ut tecum proficisci maluissemus. Sed idem fatum quo nunc sine ullâ morâ Lutetiâ cedere juberis, hac in urbe detinct. Proficiscere ergo, frater; proficiscere,*

---

[1] Your unlooked-for presence in this court would overwhelm my husband and myself with joy, did it not bring with it a great misfortune, that is, the loss not only of a brother, but also that of a friend.

amice ; proficiscere sine nobis ; proficiscentem sequuntur spes et desideria nostra." [1]

It may easily be imagined that De Mouy listened with the closest attention to these words which, although addressed to the ambassadors, were intended for him alone. Two or three times Henry had glanced indifferently over his shoulder to intimate to the young Huguenot that D'Alençon had refused; but the act, which appeared involuntary, would have been insufficient for De Mouy, had not Marguerite's words confirmed it.

While looking at Marguerite and listening with his whole soul, his piercing black eyes beneath their gray brows struck Catharine, who started as if she had had a shock of electricity, and who did not remove her eyes from him.

"What a strange face!" thought she, continuing to change her expression according as the ceremony required it. "Who is this man who watches Marguerite so attentively and whom Marguerite and Henry on their part look at so earnestly?"

The Queen of Navarre went on with her address, which from that point was a reply to the courtesies of the Polish ambassador. While Catharine was racking her brain to discover the name of this fine old man the master of ceremonies came up behind her and handed her a perfumed satin bag containing a folded paper. She opened the bag, drew out the paper, and read these words:

"*By the aid of a cordial which I have just administered to him Maurevel has somewhat recovered his strength, and has succeeded in writing the name of the man who was in the apartment of the King of Navarre. This man was Monsieur de Mouy."*

"De Mouy!" thought the queen; "well, I felt it was he. But this old man — ah! *cospetto!* — this old man is" —

She leaned toward the captain of the guard.

"Look, Monsieur de Nancey," said she, "but without attracting attention; look at Lasco who is speaking. Behind him — do you see the old man with the white beard, in the black velvet suit?"

"Yes, madame," replied the captain.

---

[1] We are heartbroken at being separated from you, when we should have preferred going with you, but the same fate which decrees that you must leave Paris without delay, retains us in this city. Go, therefore, dear brother; go, dear friend; go without us. Our hopes and our good wishes follow you.

" Well, do not lose sight of him."

" The one to whom the King of Navarre made a sign just now ? "

" Exactly. Station yourself at the door of the Louvre with ten men, and when he comes out invite him in the King's name to dinner. If he accepts, take him into some room in which you must keep him a prisoner. If he resists, seize him, dead or alive."

Fortunately Henry, who had been paying but little attention to Marguerite's address, was looking at Catharine, and had not lost a single expression of her face. Seeing the eyes of the queen mother fixed so earnestly on De Mouy, he grew uneasy ; when he saw her give an order to the captain of the guard he comprehended everything.

It was at this moment that he made the sign which had surprised Monsieur de Nancey, and which meant, " You are dis covered, save yourself! "

De Mouy understood this gesture, which was a fitting climax to the portion of Marguerite's address intended for him. He did not delay an instant, but mingled with the crowd and disappeared.

Henry, however, was not easy until Monsieur de Nancey had returned to Catharine, and he saw from the frown on the queen mother's face that the captain had not been in time.

The audience was over. Marguerite exchanged a few un official words with Lasco.

The King staggered to his feet, bowed, and went out, leaning on the arm of Ambroise Paré, who had not left him since his illness.

Catharine, pale with anger, and Henry, silent from disappointment, followed.

As to the Duc d'Alençon, he had scarcely been noticed during the ceremony, and not once had Charles, whose eyes had not left the Duc d'Anjou, glanced at him.

The new King of Poland felt himself lost. Far from his mother, carried away by those barbarians of the north, he was like Antæus, the son of Terra, who lost his strength when lifted in the arms of Hercules. Once beyond the frontier the Duc d'Anjou felt that he was forever excluded from the throne of France.

Instead of following the King he retired to his mother's apartments.

He found her no less gloomy and preoccupied than himself, for she was thinking of that fine mocking face she had not lost sight of during the ceremony, of the Béarnais for whom destiny had seemed to make way, sweeping aside kings, royal assassins, enemies, and obstacles.

Seeing her beloved son pale beneath his crown, and bent under his royal mantle, clasping his beautiful hands in silence, and holding them out to her piteously, Catharine rose and went to him.

" Oh, mother," cried the King of Poland, " I am condemned to die in exile ! "

" My son," said Catharine, " have you so soon forgotten Réné's prediction ?   Do not worry, you will not have to stay there long."

" Mother, I entreat you," said the Duc d'Anjou, " if there is the slightest hint, or the least suspicion, that the throne of France is to be vacant, send me word."

" Do not worry, my son," said Catharine.   " Until the day for which both of us are waiting, there shall always be a horse saddled in my stable, and in my antechamber a courier ready to set out for Poland."

CHAPTER XLIV.

ORESTES AND PYLADES.

HENRY OF ANJOU having departed, peace and happiness seemed to have returned to the Louvre, among this family of the Atrides.

Charles, forgetting his melancholy, recovered his vigorous health, hunting with Henry, and on days when this was not possible discussing hunting affairs with him, and reproaching him for only one thing, his indifference to hawking, declaring that he would be faultless if he knew how to snare falcons, gerfalcons, and hawks as well as he knew how to hunt brocks and hounds.

Catharine had become a good mother again.   Gentle to Charles and D'Alençon, affectionate to Henry and Marguerite, gracious to Madame de Nevers and Madame de Sauve ; and under the pretext that it was in obedience to an order from her that he had been wounded, she carried her amiabilities so far as to visit Maurevel twice during his convalescence, in his house in the Rue de la Cerisaie.

Marguerite continued to carry on her love affair after the Spanish fashion.

Every evening she opened her window and by gestures and notes kept up her correspondence with La Mole, while in each of his letters the young man reminded his lovely queen of her promise of a few moments in the Rue Cloche Percée as a reward for his exile.

Only one person was lonely and unhappy in the now calm and peaceful Louvre.

This was our friend Count Annibal de Coconnas.

It was certainly something to know that La Mole was alive; it was much to be the favorite of Madame de Nevers, the most charming and the most whimsical of women. But all the pleasure of a meeting granted him by the beautiful duchess, all the consolation offered by Marguerite as to the fate of their common friend, did not compensate in the eyes of the Piedmontese for one hour spent with La Mole at their friend La Hurière's before a bottle of light wine, or for one of those midnight rambles through that part of Paris in which an honest man ran the risk of receiving rents in his flesh, his purse, or his clothes.

To the shame of humanity it must be said that Madame de Nevers bore with impatience her rivalry with La Mole.

It was not that she hated the Provincial; on the contrary, carried away by the irresistible instinct which, in spite of herself, makes every woman a coquette with another woman's lover, especially when that woman is her friend, she had not spared La Mole the flashes of her emerald eyes, and Coconnas might have envied the frank handclasps and the amiable acts done by the duchess in favor of his friend during those days in which the star of the Piedmontese seemed growing dim in the sky of his beautiful mistress; but Coconnas, who would have strangled fifteen persons for a single glance from his lady, was so little jealous of La Mole that he had often after some indiscretions of the duchess whispered certain offers which had made the man from the Provinces blush.

At this stage of affairs it happened that Henriette, who by the absence of La Mole was deprived of all the enjoyment she had had from the company of Coconnas, that is, his never-ending flow of spirits and fun, came to Marguerite one day to beg her to do her this three-fold favor without which the heart and the mind of Coconnas seemed to be slipping away day by day.

Marguerite, always sympathetic and, besides, influenced by the prayers of La Mole and the wishes of her own heart, arranged a meeting with Henriette for the next day in the house with the double entrance, in order to discuss these matters thoroughly and uninterruptedly.

Coconnas received with rather bad grace the note from Henriette, asking him to be in the Rue Tizon at half-past nine.

Nevertheless he went to the place appointed, where he found Henriette, who was provoked at having arrived first.

"Fie, Monsieur!" she cried, "it is very bad to make — I will not say a princess — but a lady — wait in this way."

"Wait?" said Coconnas, "what an idea! I'll wager, on the contrary, that we are ahead of time."

"I was."

"Well! and I too; it cannot be more than ten o'clock at the latest."

"Well! my note said half-past nine."

"Therefore I left the Louvre at nine o'clock. I am in the service of Monsieur le Duc d'Alençon, be it said in passing, and for this reason I shall be obliged to leave you in an hour."

"Which pleases you, no doubt?"

"No, indeed! considering the fact that Monsieur d'Alençon is an ill-tempered and capricious master; moreover, if I am to be found fault with, I prefer to have it done by pretty lips like yours rather than by such sullen ones as his."

"Ah!" said the duchess, "that is a little better. You say, then, that you left the Louvre at nine o'clock."

"Yes, and with every idea of coming directly here, when at the corner of the Rue de Grenelle I saw a man who looked like La Mole."

"Good! La Mole again."

"Always, with or without permission."

"Brutal man!"

"Ah!" said Coconnas, "we are going to begin our complimentary speeches again."

"Not at all; but finish your story."

"I was not the one who wanted to tell it. It was you who asked me why I was late."

"Yes; was it my place to arrive first?"

"Well, you are not looking for any one."

"You are growing tiresome, my dear friend; but go on. At the corner of the Rue de Grenelle you saw a man who looked like La Mole — But what is that on your doublet — blood?"

"Yes, and here is more which was probably sprinkled over me as he fell."

"You had a fight?"

"I should think so."

"On account of your La Mole?"

"On whose account do you think I would fight? For a woman?"

"I thank you!"

"So I followed this man who had the impudence to look like my friend. I joined him in the Rue Coquillière, I overtook him, and stared into his face under the light from a shop. But it was not La Mole."

"Good! that was well done."

"Yes, but he did not think so. 'Monsieur,' said I to him, 'you are an ass to take it upon yourself to resemble from afar my friend Monsieur de la Mole, who is an accomplished cavalier; while on nearer view one can easily perceive that you are nothing but a vagrant.' Whereupon he drew his sword, and I mine. At the third pass he fell down, sprinkling me with his blood."

"But you assisted him at least?"

"I was about to do so when a horseman rode by. Ah! this time, duchess, I was sure that it was La Mole. Unfortunately he was galloping. I ran after him as hard as I could, and those who collected around to see the fight ran behind me. Now as I might easily have been mistaken for a thief, followed as I was by all that rabble shouting at my heels, I was obliged to turn back to scatter them, which made me lose a little time. In the meanwhile the rider disappeared; I followed, inquired of every one, gave the color of the horse; but it was useless; no one had noticed him. At last, tired out from the chase, I came here."

"Tired of the chase!" said the duchess. "How flattering you are!"

"Listen, dear friend," said Coconnas, turning nonchalantly in his chair. " You are going to bother me again on account of poor La Mole. Now, you are wrong, for friendship, you see, — I wish I had his wit or knowledge, I would then find some comparison which would make you understand how I feel — friendship, you see, is a star, while love — love — wait! I have it! — love is only a candle. You will tell me there are several varieties " —

" Of love ? "

" No! of candles, and that some are better than others. The rose, for instance, is the best; but rose as it is, the candle burns out, while the star shines forever. You will answer this by saying that when the candle is burned out, another is put in its place."

" Monsieur de Coconnas, you are a goose."

" Indeed ! "

" Monsieur de Coconnas, you are impertinent."

" Ah ? "

" Monsieur de Coconnas, you are a scoundrel."

" Madame, I warn you that you will make me trebly regret La Mole."

" You no longer love me."

" On the contrary, duchess, you do not know it, but I idolize you. But I can love and cherish and idolize you, and yet in my spare moments praise my friend."

" So you call the time spent with me spare moments, do you ? "

" What can you expect ? Poor La Mole is constantly in my thoughts."

" You prefer him to me; that is shameful! and I detest you, Annibal! Why not be frank, and tell me you prefer him to me ? Annibal, I warn you of one thing: if you prefer anything in the world to me " —

" Henriette, the loveliest of duchesses! For your own peace of mind, believe me, do not ask such unwise questions. I love you more than any woman, and I love La Mole more than any man."

" Well answered ! " said a strange voice suddenly. A damask curtain was raised in front of a great panel, which, sliding back into the wall, opened a passage between the two rooms, and showed La Mole in the doorway, like one of Titian's fine portraits in its gilded frame.

" La Mole ! " exclaimed Coconnas, without paying any attention to Marguerite or taking the time to thank her for the surprise she had arranged for him; " La Mole, my friend, my dear La Mole ! " and he rushed into the arms of his friend, upsetting the armchair in which he had been sitting and the table that stood in his way.

La Mole returned his embrace with effusion; then, turning to the Duchesse de Nevers:

"Pardon me, madame, if the mention of my name has sometimes disturbed your happiness." "Certainly," he added, glancing at Marguerite with a look of ineffable tenderness, "it has not been my fault that I have not seen you sooner."

"You see, Henriette," said Marguerite, "I have kept my word; here he is!"

"Is it, then, to the prayers of Madame la Duchesse that I owe this happiness?" asked La Mole.

"To her prayers alone," replied Marguerite.

Then, turning to La Mole, she continued:

"La Mole, I will allow you not to believe one word of what I say."

Meanwhile Coconnas pressed his friend to his heart over and over again, walked round him a dozen times, and even held a candelabrum to his face the better to see him; then suddenly turning, he knelt down before Marguerite and kissed the hem of her robe.

"Ah! that is pleasant!" said the Duchesse de Nevers. "I suppose now you will find me bearable."

"By Heaven!" cried Coconnas, "I shall find you as adorable as ever; only now I can tell you so with a lighter heart, and were there any number of Poles, Sarmatians, and other hyperborean barbarians present I should make them all admit that you were the queen of beauties."

"Gently, gently, Coconnas," said La Mole, "Madame Marguerite is here!"

"Oh! I cannot help that," cried Coconnas, with the half-comic air which belonged to him alone, "I still assert that Madame Henriette is the queen of beauties and Madame Marguerite is the beauty of queens."

But whatever he might say or do, the Piedmontese, completely carried away by the joy of having found his dear La Mole, had neither eyes nor ears for any one but him.

"Come, my beautiful queen," said Madame de Nevers, "come, let us leave these dear friends to chat awhile alone. They have a thousand things to say to each other which would be interrupted by our conversation. It is hard for us, but it is the only way. I am sure, to make Monsieur Annibal perfectly sane. Do this for me, my queen! since I am foolish enough to love this worthless fellow, as his friend La Mole calls him."

Marguerite whispered a few words to La Mole, who, anxious as he had been to see his friend, would have been glad had the affection of Coconnas for him been less exacting. Meanwhile Coconnas was endeavoring to bring back a smile and a gentle word to Henriette's lips, a result which was easily attained. Then the two women passed into the next room, where supper was awaiting them.

The young men were alone. The first questions Coconnas asked his friend were about that fatal evening which had almost cost him his life. As La Mole proceeded in his story the Piedmontese, who, however, was not easily moved, trembled in every limb.

"But why," said he, "instead of running about the country as you have done, and causing me such uneasiness, did you not seek refuge with our master? The duke who had defended you would have hidden you. I should have been near you and my grief, although feigned, would nevertheless have disturbed every simpleton at court."

"Our master!" said La Mole, in a low voice, "the Duc d'Alençon?"

"Yes. According to what he told me, I supposed it was to him you owed your life."

"I owe my life to the King of Navarre," replied La Mole.

"Oh!" exclaimed Coconnas, "are you sure?"

"Beyond a doubt."

"Oh! what a good, kind king! But what part did the Duc d'Alençon play in it all?"

"He held the rope to strangle me."

"By Heaven!" cried Coconnas, "are you sure of what you say, La Mole? What! this pale-faced, pitiful-looking cur strangle my friend! Ah! by Heaven, by to-morrow I will let him know what I think of him."

"Are you mad?"

"That is true, he would begin again. But what does it matter? Things cannot go on like this."

"Come, come, Coconnas, calm yourself and try and remember that it is half-past eleven o'clock and that you are on duty to-night."

"What do I care about my duty to him! Bah! Let him

wait! My attendance! I serve a man who has held a rope? You are joking! No! This is providential; it is said that I should find you to leave you no more. I shall stay here."

"Why, man alive, think what you are saying. You are not drunk, I hope."

"No, fortunately; if I were I would set fire to the Louvre."

"Come, Annibal," said La Mole, "be reasonable. Return to your duties. Service is a sacred thing."

"Will you return with me?"

"Impossible."

"Are they still thinking of killing you?"

"I think not. I am of too little importance for them to have any plot on hand about me. For an instant they wanted to kill me, but that was all. The princes were on a frolic that night."

"What are you going to do, then?"

"Nothing; wander about or take a walk."

"Well, I will walk, too, and wander with you. That will be charming. Then, if you are attacked, there will be two of us, and we will give them no end of trouble. Let him come, your duke! I will pin him to the wall like a butterfly!"

"But, at least, say that you are going to leave his service!"

"Yes, I am."

"In that case, tell him so."

"Well, that seems only right. I will do so. I will write to him."

"Write to him! That would be discourteous, Coconnas, to a prince of the blood."

"Yes, of the blood! of the blood of my friend. Take care," cried Coconnas, rolling his large, tragic eyes, "lest I trifle with points of etiquette!"

"Probably," said La Mole to himself, "in a few days he will need neither the prince nor any one else, for if he wants to come with us, we will take him."

Thereupon Coconnas took the pen without further opposition from his friend and hastily composed the following specimen of eloquence:

"*Monseigneur: There can be no doubt but that your highness, versed as you are in the writings of all authors of antiquity, must know the touching story of Orestes and Pylades, who were two heroes celebrated for their misfortunes and*

*their friendship. My friend La Mole is no less unfortunate
than was Orestes, while I am no less tender than Pylades.
At present he has affairs of importance which demand my aid.
It is therefore impossible for me to leave him. So with the
consent of your highness I will take a short vacation, determined as I am to attach myself to my friend's fortune, whither-
soever it may lead me. It is with the deepest grief that I tear
myself away from the service of your highness, but for this I
trust I may obtain your pardon. I venture to subscribe myself with respect, my lord,*

  " Your highness's very humble and very obedient servant,
    " ANNIBAL, COMTE DE COCONNAS,
      " The inseparable friend of Monsieur de la Mole."

This masterpiece finished, Coconnas read it aloud to La
Mole, who merely shrugged his shoulders.

"Well! what do you say to it?" asked Coconnas, who had
not seen the shrug, or who had pretended not to see it.

"I say," replied La Mole, "that Monsieur d'Alençon will
laugh at us."

"At us?"

"Both of us."

"That will be better, it seems to me, than to strangle each of
us separately."

"Bah!" said La Mole, laughing, "the one will not necessa-
rily prevent the other."

"Well! so much the worse. Come what may, I will send
the letter to-morrow morning. Where shall we sleep when
we leave here?"

"At Maître la Hurière's, in that little room in which you
tried to stab me before we were Orestes and Pylades!"

"Very well, I will send my letter to the Louvre by our host."

Just then the panel moved.

"Well!" asked both princesses at once, "where are Orestes
and Pylades?"

"By Heaven! madame," replied Coconnas, "Pylades and
Orestes are dying of hunger and love."

It was Maître la Hurière himself who, at nine o'clock the
following morning, carried to the Louvre the respectful missive
of Count Annibal de Coconnas.

CHAPTER XLV.

ORTHON.

AFTER the refusal of the Duc d'Alençon, which left every-thing in peril, even his life, Henry became more intimate with the prince than ever, if that were possible. Catharine con-cluded from the intimacy that the two princes not only under-stood each other perfectly, but also that they were planning some mutual conspiracy. She questioned Marguerite on the subject, but Marguerite was worthy of her mother, and the Queen of Navarre, whose chief talent lay in avoiding ex-planations, parried her mother's questions so cleverly that although replying to all she left Catharine more mystified than ever.

The Florentine, therefore, had nothing to guide her except the spirit of intrigue she had brought with her from Tuscany, the most interesting of the small states of that period, and the feeling of hatred she had imbibed from the court of France, which was more divided in its interests and opinions than any court at that time.

She realized that a part of the strength of the Béarnais came from his alliance with the Duc d'Alençon, and she determined to separate them.

From the moment she formed this resolution she beset her son with the patience and the wiles of an angler, who, when he has dropped his bait near the fish, unconsciously draws it in until his prey is caught.

François perceived this increase of affection on the part of his mother and made advances to her. As for Henry, he pretended to see nothing, but kept a closer watch on his ally than he had yet done.

Every one was waiting for some event.

During this state of things, one morning when the sun rose clear, giving out that gentle warmth and sweet odor which announce a beautiful day, a pale man, leaning on a cane, and walking with difficulty, came out of a small house situated behind the arsenal, and walked slowly along the Rue du Petit Muse.

At the Porte Saint Antoine he turned into the street which encircles the moat of the Bastille like a marsh, left the boulevard on his left and entered the Archery Garden, where the gatekeeper received him with every mark of respect.

There was no one in the garden, which, as its name implies, belonged to a particular society called the Taxopholites. Had there been any strollers there the pale man would have merited their sympathy, for his long mustache, his military step and bearing, though weakened by suffering, sufficiently indicated that he was an officer who had been recently wounded, and who was endeavoring to regain his strength by moderate exercise in the open air.

Yet, strange to say, when the cloak opened in which, in spite of the increasing heat, this apparently harmless man was wrapped, it displayed a pair of long pistols suspended from the silver clasps of his belt. This belt also sustained a dagger and a sword so enormously long that it seemed almost impossible to be handled, and which, completing this living arsenal, clattered against his shrunken and trembling legs.

As an additional precaution the lonely soldier glanced around at every step as though to question each turn of the path, each bush and ditch.

Having entered the garden without being molested, the man reached a sort of small arbor, facing the boulevard, from which it was separated by a thick hedge and a small ditch which formed a double inclosure. He threw himself upon a grassy bank within reach of a table on which the host of the establishment, who combined with his duties as gatekeeper the vocation of cook, at once placed a bottle of cordial.

The invalid had been there about ten minutes and had several times raised the china cup to his lips, taking little sips of its contents, when suddenly his countenance, in spite of its interesting pallor, assumed a startled expression. From the Croix Faubin, along a path which to-day is the Rue de Naples, he had perceived a cavalier, wrapped in a great cloak, stop near the moat.

Not more than five minutes had elapsed, during which the man of the pale face, whom the reader has perhaps already recognized as Maurevel, had scarcely had time to recover from the emotion caused by his unexpected presence, when the horseman was joined by a man in a close-fitting coat, like that of a page, who came by the road which is since known as the Rue des Fosses Saint Nicholas.

Hidden in his leafy arbor, Maurevel could easily see and

hear everything, and when it is known that the cavalier was
De Mouy and the young man in the tight-fitting cloak Orthon,
one may imagine whether Maurevel's eyes and ears were not
on the alert.

Both men looked very carefully around. Maurevel held his
breath.

"You may speak, monsieur," said Orthon, who being the
younger was the more confident; "no one can either see or
hear us."

"That is well," said De Mouy, "you are to go to Madame
de Sauve, and if you find her in her rooms give her this note.
If she is not there, you will place it behind the mirror where
the king is in the habit of putting his letters. Then you will
wait in the Louvre. If you receive an answer, you will bring
it you know where; if no reply is sent, you will meet me this
evening with a petronel at the spot I showed you, and from
which I have just come."

"Very well," said Orthon, "I understand."

"I will now leave you. I have much to do to-day. You
need make no haste — there is no use in it, for you do not need
to reach the Louvre until *he* is there, and I think he is taking
a lesson in hawking this morning. Now go, and show me
what you can do. You have recovered, and you apparently
are going to thank Madame de Sauve for her kindness to you
during your illness. Now go, my boy."

Maurevel listened, his eyes fixed, his hair on end, his forehead covered with perspiration. His first impulse had been
to detach one of his pistols from his belt and aim at De Mouy;
but a movement of the latter had opened his cloak and displayed a firm and solid cuirass. Therefore in all probability the
ball would flatten itself against this cuirass or strike some part
of the body wherein the wound would not be fatal. Besides, he
reflected that De Mouy, strong and well armed, would have an
advantage over him, wounded as he was. So with a sigh he
drew back the weapon which he had pointed at the Huguenot.

"How unfortunate," he murmured, "that I am unable to
stretch him dead on the spot, without other witness than that
young varlet who would have been such a good mark for my
second ball!"

But Maurevel thought that the note given to Orthon and
which he was to deliver to Madame de Sauve might perhaps
be of more importance than the life of the Huguenot chief.

" Well ! " said he, " you have escaped me again this morning; be it so. To-morrow I will have my turn at you if I have
to follow you into that hell from which you have come to ruin
me, unless I destroy you.

De Mouy raised his cloak over his face, and set out rapidly
in the direction of the Temple. Orthon took the road along
the moat which led to the banks of the river.

Then Maurevel, rising with more energy and vigor than he
had dared to hope for, regained the Rue de la Cerisaie, reached
his home, ordered a horse to be saddled, and weak as he was
and at the risk of opening his wounds again, set off at a gallop
to the Rue Saint Antoine, reached the quays, and entered the
Louvre.

Five minutes after he had passed under the gate Catharine
knew all that had just taken place, and Maurevel had received
the thousand golden crowns promised him for the arrest of
the King of Navarre.

" Oh ! " said Catharine, " either I am mistaken or this De
Mouy is the black spot that was discovered by Réné in the
horoscope of the accursed Béarnais."

A quarter of an hour after Maurevel Orthon entered the
Louvre, showed himself as De Mouy had directed, and went
to the apartments of Madame de Sauve, after having spoken
to several attendants of the palace.

Dariole was the only one in her mistress's rooms. Catharine
had asked the latter to write certain important letters, and
she had been with the queen for the last five minutes.

" No matter," said Orthon, " I will wait."

Taking advantage of his intimacy in the house, the young
man went into the sleeping-room of the baroness, and, having
assured himself that he was alone, he laid the note behind the
mirror. Just as he was removing his hand Catharine entered.

Orthon turned pale, for it seemed to him that the quick,
searching glance of the queen mother was first directed to the
mirror.

" What are you doing here, my little man ? " asked Catharine;
" looking for Madame de Sauve ? "

" Yes, madame; it is a long time since I saw her, and if I
delay any longer in thanking her I fear she will think me
ungrateful."

" You love this dear Charlotte very much, do you not ? "

" With all my heart, madame ! "

" And you are faithful, from what I hear."

" Your majesty will understand that this is very natural when you know that Madame de Sauve took more care of me than I, being only an humble servant, deserved."

" And upon what occasion did she bestow all this care on you ? " asked Catharine, pretending to be ignorant of what had happened to the youth.

" When I was wounded, madame."

" Ah, poor boy ! " said Catharine, " you were wounded ? "

" Yes, madame."

" When was that ? "

" The night they tried to arrest the King of Navarre. I was so terrified at sight of the soldiers that I called and shouted ; and one of the men gave me a blow on the head which knocked me senseless."

" Poor boy !   And are you quite recovered now ? "

" Yes, madame."

" So that you are trying to get back into the service of the King of Navarre ? "

" No, madame.   When the King of Navarre learned that I had dared to resist your majesty's order he dismissed me at once."

" Indeed ! " said Catharine, in a tone full of interest ; " well, I will see to that affair.   But if you are waiting for Madame de Sauve you will wait in vain, for she is occupied in my apartments."

Whereupon, thinking that Orthon perhaps had not had time to hide his note behind the mirror, Catharine stepped into the adjoining room in order to give him the necessary opportunity.

But just as Orthon, anxious at the unexpected arrival of the queen mother, was wondering whether her coming did not forbode some plot against his master, he heard three gentle taps against the ceiling.   This was the signal which he himself was in the habit of giving his master in case of danger when the latter was with Madame de Sauve and Orthon was keeping guard.

He started at the sound ; a light broke upon his mind ; he fancied that this time the warning had been given to him. Springing to the mirror, he removed the note he had just placed there.

Through an opening in the tapestry Catharine had followed every movement of the boy.   She saw him dart to the mirror, but she did not know whether it was to hide the note or take it away.

"Well!" murmured the impatient Florentine; "why does he not leave now?"

And she returned to the room smiling.

"Still here, my boy?" said she; "why, what do you want? Did I not tell you that I would look after your fortune? When I say a thing you do not doubt it, do you?"

"Oh, madame, God forbid!" replied Orthon.

And approaching the queen, he bent his knee, kissed the hem of her robe, and at once withdrew.

As he went through the antechamber he saw the captain of the guards, who was waiting for Catharine. The sight of this man, instead of allaying his suspicions, augmented them.

On her part, no sooner had she seen the curtains fall behind Orthon than Catharine sprang to the mirror. But in vain she sought behind it with hands trembling with impatience. She found no note.

And yet she was sure that she had seen the boy approach the mirror. It was to remove the note, therefore, and not to leave it. Fate had given to her enemies a strength equal to her own.

A child had become a man the moment he fought with her.

She moved the mirror, looked behind it, tapped it; nothing was there!

"Oh! unhappy boy!" cried she, "I wished him no ill and now by removing the note he hastens his destiny. Ho, there, Monsieur de Nancey!"

The vibrating tones of the queen mother rang through the salon and penetrated into the anteroom, where, as we have said, Monsieur de Nancey was waiting.

The captain of the guards hastened to the queen.

"Here I am, madame," said he, "what is your majesty's will?"

"Have you been in the antechamber?"

"Yes, madame."

"Did you see a young man, a child, pass through?"

"Just now."

"He cannot have gone far, can he?"

"Scarcely to the stairway."

"Call him back."

"What is his name?"

" Orthon. If he refuses to come bring him back by force; but do not frighten him unless he resists. I must speak to him at once."

The captain of the guards hurriedly withdrew.

As he had said, Orthon was scarcely half way down the stairs, for he was descending slowly, hoping to meet or see the King of Navarre or Madame de Sauve somewhere.

He heard his name and gave a start.

His first impulse was to run, but with forethought beyond his years he realized that by doing so all would be lost.

He stopped therefore.

" Who calls me ? "

" I, Monsieur de Nancey," replied the captain of the guards, hurrying down the stairs.

" But I am in haste," said Orthon.

" By order of her majesty the queen mother," said Monsieur de Nancey, as he came up to him.

The youth wiped the perspiration from his brow and turned back.

The captain followed.

Catharine's first idea had been to stop the young man, have him searched, and take possession of the note which she knew he had. She had planned to accuse him of theft, and with this end in view she had removed from the toilet table a diamond clasp which she was going to say he had taken.

But on reflection she concluded that this would be dangerous, in that it would arouse the boy's suspicions and he would inform his master, who would then begin to mistrust something, and so her enemy would gain an advantage over her.

She could, no doubt, have the young man taken to some dungeon, but the rumor of the arrest, however secretly it might be done, would spread through the Louvre, and the slightest inkling of it would put Henry on his guard. However, she must have the note, for a note from Monsieur de Mouy to the King of Navarre, a note sent with such precautions, surely meant conspiracy.

She put back the clasp from where she had taken it.

" No, no," said she, " that would be the method of a guard; it is poor. But for a note — which perhaps after all is not worth the trouble," she continued, frowning, and speaking so low that she herself could scarcely hear the sound of her words. " Well, it is not my fault, but his. Why did not the little scoundrel put the note where he should have put it? I must have this letter."

Just then Orthon entered.

Catharine's face wore such a terrible expression that the youth stopped on the threshold pale as death. He was still too young to be perfect master of himself.

"Madame," said he, "you have done me the honor of calling me back. In what can I serve your majesty?"

Catharine's face lighted up as if a ray of sunlight had touched it.

"I called you back, my child," said she, "because your face pleases me, and having promised to help you I am anxious to do so without delay. We queens are sometimes accused of being forgetful. But this is not on account of our hearts, but because our minds are filled with business. Now I remembered that kings hold men's fortunes in their hands, and so I called you back. Follow me, my child."

Monsieur de Nancey, who was taking the affair seriously, was greatly surprised at Catharine's affectionate manner.

"Can you ride, my child?" asked Catharine.

"Yes, madame."

"Then come into my room. I want to give you a message to carry to Saint Germain."

"I am at your majesty's command."

"Order a horse to be saddled, De Nancey."

Monsieur de Nancey disappeared.

"Come, boy," said Catharine, leading the way.

Orthon followed. The queen mother descended to the next floor, entered the corridor in which were the apartments of the king and the Duc d'Alençon, reached the winding staircase, again descended a flight of stairs, and opened a door leading to a circular gallery to which none but the king and herself possessed the key. Bidding Orthon pass in first, she entered after him and locked the door. This gallery formed a sort of rampart to a certain portion of the apartments of the king and the queen mother, and, like the corridor of the castle of Saint Angelo at Rome, or that of the Pitti Palace at Florence, was a safe place in case of danger. The door locked, Catharine was alone with the young man in the dark corridor. Each advanced a few steps, the queen leading the way, Orthon following.

Suddenly Catharine turned and Orthon again saw on her

face the same sinister expression which he had seen on it a few minutes before. Her eyes were as round as those of a cat or a panther and seemed to dart forth fire in the darkness.

"Stop!" she cried.

Orthon felt a shiver run through him; a deathly cold like an icy cloak seemed to fall from the ceiling. The floor felt like the covering of a tomb. Catharine's glance was so sharp that it seemed to penetrate to the very soul of the page. He recoiled and leaned against the wall, trembling from head to foot.

" Where is the note you were charged to give to the King of Navarre ? "

" The note ? " stammered Orthon.

" Yes ; which, if you did not find him, you were to place behind the mirror ? "

" I, madame," said Orthon, " I do not know what you mean."

" The note which De Mouy gave you an hour ago, behind the Archery Garden."

" I have no note," said Orthon; "your majesty must be mistaken."

" You lie," said Catharine; " give me the note, and I will keep the promise I made you."

" What promise, madame ? "

" I will make your fortune."

" I have no note, madame," repeated the child.

Catharine ground her teeth; then assuming a smile:

" Give it to me," said she, "and you shall have a thousand golden crowns."

" I have no note, madame."

" Two thousand crowns."

" Impossible ; since I have no note, how can I give it to you ? "

" Ten thousand crowns, Orthon."

Orthon, who saw the anger of the queen rising, felt that there was only one way of saving his master, and that was to swallow the note. He put his hand to his pocket, but Catharine guessed his intention and stopped him.

" There, my child," said she, laughing, " you are certainly faithful. When kings wish to attach a follower to them there is no harm in their making sure of his trustworthiness. Here, take this purse as a first reward. Go and carry your note to your master, and tell him that from to-day you are in my service. You can get out without me by the door we entered. It opens from within."

And giving the purse to the astonished youth Catharine walked on a few steps and placed her hand against the wall.

But the young man stood still, hesitating. He could not believe that the danger he had felt hovering over him was gone.

"Come, do not tremble so," said Catharine. "Have I not told you that you were free to go, and that if you wish to come back your fortune is made?"

"Thank you, madame," said Orthon. "Then you pardon me?"

"I do more, I reward you; you are a faithful bearer of notes, a gentle messenger of love. But you forget your master is waiting for you."

"Ah! that is true," said the young man, springing towards the door.

But scarcely had he advanced three steps before the floor gave way beneath his feet. He stumbled, extended both hands, gave a fearful cry, and disappeared in the dungeon of the Louvre, the spring of which Catharine had just touched.

"So," murmured the queen, "thanks to the fellow's obstinacy I shall have to descend a hundred and fifty steps."

The queen mother returned to her apartments, lighted a dark lantern, came back to the corridor, closed the spring, and opened the door of a spiral staircase which seemed to lead to the bowels of the earth. Urged on by the insatiable thirst of a curiosity which was but the minister of her hatred, she reached an iron door which turned on its hinges and admitted her to the depths of the dungeon. Bleeding, crushed, and mutilated by a fall of a hundred feet or more, but still breathing, lay poor Orthon.

Beyond the thick wall the waters of the Seine were heard roaring, brought to the foot of the stairs by a subterranean channel.

Catharine entered the damp and unwholesome place, which during her reign had witnessed many a fall similar to the one it had just seen, searched the body, seized the letter, made sure that it was the one she desired, then pushing aside the body with her foot she pressed a spring, the bottom of the dungeon sank, and the corpse, carried down by its own weight, disappeared in the direction of the river.

Closing the door again, Catharine ascended, shut herself in her closet, and read the note, which contained these words :

" This evening at ten o'clock, Rue de l'Arbre Sec, Hôtel de la Belle Étoile. If you come send no reply ; otherwise send back NO by the bearer.

"*DE MOUY DE SAINT PHALE.*"

As Catharine read this note a smile came to her lips.   She was thinking of the victory she was to gain, forgetting the price at which she had bought it.   But after all what was Orthon ? A faithful, devoted follower, a handsome young boy ; that was all.

That, one may well imagine, would not for an instant have turned the scales on which the fate of empires had been weighed.

The note read, Catharine at once went to Madame de Sauve's and placed it behind the mirror.

As she came down she found the captain of the guards at the entrance of the corridor.

"Madame," said Monsieur de Nancey, "according to your majesty's orders the horse is ready."

"My dear baron," said Catharine, "we shall not need it. I have made the boy speak, and he is really too stupid to be charged with the errand I wanted to entrust to him.   I thought he was a lackey, but he is nothing but a groom at best.   I gave him some money and dismissed him by the private gate."

"But," said Monsieur de Nancey, "the errand ? "

"The errand ? " asked Catharine.

"The one on which he was to go to Saint Germain.   Does your majesty wish me to undertake it, or shall I have one of my men attend to it ? "

"No, no," said Catharine, "this evening you and your men will have something else to do."

Whereupon the queen mother returned to her room, hoping that evening to hold in her hands the fate of the accursed King of Navarre.

CHAPTER XLVI.

THE INN OF LA BELLE ÉTOILE.

Two hours after the event we have described, no trace of which remained on Catharine's face, Madame de Sauve, having finished her work for the queen, returned to her own rooms. Henry followed her, and learning from Dariole that Orthon had been there he went directly to the mirror and found the note.

It was, as we have said, couched in these terms:

" This evening at ten o'clock, Rue de l'Arbre Sec, Hôtel de la Belle Étoile. If you come send no reply; otherwise send back NO by the bearer."

There was no address.

" Henry will not fail to keep the appointment," said Catharine, " for even had he not wished to do so there is no longer a messenger to take back his answer."

Catharine was not mistaken.

Henry inquired for Orthon. Dariole said that he had gone out with the queen mother; but as the note had been found in its place, and as the poor boy was known to be incapable of treason, Henry felt no anxiety.

He dined as usual at the table of the King, who joked him greatly on the mistakes he had made while hawking that morning.

Henry made excuses for himself, saying that he came from the mountains and not the plain, but he promised Charles to study the art. Catharine was charming, and on leaving the table begged Marguerite to pass the evening with her.

At eight o'clock Henry took two attendants, left by the Porte Saint Honoré, made a long circuit, returned by the Tour de Bois, and crossing the Seine at the ferry of Nesle, rode up the Rue Saint Jacques, where he dismissed his gentlemen, as if he were going to keep some love appointment. At the corner of the Rue des Mathurins he found a man on horseback, wrapped in a cloak. He approached him.

" Mantes ! " said the man.

" Pau ! " replied the king.

The man at once dismounted. Henry put on his splashed mantle, mounted the horse, which was covered with foam, returned by the Rue de la Harpe, crossed the Pont Saint Michel, passed down the Rue Barthélemy, again crossed the river at the Pont aux Meuniers, descended the quays, took the Rue de l'Arbre Sec, and knocked at the door of Maître la Hurière's.

La Mole was in a room writing a long love-letter — to whom may easily be imagined.

Coconnas was in the kitchen with La Hurière, watching half a dozen partridges roasting, and disputing with his friend the host as to when they should be removed from the spit. At this moment Henry knocked. Grégoire opened the door and led the horse to the stable, while the traveller entered, stamping on the floor as if to warm his benumbed feet.

" Maître La Hurière," said La Mole, as he continued to write, " here is a gentleman asking for you."

La Hurière advanced, looked at Henry from head to foot, and as his thick cloth mantle did not inspire the innkeeper with very great veneration:

" Who are you ? " he asked.

" Well, by Heaven ! " said Henry, pointing to La Mole, " monsieur has just told you ; I am a gentleman from Gascony come to court."

" What do you want ? "

" A room and supper."

" Humph ! " said La Hurière, " have you a lackey ? "

This was the question usually asked, as is well known.

" No," replied Henry, " but I hope to have one when I make my fortune."

" I do not let rooms to any one unless he has a lackey," said La Hurière.

" Even if I offered to pay you double for your supper ? "

" Oh ! you are very generous, worthy sir ! " said La Hurière, looking suspiciously at Henry.

" Not at all, but, hoping to pass the night in your hotel, which has been highly recommended by a nobleman from my county who has been here, I invited a friend to sup with me. Have you any good wine of Arbois ? "

" I have some which is better than the King of Navarre drinks."

" Good ! I will pay well for it. Ah ! here is my friend."

Just then the door opened and a gentleman entered older by

a few years than the first, and dragging a long rapier at his side.

"Ah!" said he, "you are prompt, my young friend. For a man who has just made two hundred leagues it is something to be so punctual."

"Is this your guest?" asked La Hurière.

"Yes," said the first, going up to the young man with the rapier and shaking him by the hand, "we will have our supper now."

"Here or in your room?"

"Wherever you please."

"Maître," said La Mole to La Hurière, "rid us of these Huguenot fellows. Coconnas and I cannot say a word before them."

"Carry the supper to room No. 2, on the third floor. Up-stairs, gentlemen."

The two travellers followed Grégoire, who preceded them with lights.

La Mole watched them until they had disappeared. Then turning round he saw Coconnas, whose head was thrust out of the kitchen door. Two great eyes and an open mouth gave to the latter's face a remarkable expression of astonishment.

La Mole stepped up to him.

"By Heaven!" said Coconnas, "did you see?"

"What?"

"Those two gentlemen."

"Well?"

"I would swear that it was"—

"Who?"

"Why — the King of Navarre and the man in the red cloak."

"Swear if you will, but not too loud."

"Did you recognize them too?"

"Certainly."

"What are they here for?"

"Some love affair."

"You think so?"

"I am sure of it."

"La Mole, I prefer sword-thrusts to these love affairs. I would have sworn a moment ago, now I will bet."

"What will you bet?"

"That there is some plot on hand."

"You are mad."

"I tell you" —

"I tell you that even if they are plotting it is their own affair."

"That is true. However," said Coconnas, "I no longer belong to Monsieur d'Alençon. So let them do as they see fit."

As the partridges had apparently reached the state in which Coconnas liked them, the Piedmontese, who counted on making the most of his dinner of them, called Maître la Hurière to remove them from the spit.

Meantime Henry and De Mouy were installed in their chamber.

"Well, sire," said De Mouy, when Grégoire had set the table, "have you seen Orthon ? "

"No ; but I found the note he left behind the mirror. The boy must have become frightened, I suppose, for Queen Catharine came in while he was there, so he went away without waiting for my answer."

"For a moment I felt somewhat anxious about him, as Dariole told me that the queen mother had had a long talk with him."

"Oh ! there is no danger. The boy is clever, and although the queen mother knows his profession he will not let her find out much from him, I am sure."

"But have you seen him, De Mouy ? " asked Henry.

"No, but I expect to this evening. At midnight he is to come here for me with a good petronel. He will tell me what happened as we walk along."

"And the man at the corner of the Rue des Mathurins ? "

"What man ? "

"The man who gave me his horse and cloak. Are you sure of him ? "

"He is one of our most devoted followers. Besides, he neither knows your majesty nor why he himself was there."

"Can we discuss our affairs without fear, then ? "

"Certainly. Besides, La Mole is on the watch."

"Well, sire, what says Monsieur d'Alençon ? "

"Monsieur d'Alençon will not go, De Mouy. He said so positively. The election of D'Anjou to the throne of Poland and the king's illness have changed his mind."

"So he is the one who spoiled our plan ? "

"Yes."

"Has he betrayed us ? "

" Not yet ; but he will do so at the first opportunity."

" Coward ! traitor ! Why did he not answer my letters ? "

" In order to have proofs against you, and none against him-self. Meantime, all is lost, is it not, De Mouy ? "

" On the contrary, sire, all is won. You know that the whole party, except the faction of the Prince de Condé, was for you, and used the duke, with whom it seemed to have relations, only as a safeguard. Well, since the day of the ceremony I have arranged so that everything is for you. One hundred men were enough to escape with the Duc d'Alen-çon ; I have raised fifteen hundred. In one week they will be ready and drawn up on the road to Pau. It will not be a flight but a retreat. Fifteen hundred men will suffice, sire, will they not ? Shall you feel safe with such an army ? "

Henry smiled and touched him on the shoulder.

" You know, De Mouy," said he, " and you alone know it, that Henry of Navarre is not naturally such a coward as is sup-posed."

" Yes, I know that, sire ; and I trust before long that all France will know it too."

" But where one plots one must succeed. The first condi-tion of success is decision ; and for decision to be rapid, frank, and to the point, one must be sure of success."

" Well, sire, what days do you hunt ? "

" Every week or ten days we either hunt or hawk."

" When did you hunt last ? "

" To-day."

" Then a week or ten days from now you will hunt again ? "

" No doubt ; possibly before then."

" Listen, sire; everything seems perfectly quiet. The Duc d'Anjou has left; no one thinks of him. The King is getting better every day. The persecution against us has almost ceased. Play the amiable with the queen mother and Mon-sieur d'Alençon; keep telling him that you cannot go with-out him, and try to make him believe you, which is more difficult."

" Do not worry, he will believe me."

" Do you think he has such confidence in you ? "

" No, God forbid, but he believes everything the queen says."

" And is the queen true to us ? "

" Oh ! I have proof of it. Besides, she is ambitious and is dying for this far-off crown of Navarre."

" Well! three days before the hunt send me word where it
will take place — whether it is to be at Bondy, at Saint Germain, or at Rambouillet. Monsieur de la Mole will ride ahead
of you; follow him, and ride fast. Once out of the forest if
the queen mother wants you she will have to run after you;
and I trust that her Norman horses will not see even the
hoofs of our Barbary steeds and our Spanish ponies."

" Agreed, De Mouy."

" Have you any money, sire ? "

Henry made the same grimace he made all his life at this
question.

" Not much," said he; " but I think Margot has some."

" Well! whether it is yours or hers, bring as much as you
can."

" And in the meantime what are you going to do ? "

" Having paid some attention to your majesty's affairs, as
you see, will your majesty permit me to devote a little time
to my own ? "

" Certainly, De Mouy, certainly, but what are yours ? "

" Yesterday Orthon told me (he is a very intelligent boy,
whom I recommend to your majesty) that he met that scoundrel of a Maurevel near the arsenal, that thanks to Réné he
has recovered, and that he was warming himself in the sun
like the snake that he is."

" Ah, yes, I understand," said Henry.

" Very good, then. You will be king some day, sire, and
if you have anything such as I have to avenge you can do so
in a kingly way. I am a soldier and must avenge myself like
a soldier. So while all our little affairs are being arranged,
which will give that scoundrel five or six days in which to
recover more fully, I too shall take a stroll around the arsenal,
and I will pin him to the grass with four blows of my rapier,
after which I shall leave Paris with a lighter heart."

" Attend to your affairs, my friend, by all means," said the
Béarnais. " By the way, you are pleased with La Mole, are you
not ? "

" Yes; he is a charming fellow, devoted to you body and
soul, sire, and on whom you can depend as you can on me —
brave " —

" And above all, discreet. So he must follow us to Navarre,
De Mouy; once there we will look about and see what we can
do to recompense him."

As Henry concluded these words with a sly smile, the door opened or rather was broken in, and the man they had just been praising appeared, pale and agitated.

"Quick, sire," cried he; "quick, the house is surrounded."

"Surrounded!" cried Henry, rising; "by whom?"

"By the King's guards."

"Oh!" said De Mouy, drawing his pistols from his belt, "we are to have a battle, apparently."

"Well," said La Mole, "you may well talk of pistols and battle, but what can you do against fifty men?"

"He is right," said the king; "and if there were any means of escape" —

"There is one which has already been of use to me, and if your majesty will follow me" —

"And De Mouy?"

"And De Mouy too if he wishes, but you must be quick."

Steps were heard on the stairs.

"It is too late," said Henry.

"Ah! if any one would only engage them for five minutes," cried La Mole, "I would save the king."

"Save him, then, monsieur," said De Mouy; "I will look after them. Go, sire, go."

"But what shall you do?"

"Do not fear, sire, but go."

And De Mouy began by hiding the king's plate, napkin, and goblet, so that it might seem as though he had been alone at table.

"Come, sire, come," cried La Mole, seizing the king by the arm and dragging him towards the stairway.

"De Mouy, my brave De Mouy!" exclaimed Henry, holding out his hand to the young man.

De Mouy kissed the hand, pushed Henry from the room, and closed and bolted the door after him.

"Yes, I understand," said Henry, "he will be caught, while we escape; but who the devil can have betrayed us?"

"Come, sire, come. They are on the stairs."

In fact, the light of the torches was beginning to be seen on the wall, while at the foot of the stairs sounds like the clanking of swords were heard.

"Quick, quick, sire!" cried La Mole.

And, guiding the king in the darkness, he ascended two flights, pushed open a door, which he locked behind him, and, opening the window of a closet:

"Sire," said he, "is your majesty very much afraid of a walk across the roofs?"

"I?" said Henry, "come, now; am I not a chamois hunter?"

"Well, your majesty must follow me. I know the way and will guide you."

"Go on," said Henry, "I will follow."

La Mole stepped out, went along the ledge, which formed a sort of gutter, at the end of which they came to a depression between two roofs. In this way they reached an open window leading to an empty garret.

"Sire," said La Mole, "here we are at the opening."

"Ah! so much the better," said Henry, wiping the perspiration from his pale face.

"Now," said La Mole, "it will be easier: this garret opens on to a stairway, the stairway leads to an alley, and the alley to the street. I travelled the same road, sire, on a much more terrible night than this."

"Go on, go on," said Henry.

La Mole sprang through the open window, reached the unlocked door, opened it, came to a winding stairway, and placing in the king's hand the cord that served as a baluster:

"Come, sire," said he.

Half way down the stairs Henry stopped. He was before a window which overlooked the courtyard of the *Belle Étoile*. On the opposite stairway soldiers were seen running, some carrying swords, others torches.

Suddenly in the midst of a group the King of Navarre perceived De Mouy. He had surrendered his sword and was quietly descending the stairs.

"Poor fellow," said Henry, "so brave and devoted!"

"Faith, sire," said La Mole, "your majesty is right. He certainly does seem calm; and see, he even laughs! It must be that he is planning some scheme, for you know he seldom laughs."

"And the young man who was with you?"

"Monsieur de Coconnas?" asked La Mole.

"Yes; what has become of him?"

"Oh! sire, I am not anxious about him. On seeing the soldiers he said only one word to me: 'Do we risk anything?'

"'Our heads,' I answered.

" ' Can you escape ? '

" ' I hope so.'

" ' Well, I can too,' he replied. And I promise you he will ! Sire, when Coconnas is caught it will be because he wishes to be caught."

" Then," said Henry, " all is well. Let us try to get back to the Louvre."

" That will be easy enough, sire," said La Mole. " Let us wrap ourselves in our cloaks and start. The street is full of people running to see the commotion, and we shall be taken for spectators."

The gate was open and Henry and La Mole encountered no obstacle beyond the crowds in the street.

They reached the Rue d'Avernon; but in passing by the Rue Poulies they saw De Mouy and his escort cross the Place Saint Germain l'Auxerrois, led by the captain of the guards, Monsieur de Nancey.

" Ah ! " said Henry, " they are taking him to the Louvre, apparently. The devil! the gates will be closed. They will take the names of all those who enter, and if I am seen returning after him they will think I have been with him."

" Well! but, sire," said La Mole, " enter some other way than by the gate."

" How the devil do you mean ? "

" Well, sire, there is the Queen of Navarre's window."

" *Ventre saint gris*, Monsieur de la Mole," said Henry, " you are right. I never thought of that! But how can I attract the attention of the queen ? "

" Oh," said La Mole, bowing with an air of respectful gratitude, " your majesty throws stones so well ! "

CHAPTER XLVII.

DE MOUY DE SAINT PHALE.

THIS time Catharine had taken such precautions that she felt sure of her object.

Consequently, about ten o'clock she sent away Marguerite, thoroughly convinced, as was the case, that the Queen of Navarre was ignorant of the plot against her husband, and went to the King, begging him not to retire so early.

Mystified by the air of triumph which, in spite of her usual dissimulation, appeared on his mother's face, Charles questioned Catharine, who merely answered:

"I can say only one thing to your Majesty: that this evening you will be freed from two of your bitterest enemies."

Charles raised his eyebrows like a man who says to himself:

"That is well; we shall see;" and whistling to his great boar-hound, who came to him dragging his belly along the ground like a serpent to lay his fine and intelligent head on his master's knee, he waited. At the end of a few minutes, during which Catharine sat with eyes and ears alert, a pistol-shot was heard in the courtyard of the Louvre.

"What is that noise?" asked Charles, frowning, while the hound sprang up and pricked his ears.

"Nothing except a signal," said Catharine; "that is all."

"And what is the meaning of the signal?"

"It means that from this moment, sire, your one real enemy can no longer injure you."

"Have they killed a man?" asked Charles, looking at his mother with that look of command which signifies that assassination and mercy are two inherent attributes of royal power.

"No, sire, they have only arrested two."

"Oh!" murmured Charles, "always hidden plots, always conspiracies around the King. And yet, the devil! mother, I am grown up, and big enough to look out for myself. I need neither leading-strings nor padded caps. Go to Poland with your son Henry if you wish to reign; I tell you you are wrong to play this kind of game here."

"My son," said Catharine, "this is the last time I shall meddle with your affairs. But the enterprise in which you have always thwarted me was begun long ago, and I have earnestly endeavored to prove to your Majesty that I am right."

At that moment several men stopped in the outer hall and the butt-ends of muskets were heard on the pavement. Almost at the same instant Monsieur de Nancey begged an audience of the King.

"Let him enter," said Charles, hastily.

Monsieur de Nancey appeared, saluted the King, and turning to Catharine said:

"Madame, your majesty's orders are executed; he is captured."

" What *he ?* " cried Catharine, greatly troubled. " Have you arrested only one ? "

" He was alone, madame ? "

" Did he defend himself ? "

" No, he was supping quietly in a room, and gave up his sword the moment it was demanded."

" Who ? " asked the King.

" You shall see," said Catharine. " Bring in the prisoner, Monsieur de Nancey."

Five minutes later De Mouy was there.

" De Mouy !" cried the King ; " what is the matter now, monsieur ? "

" Well, sire," said De Mouy, with perfect composure, " if your Majesty will allow me the liberty, I will ask the same of you."

" Instead of asking this question of the King," said Catharine, " have the kindness, Monsieur de Mouy, to tell my son who was the man found in the chamber of the King of Navarre a certain night, and who on that night resisted the orders of his Majesty like the rebel that he is, killed two guards, and wounded Monsieur de Maurevel ? "

" Yes," said Charles, frowning, " do you know the name of that man, Monsieur de Mouy ? "

" Yes, sire ; does your Majesty wish to hear it ? "

" That will please me, I admit."

" Well, sire, he is called De Mouy de Saint Phale."

" It was you ? "

" It was I."

Catharine, astonished at this audacity, recoiled a step.

" How did you dare resist the orders of the King ? " asked Charles.

" In the first place, sire, I did not know that there was an order from your Majesty ; then I saw only one thing, or rather one man, Monsieur de Maurevel, the assassin of my father and of the admiral. I remembered that a year and a half ago, in the very room in which we now are, on the evening of the 24th of August, your Majesty promised me to avenge us on the murderer, and as since that time very grave events have occurred I thought that in spite of himself the King had changed his mind. Seeing Maurevel within reach, I believed Heaven had sent him to me. Your Majesty knows the rest.

Sire, I sprang upon him as upon an assassin and fired at his men as I would have fired at bandits."

Charles made no reply. His friendship for Henry had for some time made him look at many things in a different light from which he had at first seen them, and more than once with terror.

In regard to Saint Bartholomew the queen mother had registered in her memory remarks which had fallen from her son's lips and which resembled remorse.

"But," observed Catharine, "what were you doing at that hour in the apartments of the King of Navarre?"

"Oh!" replied De Mouy, "it is a long story, but if his Majesty has the patience to listen" —

"Yes," said Charles; "speak, I wish to hear it."

"I will obey, sire," said De Mouy, bowing.

Catharine sat down, fixing an anxious look on the young chief.

"We are listening," said Charles. "Here, Actéon!"

The dog resumed the place he had occupied before the prisoner had been admitted.

"Sire," said De Mouy, "I came to his majesty the King of Navarre as the deputy of our brethren, your faithful subjects of the reformed religion."

Catharine signed to Charles IX.

"Be quiet, mother," said the latter. "I do not lose a word. Go on, Monsieur de Mouy, go on; why did you come?"

"To inform the King of Navarre," continued Monsieur de Mouy, "that his abjuration had lost for him the confidence of the Huguenot party; but that, nevertheless, in remembrance of his father, Antoine de Bourbon, and especially on account of his mother, the courageous Jeanne d'Albret, whose name is dear among us, the followers of the reformed religion owed him this mark of deference, to beg him to desist from his claims to the crown of Navarre."

"What did he say?" asked Catharine, unable in spite of her self-control to receive this unexpected blow calmly.

"Ah! ah!" said Charles, "and yet this crown of Navarre, which without my permission has been made to jump from head to head, seems to belong a little to me."

"The Huguenots, sire, recognize better than any one the principle of sovereignty to which your Majesty has just referred. Therefore they hope to induce your Majesty to place the crown on a head that is dear to you."

"To me!" said Charles; "on a head that is dear to me! The devil! what head do you mean, monsieur? I do not understand."

"On the head of Monsieur le Duc d'Alençon."

Catharine became as pale as death, and gave De Mouy a flashing glance.

"Did my brother D'Alençon know this?"

"Yes, sire."

"And did he accept the crown?"

"Subject to the consent of your Majesty, to whom he referred us."

"Ah!" said Charles, "it is a crown which would suit our brother D'Alençon wonderfully well. And I never thought of it! Thanks, De Mouy, thanks! When you have such ideas you will always be welcome at the Louvre."

"Sire, you would long since have been informed of this project had it not been for that unfortunate affair of Maurevel's, which made me afraid I had fallen into disgrace with your Majesty."

"Yes, but what did Henry say to this plan?" asked Catharine.

"The King of Navarre, madame, yielded to the desire of his brethren, and his renunciation was ready."

"In that case," said Catharine, "you must have the renunciation."

"It happens that I have it with me, madame, signed by him and dated."

"Dated previous to the affair in the Louvre?" said Catharine.

"Yes, the evening before, I think."

De Mouy drew from his pocket an abdication in favor of the Duc d'Alençon, written and signed in Henry's hand, and bearing the date indicated.

"Faith, yes," said Charles, "and all is in due form."

"What did Henry demand in return for this renunciation?"

"Nothing, madame; the friendship of King Charles, he told us, would amply repay him for the loss of a crown."

Catharine bit her lips in anger and wrung her beautiful hands.

"All this is perfectly correct, De Mouy," said the King.

"Then," said the queen mother, "if everything was settled between you and the King of Navarre, what was the object of your interview with him this evening?"

"I, madame! with the King of Navarre?" said De Mouy. "Monsieur de Nancey, who arrested me, will bear witness that I was alone. Your majesty can ask him."

"Monsieur de Nancey!" called the King.

The captain of the guards entered.

"Monsieur de Nancey," said Catharine, quickly, "was Monsieur de Mouy entirely alone at the inn of the *Belle Étoile?*"

"In the room, yes, madame; in the hostelry, no."

"Ah!" said Catharine, "who was his companion?"

"I do not know if he was the companion of Monsieur de Mouy, madame, but I know that a man escaped by a back door after having stretched two of my men on the floor."

"And you recognized this gentleman, no doubt?"

"No, I did not, but my guards did."

"Who was he?" asked Charles IX.

"Monsieur le Comte Annibal de Coconnas."

"Annibal de Coconnas!" exclaimed the King, gloomy and thoughtful; "the one who made such a terrible slaughter of the Huguenots during the massacre of Saint Bartholomew?"

"Monsieur de Coconnas, a gentleman in the suite of Monsieur d'Alençon," said Monsieur de Nancey.

"Very good," said Charles IX. "You may go, Monsieur de Nancey, and another time, remember one thing."

"What is it, sire?"

"That you are in my service, and that you are to obey no one but me."

Monsieur de Nancey withdrew backwards, bowing respectfully.

De Mouy smiled ironically at Catharine.

There was an instant's silence. The queen twisted the tassels of her girdle; Charles caressed his dog.

"But what was your intention, monsieur?" continued Charles; "were you acting violently?"

"Against whom, sire?"

"Why, against Henry, or François, or myself."

"Sire, we have the renunciation of your brother-in-law, the consent of your brother; and, as I have had the honor of telling you, we were on the point of soliciting your Majesty's sanction when that unfortunate affair occurred at the Louvre."

"Well, mother," said Charles, "I see nothing wrong in all this. You were right, Monsieur de Mouy, in asking for a king. Yes, Navarre may and ought to be a separate kingdom. Moreover, it seems made expressly to give to my brother D'Alençon, who has always had so great a desire for a crown that when we wear ours he cannot keep his eyes off of it. The only thing which stood in the way of this coronation was Henriot's rights; but since Henriot voluntarily abdicates " —

"Voluntarily, sire."

"It seems that it is the will of God! Monsieur de Mouy, you are free to return to your brethren, whom I have chastised somewhat roughly, perhaps, but that is between God and myself. Tell them that since they desire to have my brother d'Alençon for King of Navarre the King of France accedes to their wishes. From this moment Navarre is a kingdom, and its sovereign is called François. I ask only eight days for my brother to leave Paris with the brilliancy and pomp befitting a king. Now go, Monsieur de Mouy, go! Monsieur de Nancey, allow Monsieur de Mouy to pass; he is free."

"Sire," said De Mouy, advancing a step, "will your Majesty permit me ? "

"Yes," said the King, and he extended his hand to the young Huguenot.

De Mouy knelt and kissed the King's hand.

"By the way," said Charles, detaining him as he was about to rise, " did you not demand from me justice on that scoundrel of a Maurevel ? "

"Yes, sire."

"I do not know where he is, as he is hiding; but if you meet him, take justice into your own hands. I authorize you to do this and gladly."

"Ah! sire," cried De Mouy, "your Majesty overwhelms me. Your Majesty may rely on me. I have no idea where he is, but I will find him, you may rest assured."

De Mouy respectfully saluted King Charles and Queen Catharine, and withdrew without hindrance from the guards who had brought him thither. He passed rapidly through the corridors, reached the gate, and once outside hurried to the Place Saint Germain l'Auxerrois, to the inn of the *Belle*

Étoile. Here he found his horse, thanks to which, three hours after the scene we have just described, the young man breathed in safety behind the walls of Mantes.

Catharine, consumed with rage, returned to her apartments, whence she passed into those of Marguerite.

She found Henry there in his dressing-gown, apparently ready for bed.

"Satan!" she murmured, "aid a poor queen for whom God will do nothing more!"

CHAPTER XLVIII.

TWO HEADS FOR ONE CROWN.

"Ask Monsieur d'Alençon to come to me," said Charles as he dismissed his mother.

Monsieur de Nancey, in accordance with the remark of the King that henceforth he was to obey him alone, hastened to the duke's apartments and delivered word for word the order he had just received.

The Duc d'Alençon gave a start. He had always feared Charles, and now more than ever since by conspiring he had reason to be afraid.

Nevertheless, he went to his brother in all haste.

Charles was standing up, whistling a hunting-song.

As he entered, the Duc d'Alençon caught from the glassy eye of the King one of those bitter looks of hatred which he knew so well.

"Your Majesty has sent for me," said he. "Here I am; what does your Majesty desire?"

"I desire to tell you, my good brother, that as a reward for the great friendship you bear me I have decided to-day to do for you the thing you most want."

"For me?"

"Yes, for you. Think what for some time you have been dreaming of, without daring to ask it of me, and I will give it to you."

"Sire," said François, "I swear to you that I desire nothing but the continued good health of the King."

"In that case you will be glad to know, D'Alençon, that the indisposition I experienced at the time the Poles arrived has passed by. Thanks to Henriot, I escaped a furious wild boar, which would have ripped me open, and I am so well that I do not envy the most healthy man in my kingdom. Without being an unkind brother you can, therefore, ask for something besides the continuation of my health, which is excellent."

"I want nothing, sire."

"Yes, yes, François," said Charles, impatiently, "you desire the crown of Navarre, since you have had an understanding with Henriot and De Mouy, — with the first, that he would abdicate; with the second, that he would give it to you. Well! Henriot renounces it! De Mouy has told me of your wish, and this crown for which you are ambitious " —

"Well ? " asked D'Alençon in a trembling voice.

"Well, the devil! it is yours."

D'Alençon turned frightfully pale; then suddenly the blood rushed from his heart, which almost burst, flowed to his face, and his cheeks became suffused with a burning flush. The favor the King granted him at that moment threw him into despair.

"But, sire," said he, trembling with emotion and trying in vain to recover his self-possession, "I never desired and certainly never asked for such a thing."

"That is possible," said the King, "for you are very discreet, brother; but it has been desired and asked for you."

"Sire, I swear to you that never " —

"Do not swear."

"But, sire, are you going to exile me, then ? "

"Do you call this exile, Francois? Plague it, you are hard to please! What better do you hope for ? "

D'Alençon bit his lips in despair.

"Faith! " continued Charles, affecting kindness, "I did not think you were so popular, François, especially with the Huguenots. But they have sought you, and I have to confess to myself that I was mistaken. Besides, I could ask nothing better than to have one of my family — my brother who loves me and who is incapable of betraying me — at the head of a party which for thirty years has made war against us. This will quell everything as if by enchantment, to say nothing of the fact that we shall all be kings in the family. There will be no one except poor Henriot who will be nothing but my friend. But he is not ambitious and he shall take this title which no one else claims."

"Oh, sire! you are mistaken. I claim this title, and who

has a better right to it than I? Henry is only your brother by marriage. I am your brother by blood, and more than this, my love — Sire, I beg you, keep me near you."

"No, no, François," replied Charles; "that would be to your unhappiness."

"How so?"

"For many reasons."

"But, sire, shall you ever find as faithful a companion as I am? From my childhood I have never left your Majesty."

"I know that very well; and sometimes I have wished you farther away."

"What does your Majesty mean?"

"Nothing, nothing; I understand myself. Oh, what fine hunts you will have there, François! How I envy you! Do you know that in those devilish mountains they hunt the bear as here we do the wild boar? You will send us all such magnificent skins! They hunt there with a dagger, you know; they wait for the animal, excite him, irritate him; he advances towards the hunter, and when within four feet of him he rises on his hind legs. It is then that they plunge the steel into his heart as Henry did to the boar at our last hunt. It is dangerous sport, but you are brave, François, and the danger will be a real pleasure for you."

"Ah! your Majesty increases my grief, for I shall hunt with you no more."

"By Heaven! so much the better!" said the King. "It helps neither of us to hunt together."

"What does your Majesty mean?"

"That hunting with me causes you such pleasure and rouses in you such emotion that you who are the personification of skill, you who with any musket can bring down a magpie a hundred feet away, the last time we hunted together failed at twenty paces to hit a wild boar; but with your weapon, a weapon, too, with which you are familiar, you broke the leg of my best horse. The devil, François, that makes one reflect, you know!"

"Oh! sire, pardon me, it was from emotion," said D'Alençon, who had become livid.

"Yes," replied Charles, "I can well imagine what the emotion was; and it is on account of this emotion that I realize all that it means when I say to you: 'Believe me, François, when one has such emotions it is best for us to hunt at a distance from each other. Think about it, brother, not while you are with me, because I can see my presence troubles you, but when you are alone, and you will see that I have every reason to fear that in another hunt you might be seized with another emotion. There is nothing like emotion for causing the hand to rise, and you might kill the rider instead of the horse, the king instead of the beast. Plague it, a bullet aimed too high or too low changes an entire government. We have an example of this in our own family. When Montgommery killed our father, Henry II., by accident — emotion, perhaps — the blow placed our brother, François II., on the throne and sent our father Henry to Saint Denis. So little is necessary for Providence to effect much!"

The duke felt the perspiration running down his face at this attack, as formidable as it was unforeseen.

It would have been impossible for the King to show more clearly that he had surmised all. Veiling his anger under a jesting manner, Charles was perhaps more terrible than as if he had let himself pour forth the lava of hate which was consuming his heart; his vengeance seemed in proportion to his rancor. As the one grew sharper, the other increased, and for the first time D'Alençon felt remorse, or rather regret for having meditated a crime which had not succeeded. He had sustained the struggle as long as he could, but at this final blow he bent his head, and Charles saw dawning in his eyes that devouring fire which in beings of a tender nature ploughs the furrow from which spring tears.

But D'Alençon was one of those who weep only from anger. Charles fixed on him his vulture gaze, watching the feelings which succeeded one another across the face of the young man, and all those sensations appeared to him as accurately, thanks to the deep study he had made of his family. as if the heart of the duke had been an open book.

He left him a moment, crushed, motionless, and mute; then in a voice stamped with the firmness of hatred :

"Brother," said he, "we have declared to you our resolution ; it is immutable. You will go."

D'Alençon gave a start, but Charles did not appear to notice it, and continued :

"I wish Navarre to be proud of having for king a brother of the King of France. Gold, power, honor, all that belongs to your birth you shall have, as your brother Henry had, and like him," he added, smiling, "you will bless me from afar. But no matter, blessings know no distance."

" Sire " —

" Accept my decision, or rather, resign yourself. Once king, we shall find a wife for you worthy of a son of France, and she, perhaps, may bring you another throne."

" But," said the Duc d'Alençon, "your Majesty forgets your good friend Henry."

" Henry! but I told you that he did not want the throne of Navarre! I told you he had abdicated in favor of you! Henry is a jovial fellow, and not a pale-face like you. He likes to laugh and amuse himself at his ease, and not mope, as we who wear crowns are condemned to do."

D'Alençon heaved a sigh.

" Your Majesty orders me then to occupy myself " —

" No, not at all. Do not disturb yourself at all; I will arrange everything; rely on me, as on a good brother. And now that everything is settled, go. However, not a word of our conversation to your friends. I will take measures to give publicity to the affair very soon. Go now, François."

There was nothing further to be said, so the duke bowed and withdrew, rage in his heart.

He was very anxious to find Henry and talk with him about all that had just taken place; but he found only Catharine. As a matter of fact, Henry wished to avoid the interview, whereas the latter sought for it.

On seeing Catharine the duke swallowed his anger and strove to smile. Less fortunate than Henry of Anjou, it was not a mother he sought in Catharine, but merely an ally. He began therefore by dissimulation, for in order to make good alliances it is necessary for each party to be somewhat deceived.

He met Catharine with a face on which there remained only a slight trace of anxiety.

" Well, madame," said he, "here is great news; have you heard it? "

" I know that there is a plan on hand to make a king of you, monsieur."

" It is a great kindness on the part of my brother, madame."

" Is it not? "

" And I am almost tempted to believe that I owe a part of my gratitude to you; for it was really you who advised

Charles to make me the present of a throne; it is to you I owe it. However, I will confess that, at heart, it gives me pain thus to rob the King of Navarre."

"You love Henriot very much, apparently."

"Why, yes; we have been intimate for some time."

"Do you think he loves you as much as you love him?"

"I hope so, madame."

"Such a friendship is very edifying; do you know it? especially between princes. Court friendships mean very little, François."

"Mother, you must remember we are not only friends, but almost brothers."

Catharine smiled a strange smile.

"Ah," said she, "are there brothers among kings?"

"Oh! as to that, neither of us was a king, mother, when our intimacy began. Moreover, we never expected to be kings; that is why we loved each other."

"Yes, but things are changed."

"How changed?"

"Why, who can say now whether both of you will not be kings?"

From the nervous start of the duke and the flush which rose to his brow Catharine saw that the arrow aimed by her had hit the mark.

"He?" said he, "Henriot king? And of what kingdom, mother?"

"One of the most magnificent kingdoms in Christendom, my son."

"Oh! mother," said D'Alençon, growing pale, "what are you saying?"

"What a good mother ought to say to her son, and what you have thought of more than once, François."

"I?" said the duke; "I have thought of nothing, madame, I swear to you."

"I can well believe you, for your friend, your brother Henry, as you call him, is, under his apparent frankness, a very clever and wily person, who keeps his secrets better than you keep yours, François. For instance, did he ever tell you that De Mouy was his man of business?"

As she spoke, Catharine turned a glance upon François as though it were a dagger aimed at his very soul.

But the latter had but one virtue, or rather vice, — the art of dissimulation; and he bore her look unflinchingly.

"De Mouy!" said he in surprise, as if it were the first time he had heard the name mentioned in that connection.

"Yes, the Huguenot De Mouy de Saint Phale; the one who nearly killed Monsieur de Maurevel, and who, secretly and in various disguises, is running all over France and the capital, intriguing and raising an army to support your brother Henry against your family."

Catharine, ignorant that on this point her son François knew as much if not more than she, rose at these words and started majestically to leave the room, but François detained her.

"Mother," said he, "another word, if you please. Since you deign to initiate me into your politics, tell me how, with his feeble resources, and being so slightly known, Henry could succeed in carrying on a war serious enough to disturb my family?"

"Child," said the queen, smiling, "he is supported by perhaps more than thirty thousand men; he has but to say the word and these thirty thousand men will appear as suddenly as if they sprang from the ground; and these thirty thousand men are Huguenots, remember, that is, the bravest soldiers in the world, and then he has a protector whom you neither could nor would conciliate."

"Who is that?"

"He has the King, the King, who loves him and who urges him on; the King, who from jealousy of your brother of Poland, and from spite against you, is looking about for a successor. But, blind man that you are if you do not see it, he seeks somewhere else besides in his own family."

"The King! — you think so, mother?"

"Have you not noticed how he loves Henriot, his Henriot?"

"Yes, mother, yes."

"And how he is repaid, for this same Henriot, forgetting that his brother-in-law would have shot him at the massacre of Saint Bartholomew, grovels to the earth like a dog which licks the hand that has beaten him."

"Yes, yes," murmured François, "I have already noticed that Henry is very humble with my brother Charles."

"Clever in trying to please him in everything."

"So much so that because of being always rallied by the King as to his ignorance of hawking he has begun to study it;

and yesterday, yes, it was only yesterday, he asked me if I had not some books on that sport."

"Well," said Catharine, whose eyes sparkled as if an idea had suddenly come to her, "what did you answer him?"

"That I would look in my library."

"Good," said Catharine, "he must have this book."

"But I looked, madame, and found nothing."

"I will find one — and you shall give it to him as though it came from you."

"And what will come of this?"

"Have you confidence in me, D'Alençon?"

"Yes, mother."

"Will you obey me blindly so far as Henry is concerned? For whatever you may have said you do not love him."

D'Alençon smiled.

"And I detest him," continued Catharine.

"Yes, I will obey you."

"Well, the day after to-morrow come here for the book; I will give it to you, you shall take it to Henry, and " —

"And?"

"Leave the rest to Providence or to chance."

François knew his mother well enough to realize that she was not in the habit of leaving to Providence or to chance the care of friendships or hatreds. But he said nothing, and bowing like a man who accepts the commission with which he is charged, he returned to his own apartments.

"What does she mean?" thought the young man as he mounted the stairs. "I cannot see. But what I do understand in all this is that she acts like our common enemy. Well, let her go ahead."

Meantime Marguerite, through La Mole, had received a letter from De Mouy to the King of Navarre. As in politics the two illustrious allies had no secrets, she opened the letter and read it.

The letter must have interested her, for, taking advantage of the darkness which was beginning to overshadow the walls of the Louvre, Marguerite at once hurried along the secret corridor, ascended the winding stairway, and, having looked carefully about on all sides, glided on like a shadow and disappeared within the antechamber of the King of Navarre.

This room had been unguarded since the disappearance of Orthon.

This circumstance, of which we have not spoken since the reader learned of the tragic fate of poor Orthon, had greatly troubled Henry. He had spoken of it to Madame de Sauve and to his wife, but neither of them knew any more about it than he did. Madame de Sauve had given him some information from which it was perfectly clear to Henry's mind that the poor boy had been a victim of some machination of the queen mother, and that this was why he himself had been interrupted with De Mouy in the inn of the *Belle Étoile.* Any other than Henry would have kept silence, fearing to speak, but Henry calculated everything. He realized that his silence would betray him. One does not as a rule lose one's servitor and confidant thus, without making inquiries about him and looking for him. So Henry asked and searched even in the presence of the King and the queen mother, and of every one, from the sentinel who walked before the gate of the Louvre to the captain of the guards, keeping watch in the antechamber of the King; but all inquiry and search was in vain, and Henry seemed so affected by the circumstance and so attached to the poor absent servitor that he said he would not put another in his place until he was perfectly sure that Orthon had disappeared forever.

So the antechamber, as we have said, was empty when Marguerite reached it.

Light as were the steps of the queen, Henry heard them and turned round.

"You, madame!" he exclaimed.

"Yes," said Marguerite. "Quick! Read this!" and she handed him the open letter.

It contained these lines:

" *Sire: The moment has come for putting our plan of flight into execution. The day after to-morrow there will be hunting along the Seine, from Saint Germain to Maisons, that is, all long the forest.*

" *Go to the hunt, although it is hawking; wear a good coat of mail under your suit; take your best sword and ride the best horse in your stable. About noon, when the chase is at its height, and the King is galloping after the falcon, escape alone if you come alone; with the Queen of Navarre if the queen will follow you.*

" *Fifty of our men will be hidden in the Pavilion of François*

I., *of which we have the key; no one will know that they will be there, for they will have come at night, and the shutters will be closed.*

"*You will pass by the Alley of the Violettes, at the end of which I shall be watching; at the right of this alley in an open space will be Messieurs de la Mole and Coconnas, with two horses. These horses are intended to replace yours and that of her majesty the Queen of Navarre, if necessary.*

"*Adieu, sire; be ready, as we shall be.*"

" You will be," said Marguerite, uttering after sixteen hundred years the same words that Cæsar spoke on the banks of the Rubicon.

" Be it so, madame," replied Henry; " I will not fail you."

" Now, sire, be a hero; it is not difficult. You have but to follow the path that is indicated, and make a beautiful throne for me," said the daughter of Henry II.

An imperceptible smile rose to the thin lips of the Béarnais. He kissed Marguerite's hand, and went out to explore the corridor, whistling the refrain of an old song:

> " *Cil qui mieux battit la muraille*
> *N'entra pas dedans le chasteau.*"[1]

The precaution was wise, for just as he opened the door of his sleeping-room the Duc d'Alençon opened that of his antechamber. Henry motioned to Marguerite, and then, aloud, said:

" Ah! is it you, brother? Welcome."

At the sign from her husband the queen had understood everything, and stepped hurriedly into a dressing-closet, in front of the door of which hung a thick tapestry. The Duc d'Alençon entered with a timorous step and looked around him.

" Are we alone, brother? " asked he in a whisper.

"Entirely. But what is the matter? You seem disturbed."

" We are discovered, Henry."

" How? — discovered? "

" Yes, De Mouy has been arrested."

" I know it."

" Well, De Mouy has told the King all."

" What has he told him? "

" He has told him that I desire the throne of Navarre, and that I have conspired to obtain it."

---

[1] He who beats on the wall will never get into the castle.

" Ah, the stupid!" cried Henry, " so that now you are compromised, my poor brother! How is it, then, that you have not been arrested?"

" I do not know. The King joked with me by pretending to offer me the throne of Navarre. He hoped, no doubt, to draw some confession from me, but I said nothing."

" And you did well, *ventre saint gris!* " said the Béarnais. " Stand firm, for our lives depend on that."

" Yes," said François, "the position is unsafe, I know. That is why I came to ask your advice, brother; what do you think I ought to do — run or stay?"

" You must have seen the King, since he spoke to you?"

" Yes, of course."

" Well! you must have read his thoughts. So follow your inspiration."

" I prefer to remain," replied François.

Notwithstanding the fact that he was almost thorough master of himself, Henry could not prevent a movement of joy from escaping him, and slight as it was, François saw it.

" Remain, then," said Henry.

" But you?"

" Why!" replied Henry, " if you remain, I have no motive for leaving. I was going only to follow you from devotion, in order not to be separated from my brother."

" So," said D'Alençon, " there is an end to all our plans; you give up without a struggle at the first stroke of ill luck?"

" I do not look upon it as a stroke of ill luck to remain here," said Henry. " Thanks to my careless disposition, I am contented everywhere."

" Well, then," said D'Alençon, " we need say no more about it, only in case you decide anything different let me know."

" By Heaven! I shall not fail to do that, you may be sure," replied Henry. " Was it not agreed that we were to have no secrets from each other?"

D'Alençon said no more, but withdrew, pondering, however; for at one time he thought he had seen the tapestry in front of the closet move.

Scarcely was the duke gone when the curtain was raised and Marguerite reappeared.

" What do you think of this visit?" asked Henry.

" That there is something new and important on hand."

" What do you think it is?"

"I do not know yet; but I will find out."

"In the meanwhile?"

"In the meanwhile do not fail to come to my room to-morrow evening."

"Indeed I will not fail, madame!" said Henry, gallantly kissing the hand of his wife.

With the same caution she had used in coming Marguerite returned to her own apartments.

CHAPTER XLIX.

THE TREATISE ON HUNTING.

THREE days had elapsed since the events we have just related. Day was beginning to dawn, but every one was already up and awake at the Louvre as usual on hunting days, when the Duc d'Alençon entered the apartments of the queen mother in answer to the invitation he had received. Catharine was not in her bedroom; but she had left orders that if her son came he was to wait for her.

At the end of a few minutes she came out of a private closet, to which no one but herself had admission, and in which she carried on her experiments in chemistry. As Catharine entered the room there came either from the closet or from her clothes the penetrating odor of some acrid perfume, and through the open door D'Alençon perceived a thick vapor, as of some burnt aromatic substance, floating in the laboratory like a white cloud.

The duke could not repress a glance of curiosity.

"Yes," said Catharine de Médicis, "I have been burning several old parchments which gave out such an offensive smell that I put some juniper into the brazier, hence this odor."

D'Alençon bowed.

"Well," said the queen, concealing under the wide sleeves of her dressing-gown her hands, which here and there were stained with reddish spots, "is there anything new since yesterday?"

"Nothing, mother."

"Have you seen Henry?"

"Yes."

"Does he still refuse to leave?"

" Absolutely."

" The knave ! "

" What do you say, madame ? "

" I say that he will go."

" You think so ? "

" I am sure of it."

" Then he will escape us ? "

." Yes," said Catharine.

" And shall you let him go ? "

" Not only that, but I tell you he must go."

" I do not understand, mother."

" Listen well to what I am about to tell you, François. A very skilful physician, the one who let me take the book on hunting which you are to give him, has told me that the King of Navarre is on the point of being attacked with consumption, one of those incurable diseases for which science has no remedy. Now, you understand that if he has to die from such a cruel malady it would be better for him to die away from us than among us here at court."

" In fact," said the duke, " that would cause us too much pain."

" Especially your brother Charles," said Catharine; " whereas, if he dies after having betrayed him the King will regard his death as a punishment from Heaven."

" You are right, mother," said François in admiration, " he must leave. But are you sure that he will ? "

" All his plans are made. The meeting-place is in the forest of Saint Germain. Fifty Huguenots are to escort him as far as Fontainebleau, where five hundred others will await him."

" And," said D'Alençon, with a slight hesitation and visible pallor, " will my sister Margot accompany him ? "

" Yes," replied Catharine, " that is agreed on. But at Henry's death Margot is to return to court a widow and free."

" And Henry will die, madame ? Are you sure of this ? "

" The physician who gave me the book assured me of it."

" Where is this book, madame ? "

Catharine went slowly towards the mysterious closet, opened the door, entered, and a moment later appeared with the book in her hand.

" Here it is," said she.

D'Alençon looked at the volume with a certain feeling of terror.

"What is this book, madame?" he asked, shuddering.

"I have already told you, my son. It is a treatise on the art of raising and training falcons, gerfalcons, and hawks, written by a very learned scholar for Lord Castruccio Castracani, tyrant of Lucca."

"What must I do with it?"

"Take it to your good friend Henriot, who you told me had asked you for a treatise on the art of hunting. As he is going hawking to-day with the King he will not fail to read some of it, in order to prove to Charles that he has followed his advice and taken a lesson or two. The main thing is to give it into Henry's own hands."

"Oh! I do not dare!" said D'Alençon, shuddering.

"Why not?" asked Catharine; "it is a book like any other except that it has been packed away for so long that the leaves stick together. Do not attempt to read it, François, for it can be read only by wetting the finger and turning over each leaf, and this takes time and trouble."

"So that only a man who is very anxious to be instructed in the sport of hawking would waste his time and go to this trouble?" asked D'Alençon.

"Exactly, my son; you understand."

"Oh!" said D'Alençon; "there is Henriot in the court-yard. Give me the book, madame. I will take advantage of his absence and go to his room with it. On his return he will find it."

"I should prefer you to give it to him yourself, François, that would be surer."

"I have already said that I do not dare, madame," replied the duke.

"Very well; but at least put it where he can see it."

"Open? Is there any reason why it should not be open?"

"None."

"Then give it to me."

D'Alençon tremblingly took the book, which Catharine with a firm hand held out to him.

"Take it," said the queen, "there is no danger — I touch it; besides, you have gloves on."

This precaution was not enough for D'Alençon, who wrapped the volume in his cloak.

"Make haste," said Catharine; "Henry may return at any moment."

"You are right, madame. I will go at once."

The duke went out, trembling with fright.

We have often introduced the reader into the apartments of the King of Navarre, and he has been present at the events which have taken place in them, events bright or gloomy, according to the smile or frown of the protecting genius of the future king of France.

But perhaps never had these walls, stained with the blood of murders, sprinkled with the wine of orgies, scented with the perfumes of love, — perhaps never had this corner of the Louvre seen a paler face than that of the Duc d'Alençon, as with book in hand he opened the door of the bedchamber of the King of Navarre. And no one, as the duke had expected, was in the room to question with curious or anxious glances what he was about to do. The first rays of the morning sun alone were lighting up the vacant chamber.

On the wall in readiness hung the sword which Monsieur de Mouy had advised Henry to take with him. Some links of a coat of mail were scattered on the floor. A well-filled purse and a small dagger lay on a table, and some light ashes in the fireplace, joined to the other evidence, clearly showed D'Alençon that the King of Navarre had put on the shirt of mail, collected some money from his treasurer, and burned all papers that might compromise him.

"My mother was not mistaken," said D'Alençon · "the knave would have betrayed me."

Doubtless this conviction gave added strength to the young man. He sounded the corners of the room at a glance, raised the portieres, and realizing from the loud noise in the court-yard below and the dense silence in the apartments that no one was there to spy on him, he drew the book from under his cloak, hastily laid it on the table, near the purse, propping it up against a desk of sculptured oak; then drawing back, he reached out his arm, and, with a hesitation which betrayed his fears, with his gloved hand he opened the volume to an engraving of a hunt. This done, D'Alençon again stepped back, and drawing off his glove threw it into the still warm fire, which had just consumed the papers. The supple leather crackled over the coals, twisted and flattened itself out like the body of a great reptile, leaving nothing but a burned and blackened lump.

D'Alençon waited until the flame had consumed the glove, then rolling up the cloak which had been wrapped around the book, he put it under his arm, and hastily returned to his own apartments. As he entered with beating heart, he heard steps on the winding stairs, and not doubting but that it was Henry he quickly closed his door. Then he stepped to the window, but he could see only a part of the court-yard of the Louvre. Henry was not there, however, and he felt convinced that it was the King of Navarre who had just returned.

The duke sat down, opened a book, and tried to read. It was a history of France from Pharamond to Henry II., for which, a few days after his accession to the throne, Henry had given a license.

But the duke's thoughts were not on what he was reading; the fever of expectation burned in his veins. His temples throbbed clear to his brain, and as in a dream or some magnetic trance, it seemed to François that he could see through the walls. His eyes appeared to probe into Henry's chamber, in spite of the obstacles between.

In order to drive away the terrible object before his mind's eye the duke strove to fix his attention on something besides the terrible book opened on the oak desk; but in vain he looked at his weapons, his ornaments; in vain he gazed a hundred times at the same spot on the floor; every detail of the picture at which he had merely glanced remained graven on his memory. It consisted of a gentleman on horseback fulfilling the duties of a beater of hawking, throwing the bait, calling to the falcon, and galloping through the deep grass of a swamp. Strong as was the duke's will, his memory triumphed over it.

Then it was not only the book he saw, but the King of Navarre approaching it, looking at the picture, trying to turn the pages, finally wetting his thumb and forcing the leaves apart. At this sight, fictitious and imaginary as it was, D'Alençon staggered and was forced to lean one hand against a table, while with the other he covered his eyes, as if by so doing he did not see more clearly than before the vision he wished to escape. This vision was in his own thoughts.

Suddenly D'Alençon saw Henry cross the court; he stopped a few moments before the men who were loading two mules with the provisions for the chase — none other than the money and other things he wished to take with him; then, having given his orders, he crossed the court diagonally and advanced towards the door.

D'Alençon stood motionless. It was not Henry, then, who had mounted the secret staircase. All the agony he had undergone during the last quarter of an hour had been useless. What he thought was over or almost over was only beginning.

François opened the door of his chamber, then holding it so he listened. This time he could not be mistaken, it was Henry himself; he recognized his step and the peculiar jingle of his spurs.

Henry's door opened and closed.

D'Alençon returned to his room and sank into an armchair.

"Good!" said he, "this is what is now taking place: he has passed through the antechamber, the first room, the sleeping-room; then he glances to see if his sword, his purse, his dagger are there; at last he finds the book open on his table.

"'What book is this?' he asks himself. 'Who has brought it?'

"Then he draws nearer, sees the picture of the horseman calling his falcon, wants to read, tries to turn the leaves."

A cold perspiration started to the brow of François.

"Will he call? Is the effect of the poison sudden? No, no, for my mother said he would die of slow consumption."

This thought somewhat reassured him.

Ten minutes passed thus, a century of agony, dragging by second after second, each supplying all that the imagination could invent in the way of maddening terror, a world of visions.

D'Alençon could stand it no longer. He rose and crossed the antechamber, which was beginning to fill with gentlemen.

"Good morning, gentlemen," said he, "I am going to the King."

And to distract his consuming anxiety, and perhaps to prepare an *alibi*, D'Alençon descended to his brother's apartments. Why did he go there? He did not know. What had he to say? Nothing! It was not Charles he sought — it was Henry he fled.

He took the winding staircase and found the door of the King's apartments half opened. The guards let the duke enter without opposition. On hunting days there was neither etiquette nor orders.

François traversed successively the antechamber, the salon, and the bedroom without meeting any one. He thought

Charles must be in the armory and opened the door leading thither.

The King was seated before a table, in a deep carved armchair. He had his back to the door, and appeared to be absorbed in what he was doing.

The duke approached on tiptoe; Charles was reading.

" By Heaven!" cried he, suddenly, "this is a fine book. I had heard of it, but I did not know it could be had in France."

D'Alençon listened and advanced a step.

"Cursed leaves!" said the King, wetting his thumb and applying it to the pages; "it looks as though they had been stuck together on purpose to conceal the wonders they contain from the eyes of man."

D'Alençon bounded forward. The book over which Charles was bending was the one he had left in Henry's room. A dull cry broke from him.

"Ah, is it you, François?" said Charles, "you are welcome; come and see the finest book on hunting which ever came from the pen of man."

D'Alençon's first impulse was to snatch the volume from the hands of his brother; but an infernal thought restrained him; a frightful smile passed over his pallid lips, and he rubbed his hand across his eyes like a man dazed. Then recovering himself by degrees, but without moving:

"Sire," he asked, "how did this book come into your Majesty's possession?"

"I went into Henriot's room this morning to see if he was ready; he was not there, he was probably strolling about the kennels or the stables; at any rate, instead of him I found this treasure, which I brought here to read at my leisure."

And the King again moistened his thumb, and again turned over an obstinate page.

"Sire," stammered D'Alençon, whose hair stood on end, and whose whole body was seized with a terrible agony. "Sire, I came to tell you" —

"Let me finish this chapter, François," said Charles, "and then you shall tell me anything you wish. I have read or rather devoured fifty pages."

"He has tasted the poison twenty-five times," murmured François; "my brother is a dead man!"

Then the thought came to him that there was a God in heaven who perhaps after all was not chance.

With trembling hand the duke wiped away the cold perspiration which stood in drops on his brow, and waited in silence, as his brother had bade him do, until the chapter was finished.

CHAPTER L.

HAWKING.

CHARLES still read. In his curiosity he seemed to devour the pages, and each page, as we have said, either because of the dampness to which it had been exposed for so long or from some other cause, adhered to the next.

With haggard eyes D'Alençon gazed at this terrible spectacle, the end of which he alone could see.

"Oh!" he murmured, "what will happen? I shall go away, into exile, and seek an imaginary throne, while at the first news of Charles's illness Henry will return to some fortified town near the capital, and watch this prey sent us by chance, able at a single stride to reach Paris; so that before the King of Poland even hears the news of my brother's death the dynasty will be changed. This cannot be!"

Such were the thoughts which dominated the first involuntary feeling of horror that had urged François to warn Charles. It was the never-failing fatality which seemed to preserve Henry and follow the Valois which the duke was again going to try to thwart. In an instant his whole plan with regard to Henry was altered. It was Charles and not Henry who had read the poisoned book. Henry was to have gone, and gone condemned to die. The moment fate had again saved him, Henry must remain; for Henry was less to be feared in the Bastille or as prisoner at Vincennes than as the King of Navarre at the head of thirty thousand men.

The Duc d'Alençon let Charles finish his chapter, and when the King had raised his head:

"Brother," said the duke, "I have waited because your Majesty ordered me to do so, but I regret it, because I have something of the greatest importance to say to you."

"Go to the devil!" said Charles, whose cheeks were slowly turning a dull red, either because he had been too much engrossed in his reading or because the poison had begun to act.

"Go to the devil! If you have come to discuss that same subject again, you shall leave as did the King of Poland. I rid myself of him, and I will do the same to you without further talk about it."

"It is not about my leaving, brother, that I want to speak to you, but about some one else who is going away. Your Majesty has touched me in my most sensitive point, my love for you as a brother, my devotion to you as a subject; and I hope to prove to you that I am no traitor."

"Well," said Charles, as he leaned his elbow on the book, crossed his legs, and looked at D'Alençon like a man who is trying to be patient. "Some fresh report, some accusation?"

"No, sire, a certainty, a plot, which my foolish scruples alone prevented my revealing to you before."

"A plot?" said Charles, "well, let us hear about it."

"Sire," said François, "while your Majesty hawks near the river in the plain of Vesinet the King of Navarre will escape to the forest of Saint Germain, where a troop of friends will be waiting to flee with him."

"Ah, I knew it," said Charles, "another calumny against my poor Henry! When will you be through with him?"

"Your Majesty need not wait long at least to find out whether or not what I have just had the honor of telling you is a calumny."

"How so?"

"Because this evening our brother-in-law will be gone."

Charles rose.

"Listen," said he, "I will try for the last time to believe you; but I warn you, both you and your mother, that it will be the last time."

Then raising his voice:

"Summon the King of Navarre!" he cried.

A guard started to obey, but François stopped him with a gesture.

"This is a poor way, brother, to learn anything," said he. "Henry will deny, will give a signal, his accomplices will be warned and will disappear. Then my mother and myself will be accused not only of being visionary but of being calumniators."

"What do you want, then?"

"In the name of our brotherly love I ask your Majesty to listen to me, in the name of my devotion, which you will realize, I want you to do nothing hastily. Act so that the real culprit, who for two years has been betraying your Majesty in will as well as in deed, may at last be recognized as guilty by an infallible proof, and punished as he deserves."

Charles did not answer, but going to a window raised it. The blood was rushing to his head.

Then turning round quickly :

" Well ! " said he, " what would you do ? Speak, François."

" Sire," said D'Alençon, " I would surround the forest of Saint Germain with three detachments of light horse, who at a given hour, eleven o'clock, for instance, should start out and drive every one in the forest to the Pavilion of Francis I., which I would, as if by chance, have indicated as the meeting-place. Then I would spur on, as if following my falcon, to the meeting-place, where Henry should be captured with his companions."

" The idea is good," said the King ; " summon the captain of the guards."

D'Alençon drew from his doublet a silver whistle, sus-pended from a gold chain, and raised it to his lips.

De Nancey appeared.

Charles gave him some orders in a low tone.

Meanwhile Actéon, the great greyhound, had dragged a book from the table, and was tossing it about the room, mak-ing great bounds after it.

Charles turned round and uttered a terrible oath. The book was the precious treatise on hunting, of which there existed only three copies in the world.

The punishment was proportionate to the offence.

Charles seized a whip and gave the dog three whistling blows.

Actéon uttered a howl, and fled under a table covered with a large cloth which served him as a hiding-place.

Charles picked up the book and saw with joy that only one leaf was gone, and that was not a page of the text, but an engraving. He placed the volume carefully away on a shelf where Actéon could not reach it. D'Alençon looked anxiously at him. Now that the book had fulfilled its dread mission he would have liked to see it out of Charles's hands.

Six o'clock struck. It was time for the King to descend to the court-yard, already filled with horses richly caparisoned, and elegantly dressed ladies and gentlemen. The hunters held on their wrists their hooded falcons ; some outriders carried horns wound with scarfs, in case the King, as sometimes happened, grew weary of hawking, and wished to hunt a deer or a chamois.

Charles closed the door of his armory and descended D'Alençon watched each movement closely, and saw him put the key in his pocket.

As he went down the stairs Charles stopped and raised his hand to his head.

The limbs of the Duc d'Alençon trembled no less than did those of the King.

"It seems to me," said the duke, "that there is going to be a storm."

"A storm in January!" said Charles; "you are mad. No, I am dizzy, my skin is dry, I am weak, that is all."

Then in a low tone:

"They will kill me," he murmured, "with their hatred and their plots."

But on reaching the court the fresh morning air, the shouts of the hunters, the loud greetings of the hundred people gathered there, produced their usual effect on Charles.

He breathed freely and happily. His first thought was for Henry, who was beside Marguerite.

This excellent couple seemed to care so much for each other that they were unable to be apart.

On perceiving Charles, Henry spurred his horse, and in three bounds was beside him.

"Ah, ah!" said Charles, "you are mounted as if you were going to hunt the stag, Henriot; but you know we are going hawking to-day."

Then without waiting for a reply:

"Forward, gentlemen, forward! we must be hunting by nine o'clock!" and Charles frowned and spoke in an almost threatening tone.

Catharine was watching everything from a window, behind which a curtain was drawn back, showing her pale face. She herself was dressed in black and was hidden from view.

At the order from Charles all this gilded, embroidered, perfumed crowd, with the King at its head, lengthened out to pass through the gate of the Louvre, and swept like an avalanche along the road to Saint Germain, amid the shouts of the people, who saluted the young King as he rode by, thoughtful and pensive, on his white horse.

"What did he say to you?" asked Marguerite of Henry.

"He congratulated me on the speed of my horse."

"Was that all?"

"Yes."

"Then he suspects something."

"I fear so."

"Let us be cautious."

Henry's face lighted up with one of his beautiful smiles, which meant especially to Marguerite, " Be easy, my love." As to Catharine, scarcely had the cortège left the court of the Louvre before she dropped the curtain.

But she had not failed to see one thing, namely, Henry's pallor, his nervousness, and his low-toned conversation with Marguerite.

Henry was pale because, not having physical courage, his blood, under all circumstances in which his life was at stake, instead of rushing to his head, as is usually the case, flowed to his heart. He was nervous because the manner in which he had been received by Charles, so different from usual, had made a deep impression on him. Finally, he had conferred with Marguerite because, as we know, the husband and wife had formed, so far as politics were concerned, an alliance offensive and defensive.

But Catharine had interpreted these facts differently.

" This time," she murmured, with her Florentine smile, " I think I may rely on my dear Henriot."

Then to satisfy herself, having waited a quarter of an hour to give the party time to leave Paris, she went out of her room, mounted the winding staircase, and with the help of her pass-key opened the door of the apartments of the King of Navarre. She searched, but in vain, for the book. In vain she looked on every table, shelf, and in every closet; nowhere could she find it.

" D'Alençon must have taken it away," said she, " that was wise."

And she descended to her own chamber, quite sure this time that her plan would succeed.

The King went on towards Saint Germain, which he reached after a rapid ride of an hour and a half. They did not ascend to the old castle, which rose dark and majestic in the midst of the houses scattered over the mountain. They crossed the wooden bridge, which at that time was opposite the tree

AS THOUGH IT UNDERSTOOD THE WORDS, THE NOBLE BIRD ROSE
LIKE AN ARROW.

to-day called the " Sully Oak." Then they signed for the boats adorned with flags which followed the hunting-party to aid the King and his suite in crossing the river. This was done. Instantly all the joyous procession, animated by such varied interests, again began to move, led by the King, over the magnificent plain which stretched from the wooded summit of Saint Germain, and which suddenly assumed the appearance of a great carpet covered with people, dotted with a thousand colors, and of which the river foaming along its banks seemed a silver fringe.

Ahead of the King, still on his white horse and holding his favorite falcon, rode the beaters, in their long green close-fitting coats and high boots, calling now and then to the half dozen great dogs, and beating, with their whips, the reeds which grew along the river banks.

At that moment the sun, until then hidden behind a cloud, suddenly burst forth and lighted with one of its rays all that procession of gold, all the ornaments, all the glowing eyes, and turned everything into a torrent of flame. Then, as if it had waited for that moment so that the sun might shine on its defeat, a heron rose from the midst of the reeds with a prolonged and plaintiff cry.

"Haw! Haw!" cried Charles, unhooding his falcon and sending it after the fugitive.

" Haw ! Haw ! " cried every voice to encourage the bird.

The falcon, dazzled for an instant by the light, turned, described a circle, then suddenly perceiving the heron, dashed after it.

But the heron, like a prudent bird, had risen a hundred yards before the beaters, and while the King had been unhooding his falcon, and while the latter had been growing accustomed to the light, it had gained a considerable height, so that by the time its enemy saw it, it had risen more than five hundred feet, and finding in the higher zones the air necessary for its powerful wings, continued to mount rapidly.

"Haw! Haw! Iron Beak!" cried Charles, cheering his falcon. "Show us that you are a thoroughbred! Haw! Haw ! "

As if it understood the words the noble bird rose like an arrow, described a diagonal line, then a vertical one, as the heron had done, and mounted higher and higher as though it would soon disappear in the upper air.

"Ah! coward!" cried Charles, as if the fugitive could hear him, and, spurring his horse, he followed the flight of the birds as far as he could, his head thrown back so as not to lose sight of them for an instant. "Ah! double coward! You run! My Iron Beak is a thoroughbred; on! on! Haw, Iron Beak! Haw!"

The contest was growing exciting. The birds were beginning to approach each other, or rather the falcon was nearing the heron. The only question was which could rise the higher.

Fear had stronger wings than courage. The falcon passed under the heron, and the latter, profiting by its advantage, dealt a blow with its long beak.

The falcon, as though hit by a dagger, described three circles, apparently overcome, and for an instant it looked as if the bird would fall. But like a warrior, who when wounded rises more terrible than before, it uttered a sharp and threatening cry, and went after the heron. The latter, making the most of its advantage, had changed the direction of its flight and turned toward the forest, trying this time to gain in distance instead of in height, and so escape. But the falcon was indeed a thoroughbred, with the eye of a gerfalcon.

It repeated the same manœuvre, rose diagonally after the heron, which gave two or three cries of distress and strove to rise perpendicularly as at first.

At the end of a few seconds the two birds seemed again about to disappear. The heron looked no larger than a lark, and the falcon was a black speck which every moment grew smaller.

Neither Charles nor his suite any longer followed the flight of the birds. Each one stopped, his eyes fixed on the clouds.

"Bravo! Bravo! Iron-beak!" cried Charles, suddenly. "See, see, gentlemen, he is uppermost! Haw! haw!"

"Faith, I can see neither of them," said Henry.

"Nor I," said Marguerite.

"Well, but if you cannot see them, Henry, you can hear them," said Charles, "at least the heron. Listen! listen! he asks quarter!"

Two or three plaintive cries were heard which a practised ear alone could detect.

"Listen!" cried Charles, "and you will see them come down more quickly than they went up."

As the King spoke, the two birds reappeared. They were still only two black dots, but from the size of the dots the falcon seemed to be uppermost.

" See ! see ! " cried Charles, " Iron Beak has him ! "

The heron, outwitted by the bird of prey, no longer strove to defend itself. It descended rapidly, constantly struck at by the falcon, and answered only by its cries. Suddenly it folded its wings and dropped like a stone ; but its adversary did the same, and when the fugitive again strove to resume its flight a last blow of the beak finished it ; it continued to fall, turning over and over, and as it touched the earth the falcon swooped down and uttered a cry of victory which drowned the cry of defeat of the vanquished.

"" To the falcon ! the falcon ! " shouted Charles, spurring his horse to the place where the birds had fallen. But suddenly he reined in his steed, uttered a cry, dropped his bridle, and grasping his horse's mane with one hand pressed the other to his stomach as though he would tear out his very vitals.

All the courtiers hastened to him.

" It is nothing, nothing," said Charles, with inflamed face and haggard eye ; " it seemed as if a red-hot iron were passing through me just now ; but forward ! it is nothing."

And Charles galloped on.

D'Alençon turned pale.

" What now ? " asked Henry of Marguerite.

" I do not know," replied she ; " but did you see ? My brother was purple in the face."

" He is not usually so," said Henry.

The courtiers glanced at one another in surprise and followed the King.

They arrived at the scene of combat. The falcon had already begun to peck at the head of the heron.

Charles sprang from his horse to obtain a nearer view ; but on alighting he was obliged to seize hold of the saddle. The ground seemed to spin under him. He felt very sleepy.

" Brother ! Brother ! " cried Marguerite ; " what is the matter ? "

" I feel," said Charles, " as Portia must have felt when she swallowed her burning coals. I am burning up and my breath seems on fire."

Charles exhaled his breath and seemed surprised not to see fire issue from his lips.

The falcon had been caught and hooded again, and every one had gathered around the King.

"Why, what does it mean? Great Heavens! It cannot be anything, or if it is it must be the sun which is affecting my head and blinding my eyes. So on, on, to the hunt, gentlemen! There is a whole flight of herons. Unhood the falcons, all of them, by Heaven! now for some sport!"

Instantly five or six falcons were unhooded and let loose. They rose in the direction of the prey, while the entire party, the King at their head, reached the bank of the river.

"Well! what do you say, madame?" asked Henry of Marguerite.

"That the moment is favorable, and that if the King does not look back we can easily reach the forest from here."

Henry called the attendant who was carrying the heron, and while the noisy, gilded avalanche swept along the road which to-day is a terrace he remained behind as if to examine the dead bird.

CHAPTER LI.

THE PAVILION OF FRANÇOIS I.

HAWKING was a beautiful sport as carried on by kings, when kings were almost demi-gods, and when the chase was not only a pastime but an art.

Nevertheless we must leave the royal spectacle to enter a part of the forest where the actors in the scene we have just described will soon join us.

The Allée des Violettes was a long, leafy arcade and mossy retreat in which, among lavender and heather, a startled hare now and then pricked up its ears, and a wandering stag raised its head heavy with horns, opened its nostrils, and listened. To the right of this alley was an open space far enough from the road to be invisible, but not so far but that the road could be seen from it.

In the middle of the clearing two men were lying on the grass. Under them were travellers' cloaks, at their sides long swords, and near each of them a musketoon (then called a petronel) with the muzzle turned from them. In the richness of their costume they resembled the joyous characters of the

"Decameron;" on closer view, by the threatening aspect of their
weapons, they seemed like those forest robbers whom a hundred
years later Salvator Rosa painted from nature in his landscapes.
One of them was leaning on his hand and on one knee, listening as attentively as the hare or deer we mentioned above.

"It seems to me," said this one, "that the hunt was very
near us just now. I heard the cries of the hunters cheering
the falcon."

"And now," said the other, who seemed to await events with
much more philosophy than his companion, "now I hear nothing more; they must have gone away. I told you this was a
poor place from which to see anything. We cannot be seen,
it is true; but we cannot see, either."

"The devil! my dear Annibal," said the first speaker, "we
had to put our horses somewhere, as well as the mules, which,
by the way, are so heavily laden that I do not see how they
can follow us. Now I know that these old beeches and oaks
are perfectly suited to this difficult task. I should venture to
say that far from blaming Monsieur de Mouy as you are doing,
I recognize in every detail of the enterprise he is directing
the common sense of a true conspirator."

"Good!" said the second gentleman, whom no doubt our
reader has already recognized as Coconnas; "good! that is the
word! I expected it! I relied on you for it! So we are conspiring?"

"We are not conspiring; we are serving the king and the
queen."

"Who are conspiring and which amounts to the same for us."

"Coconnas, I have told you," said La Mole, "that I do not
in the least force you to follow me in this affair. I have under-
taken it only because of a particular sentiment, which you
can neither feel nor share."

"Well, by Heaven! Who said that you were forcing me?
In the first place, I know of no one who could compel Coconnas,
to do what he did not wish to do; but do you suppose that I
would let you go without following you, especially when I see
that you are going to the devil?"

"Annibal! Annibal!" said La Mole, "I think that I see
her white palfrey in the distance. Oh! it is strange how my
heart throbs at the mere thought of her coming!"

"Yes, it is strange," said Coconnas, yawning; "my heart
does not throb in the least."

"It is not she," said La Mole. "What can have happened? They were to be here at noon, I thought."

"It happens that it is not noon," said Coconnas, "that is all, and, apparently, we still have time to take a nap."

So saying, Coconnas stretched himself on his cloak like a man who is about to add practice to precept; but as his ear touched the ground he raised his finger and motioned La Mole to be silent.

"What is it?" asked the latter.

"Hush! this time I am sure I hear something."

"That is singular; I have listened, but I hear nothing."

"Nothing?"

"No."

"Well!" said Coconnas, rising and laying his hand on La Mole's arm, "look at that deer."

"Where?"

"Yonder."

Coconnas pointed to the animal.

"Well?"

"Well, you will see."

La Mole watched the deer. With head bent forward as though about to browse it listened without stirring. Soon it turned its head, covered with magnificent branching horns, in the direction from which no doubt the sound came. Then suddenly, without apparent cause, it disappeared like a flash of lightning.

"Oh!" said La Mole, "I believe you are right, for the deer has fled."

"Because of that," said Coconnas, "it must have heard what you have not heard."

In short, a faint, scarcely perceptible sound quivered vaguely through the passes; to less practised ears it would have seemed like the breeze; for the two men it was the far-off galloping of horses. In an instant La Mole was on his feet.

"Here they are!" said he; "quick."

Coconnas rose, but more calmly. The energy of the Piedmontese seemed to have passed into the heart of La Mole, while on the other hand the indolence of the latter seemed to have taken possession of his friend. One acted with enthusiasm; the other with reluctance. Soon a regular and measured sound struck the ear of the two friends. The neighing of a horse made the coursers they had tied ten paces away prick up their ears, as through the alley there passed like a white shadow a woman who, turning towards them, made a strange sign and disappeared.

"The queen!" they exclaimed together.

"What can it mean?" asked Coconnas.

"She made a sign," said La Mole, "which meant 'presently.'"

"She made a sign," said Coconnas, "which meant 'flee!'"

"The signal meant 'wait for me.'"

"The signal meant 'save yourself.'"

"Well," said La Mole, "let each act on his own conviction; you leave and I will remain."

Coconnas shrugged his shoulders and lay down again.

At that moment in the opposite direction from that in which the queen was going, but in the same alley, there passed at full speed a troop of horsemen whom the two friends recognized as ardent, almost rabid Protestants. Their steeds bounded like the locusts of which Job said, 'They came and went.'"

"The deuce! the affair is growing serious," said Coconnas, rising. "Let us go to the pavilion of François I."

"No," said La Mole; "if we are discovered it will be towards the pavilion that the attention of the King will be at first directed, since that is the general meeting-place."

"You may be right, this time," grumbled Coconnas.

Scarcely had Coconnas uttered these words before a horseman passed among the trees like a flash of lightning, and leaping ditches, bushes, and all barriers reached the two gentlemen.

He held a pistol in each hand and with his knees alone guided his horse in its furious chase.

"Monsieur de Mouy!" exclaimed Coconnas, uneasy and now more on the alert than La Mole; "Monsieur de Mouy running away! Every one for himself, then!"

"Quick! quick!" cried the Huguenot; "away! all is lost! I have come around to tell you so. Away!"

As if he had not stopped to utter these words, he was gone almost before they were spoken, and before La Mole and Coconnas realized their meaning.

"And the queen?" cried La Mole.

But the young man's voice was lost in the distance; De Mouy was too far away either to hear or to answer him.

Coconnas had speedily made up his mind. While La Mole stood motionless, gazing after De Mouy, who had disappeared among the trees, he ran to the horses, led them out, sprang on his own, and, throwing the bridle of the other to La Mole, prepared to gallop off.

"Come! come!" cried he; "I repeat what De Mouy said: Let us be off! De Mouy knows what he is doing. Come, La Mole, quick!"

"One moment," said La Mole; "we came here for something."

"Unless it is to be hanged," replied Coconnas, "I advise you to lose no more time. I know you are going to parse some rhetoric, paraphrase the word 'flee,' speak of Horace, who hurled his buckler, and Epaminondas, who was brought back on his. But I tell you one thing, when Monsieur de Mouy de Saint Phale flees all the world may run too."

"Monsieur de Mouy de Saint Phale," said La Mole, "was not charged to carry off Queen Marguerite! Nor does Monsieur de Mouy de Saint Phale love Queen Marguerite!"

"By Heaven! he is right if this love would make him do such foolish things as you plan doing. May five hundred thousand devils from hell take away the love which may cost two brave gentlemen their heads! By Heaven! as King Charles says, we are conspiring, my dear fellow; and when plans fail one must run. Mount! mount, La Mole!"

"Mount yourself, my dear fellow, I will not prevent you. I even urge you to do so. Your life is more precious than mine. Defend it, therefore."

"You must say to me: 'Coconnas, let us be hanged together,' and not 'Coconnas, save yourself.'"

"Bah! my friend," replied La Mole, "the rope is made for clowns, not for gentlemen like ourselves."

"I am beginning to think," said Coconnas, "that the precaution I took is not bad."

"What precaution?"

"To have made friends with the hangman."

"You are sinister, my dear Coconnas."

"Well, what are we going to do?" cried the latter, impatiently.

"Set out and find the queen."

"Where?"

"I do not know — seek the king."

" Where ? "

" I have not the least idea; but we must find him, and we two by ourselves can do what fifty others neither could nor would dare to do."

" You appeal to my pride, Hyacinthe; that is a bad sign."

" Well! come; to horse and away ! "

" A good suggestion ! "

La Mole turned to seize the pommel of his saddle, but just as he put his foot in the stirrup an imperious voice was heard:

" Halt there! surrender ! "

At the same moment the figure of a man appeared behind an oak, then another, then thirty. They were the light-horse, who, dismounted, had glided on all fours in and out among the bushes, searching the forest.

" What did I tell you ? " murmured Coconnas, in a low tone.

A dull groan was La Mole's only answer.

The light-horse were still thirty paces away from the two friends.

" Well! " continued the Piedmontese, in a loud tone, to the lieutenant of the dragoons. " What is it, gentlemen ? "

The lieutenant ordered his men to aim.

Coconnas continued under breath:

" Mount, La Mole, there is still time. Spring into your saddle as I have seen you do hundreds of times, and let us be off."

Then turning to the light-horse:

" The devil, gentlemen, do not fire; you would kill friends."

Then to La Mole:

" Between the trees they cannot aim well; they will fire and miss us."

" Impossible," said La Mole, " we cannot take Marguerite's horse with us or the two mules. They would compromise us, whereas by my replies I can avert all suspicion. Go, my friend, go ! "

" Gentlemen," said Coconnas, drawing his sword and rais-ing it, " gentlemen, we surrender."

The light-horse dropped their muskets.

" But first tell us why we must do so ? "

" You must ask that of the King of Navarre."

" What crime have we committed ? "

" Monsieur d'Alençon will inform you."

Coconnas and La Mole looked at each other. The name of their enemy at such a moment did not greatly reassure them.

Yet neither of them made any resistance. Coconnas was asked to dismount, a manœuvre which he executed without a word. Then both were placed in the centre of the light-horse and took the road to the pavilion.

" You always wanted to see the pavilion of François I.," said Coconnas to La Mole, perceiving through the trees the walls of a beautiful Gothic structure ; "now it seems you will."

La Mole made no reply, but merely extended his hand to Coconnas.

By the side of this lovely pavilion, built in the time of Louis XII., and named after François I., because the latter always chose it as a meeting-place when he hunted, was a kind of hut built for prickers, partly hidden behind the muskets, halberds, and shining swords like an ant-hill under a whitening harvest.

The prisoners were conducted to this hut.

We will now relate what had happened and so throw some light on the situation, which looked very dark, especially for the two friends.

The Protestant gentlemen had assembled, as had been agreed on, in the pavilion of François I., of which, as we know, De Mouy had the key.

Masters of the forest, or at least so they had believed, they had placed sentinels here and there whom the light-horse, having exchanged their white scarfs for red ones (a precaution due to the ingenious zeal of Monsieur de Nancey), had surprised and carried away without a blow.

The light-horse had continued their search surrounding the pavilion ; but De Mouy, who, as we know, was waiting for the king at the end of the Allée des Violettes, had perceived the red scarfs stealing along and had instantly suspected them. He sprang to one side so as not to be seen, and noticed that the vast circle was narrowing in such a way as to beat the forest and surround the meeting-place. At the same time, at the end of the principal alley, he had caught a glimpse of the white aigrettes and the shining arquebuses of the King's bodyguard. Finally he saw the King himself, while in the opposite direction he perceived the King of Navarre.

Then with his hat he had made a sign of the cross, which was the signal agreed on to indicate that all was lost.

At this signal the king had turned back and disappeared. De Mouy at once dug the two wide rowels of his spurs into the sides of his horse and galloped away, shouting as he went the words of warning which we have mentioned, to La Mole and Coconnas.

Now the King, who had noticed the absence of Henry and Marguerite, arrived, escorted by Monsieur d'Alençon, just as the two men came out of the hut to which he had said that all those found, not only in the pavilion but in the forest, were to be conducted.

D'Alençon, full of confidence, galloped close by the King, whose sharp pains were augmenting his ill humor. Two or three times he had nearly fainted and once he had vomited blood.

"Come," said he on arriving, "let us make haste; I want to return to the Louvre. Bring out all these rascals from their hole. This is Saint Blaise's day; he was cousin to Saint Bartholomew."

At these words of the King the entire mass of pikes and muskets began to move, and one by one the Huguenots were forced out not only from the forest and the pavilion but from the hut.

But the King of Navarre, Marguerite, and De Mouy were not there.

"Well," said the King, "where is Henry? Where is Margot? You promised them to me, D'Alençon, and, by Heaven, they will have to be found!"

"Sire, we have not even seen the King and the Queen of Navarre."

"But here they are," said Madame de Nevers.

At that moment, at the end of an alley leading to the river, Henry and Margot came in sight, both as calm as if nothing had happened; both with their falcons on their wrists, riding lovingly side by side, so that as they galloped along their horses, like themselves, seemed to be caressing each other.

It was then that D'Alençon, furious, commanded the forest to be searched, and that La Mole and Coconnas were found within their ivy bower. They, too, in brotherly proximity entered the circle formed by the guards; only, as they were not sovereigns, they could not assume so calm a manner as Henry and Marguerite. La Mole was too pale and Coconnas too red.

CHAPTER LII.

THE EXAMINATION.

THE spectacle which struck the young men as they entered the circle, although seen but for a few moments, was one never to be forgotten.

As we have said, Charles IX. had watched the gentlemen as the guards led them one by one from the pricker's hut.

Both he and D'Alençon anxiously followed every movement, waiting to see the King of Navarre come out. Both, however, were doomed to disappointment. But it was not enough to know that the king was not there, it was necessary to find out what had become of him.

Therefore when the young couple were seen approaching from the end of the alley, D'Alençon turned pale, while Charles felt his heart grow glad; he instinctively desired that everything his brother had forced him to do should fall back on the duke.

" He will outwit us again," murmured François, growing still paler.

At that moment the King was seized with such violent pains that he dropped his bridle, pressed both hands to his sides, and. shrieked like a madman.

Henry hastily approached him, but by the time he had traversed the few hundred feet which separated them, Charles had recovered.

" Whence do you come, monsieur ? " said the King, with a sternness that frightened Marguerite.

" Why, from the hunt, brother," replied she.

" The hunt was along the river bank, and not in the forest."

" My falcon swooped down on a pheasant just as we stopped behind every one to look at the heron."

" Where is the pheasant ? "

" Here; a beautiful bird, is it not ? "

And Henry, in perfect innocence, held up his bird of purple, blue, and gold plumage.

" Ah ! " said Charles, " and this pheasant caught, why did you not rejoin me ? "

" Because the bird had directed its flight towards the park, sire, and when we returned to the river bank we saw you half

a mile ahead of us, riding towards the forest. We set out to
gallop after you, therefore, for being in your Majesty's hunting-
party we did not wish to lose you."

" And were all these gentlemen invited also ? " said Charles.

" What gentlemen ? " asked Henry, casting an inquiring
look about.

" Why, your Huguenots, by Heaven ! " said Charles; " at
all events if they were invited it was not by me."

" No, sire," replied Henry, " but possibly Monsieur d'Alençon asked them."

" Monsieur d'Alençon ? How so ? "

" I ? " said the duke.

" Why, yes, brother," said Henry; " did you not announce
yesterday that you were King of Navarre ? The Huguenots
who demanded you for their king have come to thank you for
having accepted the crown, and the King for having given it.
Is it not so, gentlemen ? "

" Yes ! yes ! " cried twenty voices. " Long live the Duc
d'Alençon ! Long live King Charles ! "

" I am not king of the Huguenots," said François, white
with anger; then, glancing stealthily at Charles, " and I sin-
cerely trust I never shall be ! "

" No matter ! " said Charles, " but you must know, Henry,
that I consider all this very strange."

" Sire," said the King of Navarre, firmly, " God forgive me,
but one would say that I were undergoing an examination."

" And if I should tell you that you were, what would you
answer ? "

" That I am a king like yourself, sire," replied Henry,
proudly, " for it is not the crown but birth that makes royalty,
and that I would gladly answer any questions from my brother
and my friend, but never from my judge."

" And yet," murmured Charles, " I should really like to know
for once in my life how to act."

" Let Monsieur de Mouy be brought out," said D'Alençon,
" and then you will know. Monsieur de Mouy must be among
the prisoners."

" Is Monsieur de Mouy here ? " asked the King.

Henry felt a moment's anxiety and exchanged glances with
Marguerite; but his uneasiness was of short duration.

No voice replied.

" Monsieur de Mouy is not among the prisoners," said Monsieur de Nancey; " some of our men think they saw him, but no one is sure of it."

D'Alençon uttered an oath.

" Well!" said Marguerite, pointing to La Mole and Coconnas, who had heard all that had passed, and on whose intelligence she felt she could depend, " there are two gentlemen in the service of Monsieur d'Alençon; question them; they will answer."

The duke felt the blow.

" I had them arrested on purpose to prove that they do not belong to me," said he.

The King looked at the two friends and started on seeing La Mole again.

"Ah! that Provençal here ? " said he.

Coconnas bowed graciously.

" What were you doing when you were arrested? " asked the King.

" Sire, we were planning deeds of war and of love."

" On horseback, armed to the teeth, ready for flight!"

" No, sire," said Coconnas; "your Majesty is misinformed. We were lying under the shade of a beech tree — *sub tegmine fagi.*"

" Ah ! so you were lying under the shade of a beech tree ? "

" And we might easily have escaped had we thought that in any way we had roused your Majesty's anger. Now, gentlemen, on your honor as soldiers," continued Coconnas, turning to the light-horse, " do you not think that had we so wished we could have escaped? "

" The fact is," said the lieutenant, " that these gentlemen did not even attempt to run."

" Because their horses were too far away," said the Duc d'Alençon.

" I humbly beg monseigneur's pardon," said Coconnas; "but I was on mine, and my friend the Comte Lérac de la Mole was holding his by the bridle."

" Is this true, gentlemen ? " said the King.

" Yes, sire," replied the lieutenant; " on seeing us Monsieur de Coconnas even dismounted."

Coconnas smiled in a way which signified, " You see, sire ! "

" But the other horses, the mules, and the boxes with which they were laden ? " asked François.

"Well," said Coconnas, " are we stable boys ? Send for the groom who had charge of them."

" He is not here," exclaimed the duke, furious.

" Then he must have become frightened and run away," said Coconnas ; " one cannot expect a clown to have the manners of a gentleman."

"Always the same system," said D'Alençon, gnashing his teeth. "Fortunately, sire, I told you that for some time these gentlemen have not been in my service."

" I ! " exclaimed Coconnas, "am I unfortunate enough no longer to belong to your highness ? "

" By Heaven ! monsieur, you ought to know that better than any one, since you yourself gave me your dismissal, in a letter so impertinent that, thank God, I kept it, and fortunately have it with me."

" Oh ! " exclaimed Coconnas, " I had hoped that your highness would forgive me for a letter written under the first impulse of anger. I had been told that your highness had tried to strangle my friend La Mole in one of the corridors of the Louvre."

" What is he saying ? " interrupted the King.

" At first I thought your highness was alone," continued Coconnas, ingenuously, " but afterwards I learned that three others " —

" Silence ! " exclaimed Charles ; " we have heard enough. Henry," said he to the King of Navarre, " your word not to try to escape."

" I give it to your Majesty, sire."

" Return to Paris with Monsieur de Nancey, and remain in your chamber under arrest. You, gentlemen," continued he, addressing the two friends, " give up your swords."

La Mole looked at Marguerite. She smiled. La Mole at once handed his sword to the nearest officer. Coconnas did the same.

" Has Monsieur de Mouy been found ? " asked the King.

" No, sire," said Monsieur de Nancey ; " either he was not in the forest or he escaped."

" So much the worse," said the King ; " but let us return. I am cold and dizzy."

" Sire, it is from anger, probably," said François.

" Possibly ; but my eyes trouble me. Where are the prisoners ? I cannot see them. Is it night already? Oh! mercy! I am burning up! Help! Help!"

The unfortunate King dropped the bridle of his horse, stretched out his arms, and fell backward. The courtiers, frightened at this second attack, caught him as he fell.

François, standing apart, wiped the perspiration from his brow, for he alone knew the cause of the trouble from which his brother was suffering.

On the other side the King of Navarre, already under the guard of Monsieur de Nancey, looked upon the scene with growing astonishment.

"Well! well!" murmured he, with that wonderful intuition which at times made him seem inspired, "was I perhaps fortunate in having been stopped in my flight ?"

He glanced at Margot, whose great eyes, wide open with surprise, were looking first at him and then at the King.

This time Charles was unconscious. A litter was brought and he was laid on it. They covered him with a cloak, taken from the shoulders of one of the courtiers. The procession silently set out in the direction of Paris, whence that morning light-hearted conspirators and a happy King had started forth, and to which now a dying King was returning, surrounded by rebel prisoners.

Marguerite, who throughout all this had lost neither the control of her mind nor body, gave her husband a look of intelligence; then, passing so close to La Mole that the latter was able to catch the following two Greek words, she said:

"*Me deide*," which meant, "Fear nothing."

"What did she say ?" asked Coconnas.

"She told me to fear nothing," replied La Mole.

"So much the worse," murmured the Piedmontese, "so much the worse; that means that it is not good for us to be here. Every time that word has been said to me in an encouraging tone I have either received a bullet or a sword-thrust in my body, or a flower pot on my head. 'Fear nothing,' whether in Hebrew, Greek, Latin, or French, has always meant for me: ' Take care ! ' "

"Forward, gentlemen!" said the lieutenant of the light-horse.

"Without being indiscreet, monsieur," said Coconnas, "may we know where we are going ?"

"To Vincennes, I think," said the lieutenant.

"I would rather go elsewhere," said Coconnas; "but one does not always go just where one wishes."

On the way the King recovered conscicusness and some strength.

At Nanterre he even wanted to ride, but this was not allowed.

"Summon Maître Ambroise Paré," said Charles, on reaching the Louvre.

He descended from his litter, ascended the stairs, leaning on the arm of Tavannes, and entered his apartment, giving orders that no one be allowed to follow him.

Every one had noticed that he seemed very grave. During the journey he had been in a deep study, not addressing a word to any one, concerned neither with conspiracy nor conspirators. It was evident that he was occupied with his illness; a malady so sudden, so strange, so severe, some of the symptoms of which had been noticed in his brother François II. a short time before his death.

So the order to admit no one whomsoever to his rooms, except Maître Paré, caused no surprise. It was well known that the prince was a misanthrope. Charles entered his sleeping-room, seated himself in a folding-chair, and leaned his head against the cushions. Then reflecting that Maître Ambroise Paré might not be at home, and that there might be some delay before he saw him, he decided to employ the intervening time.

He clapped his hands, thus summoning a guard.

"Say to the King of Navarre that I wish to speak with him," said Charles.

The man bowed and withdrew.

Just then Charles's head fell back, a great weight seemed to oppress him; his ideas grew confused; it was as if a sort of bloody vapor were floating before his eyes; his mouth was dry, although he had already swallowed a whole carafe of water.

While he was in this drowsy state the door opened and Henry appeared. Monsieur de Nancey had followed him, but stopped in the antechamber.

The King of Navarre waited until the door was closed. Then he advanced.

"Sire," said he, "you sent for me; I am here."

The King started at the voice and mechanically extended his hand.

" Sire," said Henry, letting his arms hang at his side, "your Majesty forgets that I am no longer your brother but your prisoner."

" Ah! that is true," said Charles. " Thank you for having reminded me of it. Moreover, it seems to me that when we last spoke together you promised to answer frankly what I might ask you."

" I am ready to keep my word, sire. Ask your questions."

The King poured some cold water into his hand and applied it to his forehead.

" Tell me, Henry, how much truth is there in the accusation brought against you by the Duc d'Alençon? "

" Only a little. It was Monsieur d'Alençon who was to have fled, and I who was to have accompanied him."

" And why should you have gone with him? Are you dissatisfied with me, Henry? "

" No, sire; on the contrary, I have only praise for your majesty; and God, who reads our hearts, knows how deeply I love my brother and my King."

" It seems to me," said Charles, " that it is not natural to flee from those we love and who love us "

" I was not fleeing from those who love me; I was fleeing from those who hate me. Will your Majesty permit me to speak openly? "

" Speak, monsieur."

" Those who hate me, sire, are Monsieur d'Alençon and the queen mother."

" As for Monsieur d'Alençon I will not answer; but the queen mother overwhelms you with attentions."

" That is just why I mistrust her, sire. And I do well to do so."

" Mistrust her? "

" Her, or those about her. You know, sire, that the misfortune of kings is not always that they are too little but that they are too well served."

" Explain yourself; you promised to tell me everything."

" Your Majesty will see that I will do so."

" Continue."

" Your Majesty loves me, you have said."

" I loved you before your treason, Henry."

" Pretend that you still love me, sire."

" Very well."

" If you love me you must want me to live, do you not ? "

" I should be wretched were any harm to befall you."

" Well, sire, twice your Majesty has just escaped being wretched."

" How so ? "

" Twice Providence has saved my life. It is true that the second time Providence assumed the features of your Majesty ? "

" What form did it assume the first time ? "

" That of a man who would be greatly surprised to see himself mistaken for Providence; I mean Réné. You, sire, saved me from steel."

Charles frowned, for he remembered the night when he had taken Henry to the Rue des Barres.

" And Réné ? " said he.

" Réné saved me from poison."

" The deuce, Henriot, you have luck," said the King, trying to smile. But a quick spasm of pain changed the effort into a nervous contraction of the lips. " That is not his profession."

" Two miracles saved me, sire. A miracle of repentance on the part of the Florentine, and a miracle of goodness on your part. Well ! I will confess to your Majesty that I am afraid Heaven will grow weary of working miracles, and I tried to run away, because of the proverb : ' Heaven helps those who help themselves.' "

" Why did you not tell me this sooner, Henriot ? "

" Had I uttered these words yesterday I should have been a denunciator."

" And to-day ? "

" To-day is different — I am accused and I am defending myself."

" Are you sure of the first attempt, Henriot ? "

" As sure as I am of the second."

" And they tried to poison you ? "

" Yes."

" With what ? "

" With an opiate."

" How could they poison you with an opiate ? "

" Why, sire, ask Réné; poisoning is done with gloves " —

Charles frowned; then by degrees his brow cleared.

" Yes," said he, as if speaking to himself. " It is the nature of wild creatures to flee from death. Why, then, should not knowledge do what instinct does?"

"Well, sire!" said Henry, "is your Majesty satisfied with my frankness, and do you believe that I have told you everything?"

"Yes, Henriot, and you are a good fellow. Do you think that those who hate you have grown weary, or will new attempts be made on your life?"

"Sire, every evening I am surprised to find myself still living."

"It is because they know I love you, Henriot, that they wish to kill you. But do not worry. They shall be punished for their evil intentions. Meanwhile you are free."

"Free to leave Paris, sire?" asked Henry.

"No; you well know that I cannot possibly do without you. In the name of a thousand devils! I must have some one here who loves me."

"Then, sire, if your Majesty keep me with you, will you grant me a favor" —

"What is it?"

"Not to keep me as a friend, but as a prisoner. Yes; does not your Majesty see that it is your friendship for me that is my ruin?"

"Would you prefer my hatred?"

"Your apparent hatred, sire. It will save me. As soon as they think I am in disgrace they will be less anxious for my death."

"Henriot," said Charles, "I know neither what you desire, nor what object you seek; but if your wishes do not succeed, and if your object is not accomplished, I shall be greatly surprised."

"I may, then, count on the severity of the King?"

"Yes."

"In that case I shall be less uneasy. Now what are your Majesty's commands?"

"Return to your apartments, Henriot, I am in pain. I will see my dogs and then go to bed."

"Sire," said Henry, "your Majesty ought to send for a physician. Your trouble is perhaps more serious than you imagine."

"I have sent for Maître Ambroise Paré, Henriot."

"Then I shall retire more satisfied."

"Upon my soul," said the King, "I believe that of all my family you are the only one who really loves me."

"Is this indeed your opinion, sire?"

"On the word of a gentleman."

"Then commend me to Monsieur de Nancey as a man your deep anger may not allow to live a month. By this means you will have me many years to love you."

"Monsieur de Nancey!" cried Charles.

The captain of the guards entered.

"I commit into your hands the most guilty man of my kingdom. You will answer for him with your life."

Henry assumed an air of consternation, and followed Monsieur de Nancey.

CHAPTER LIII.

ACTÉON.

CHARLES, left alone, wondered greatly at not having seen either of his favorites, his nurse Madeleine or his greyhound Actéon.

"Nurse must have gone to chant psalms with some Huguenot of her acquaintance," said he to himself; "and Actéon is probably still angry with me for the whipping I gave him this morning."

Charles took a candle and went into his nurse's room. The good woman was not there. From her chamber a door opened into the armory, it may be remembered. The King started towards this door, but as he did so he was seized with one of those spasms he had already felt, and which seemed to attack him suddenly. He felt as if his entrails were being run through with a red-hot iron, and an unquenchable thirst consumed him. Seeing a cup of milk on the table, he swallowed it at a gulp, and felt somewhat relieved.

Taking the candle he had set down, he entered the armory.

To his great astonishment Actéon did not come to meet him. Had he been shut up? If so, he would have known that his master had returned from hunting, and would have barked.

Charles called and whistled, but no animal appeared. He advanced a few steps, and as the light from the candle fell upon a corner of the room, he perceived an inert something lying there on the floor.

"Why! hello, Actéon!" cried Charles. He whistled again, but the dog did not stir. Charles hastened forward and touched him; the poor beast was stiff and cold. From his throat, contracted by pain, several drops of gall had fallen, mixed with foamy and bloody saliva. The dog had found an old cap of his master's in the armory, and had died with his head resting on this object, which represented a friend.

At the sight, which made him forget his own pain and restored all his energy, rage boiled in Charles's veins. He would have cried out; but, restrained as they are in their greatness, kings are not free to yield to that first impulse which every man turns to the profit of his passion or to his defence. Charles reflected that there had been some treason, and was silent.

Then he knelt down before his dog and with experienced eye examined the body. The eyes were glassy, the tongue red and covered with pustules. It was a strange disease, and one which made Charles shudder. The King put on his gloves, which he had taken off and slipped into his belt, opened the livid lips of the dog to examine his teeth, and perceived in the interstices some white-looking fragments clinging to the sharp points of the molars. He took out these pieces, and saw that they were paper. Near where the paper had been the swelling was greater, the gums were swollen, and the skin looked as if it had been eaten by vitriol.

Charles gazed carefully around him. On the carpet lay two or three bits of the paper similar to that which he had already recognized in the dog's mouth. One of the pieces, larger than the others, showed the marks of a woodcut. Charles's hair stood on end, for he recognized a fragment of the picture which represented a gentleman hawking, and which Actéon had torn from the treatise on hunting.

"Ah!" said he, turning pale; "the book was poisoned!"

Then, suddenly remembering:

"A thousand devils!" he exclaimed, "I touched every page with my finger, and at every page I raised my finger to my lips. These fainting-spells, these attacks of pain and vomiting! I am a dead man!"

For an instant Charles remained motionless under the weight of this terrible thought. Then, rising with a dull groan, he hastened to the door of the armory.

" Maître Réné ! " he cried, " I want Maître Réné, the
Florentine; send some one as quickly as possible to the Pont
Saint Michel and bring him to me! He must be here within
ten minutes. Let some one mount a horse and lead another
that he may come more quickly. If Maître Ambroise Paré
arrives have him wait."

A guard went instantly to carry out the King's commands.

" Oh ! " murmured Charles, " if I have to put everybody to
the torture, I will know who gave this book to Henriot ; " and
with perspiration on his brow, clenched hands, and heaving
breast, he stood with his eyes fixed on the body of his dead dog.

Ten minutes later the Florentine knocked timidly and not
without some anxiety at the door of the King's apartments.
There are some consciences to which the sky is never clear.

" Enter ! " said Charles.

The perfumer appeared. Charles went towards him with
imperious air and compressed lip.

" Your Majesty sent for me," said Réné, trembling.

" You are a skilful chemist, are you not ? "

" Sire " —

" And you know all that the cleverest doctors know ? "

" Your Majesty exaggerates."

" No; my mother has told me so. Besides, I have confidence
in you, and I prefer to consult you rather than any one else.
See," he continued, pointing to the dog, " look at what this
animal has between his teeth, I beg you, and tell me of what
he died."

While Réné, candle in hand, bent over the floor as much to
hide his emotion as to obey the King, Charles stood up, his
eyes fixed on the man, waiting with an impatience easy to
understand for the reply which was to be his sentence of death
or his assurance of safety.

Réné drew a kind of scalpel from his pocket, opened it, and
with the point detached from the mouth of the greyhound
the particles of paper which adhered to the gums; then he
looked long and attentively at the humor and the blood which
oozed from each wound.

" Sire," said he, trembling, " the symptoms are very bad."

Charles felt an icy shudder run through his veins to his
very heart.

" Yes," said he, " the dog has been poisoned, has he not ? "

" I fear so, sire."

"With what sort of poison?"

"With mineral poison, I think."

"Can you ascertain positively that he has been poisoned?"

"Yes, certainly, by opening and examining the stomach."

"Open it. I wish there to be no doubt."

"I must call some one to assist me."

"I will help you," said Charles.

"You, sire!"

"Yes. If he has been poisoned, what symptoms shall we find?"

"Red blotches and herborizations in the stomach."

"Come, then," said Charles, "begin."

With a stroke of the scalpel Réné opened the hound's body and with his two hands removed the stomach, while Charles, one knee on the floor, held the light with clenched and trembling hand.

"See, sire," said Réné; "here are evident marks. These are the red spots I spoke of; as to these bloody veins, which seem like the roots of a plant, they are what I meant by herborizations. I find here everything I looked for."

"So the dog was poisoned?"

"Yes, sire."

"With mineral poison?"

"In all probability."

"And what symptoms would a man have who had inadvertently swallowed some of the same poison?"

"Great pain in the head, internal burning as if he had swallowed hot coals, pains in the bowels, and vomiting."

"Would he be thirsty?" asked Charles.

"Intensely thirsty."

"That is it! that is it!" murmured the King.

"Sire, I seek in vain for the motive for all these questions."

"Of what use to seek it? You need not know it. Answer my questions, that is all."

"Yes, sire."

"What is the antidote to give a man who may have swallowed the same substance as my dog?"

Réné reflected an instant.

"There are several mineral poisons," said he; "and before answering I should like to know what you mean. Has your Majesty any idea of the way in which your dog was poisoned?"

" Yes," said Charles; " he chewed the leaf of a book."

" The leaf of a book ? "

" Yes."

" Has your Majesty this book ? "

" Here it is," said Charles, and, taking the volume from the shelf where he had placed it, he handed it to Réné.

The latter gave a start of surprise which did not escape the King.

" He ate a leaf of this book ? " stammered Réné.

" Yes, this one," and Charles pointed to the torn page.

" Will you allow me to tear out another, sire ? "

" Do so."

Réné tore out a leaf and held it over the candle. The paper caught fire, filling the room with a strong smell of garlic.

" He has been poisoned with a preparation of arsenic," said he.

" You are sure ? "

" As sure as if I had prepared it myself."

" And the antidote ? "

Réné shook his head.

" What ! " said Charles in a hoarse voice, " you know no remedy ? "

" The best and most efficacious is the white of eggs beaten in milk ; but " —

" But what ? "

" It must be administered at once ; otherwise " —

" Otherwise ? "

" Sire, it is a terrible poison," said René, again.

" Yet it does not kill immediately," said Charles.

" No, but it kills surely, no matter how long the time, though even this may sometimes be calculated."

Charles leaned against the marble table.

" Now," said he, putting his hand on Réné's shoulder, " you know this book ? "

" I, sire ? " said Réné, turning pale.

" Yes, you ; on seeing it you betrayed yourself."

" Sire, I swear to you " —

" Réné," said Charles, " listen to me. You poisoned the Queen of Navarre with gloves; you poisoned the Prince of Porcion with the smoke from a lamp; you tried to poison Monsieur de Condé with a scented apple. Réné, I will have your skin removed with red-hot pincers, bit by bit, if you do not tell me to whom this book belongs."

The Florentine saw that he could not dally with the anger of Charles IX., and resolved to be bold.

" If I tell the truth, sire, who will guarantee that I shall not be more cruelly punished than if I keep silent ? "

" I will."

" Will you give me your royal word ? "

" On my honor as a gentleman your life shall be spared," said the King.

" The book belongs to me, then," said Réné.

" To you ! " cried Charles, starting back and looking at the poisoner with haggard eyes.

" Yes, to me."

" How did it leave your possession ? "

" Her majesty the queen mother took it from my house."

" The queen mother ! " exclaimed Charles.

" Yes."

" With what object ? "

" With the intention, I think, of having it sent to the King of Navarre, who had asked the Duc d'Alençon for a book of the kind in order to study the art of hawking."

" Ah ! " cried Charles, " that is it. I see it all. The book indeed was in Henriot's room. There is a destiny about this and I submit to it."

At that moment Charles was seized with a violent fit of coughing, followed by fresh pain in the bowels. He gave two or three stifled cries, and fell back in his chair.

" What is the matter, sire ? " asked Réné in a frightened voice.

" Nothing," said Charles, " except that I am thirsty. Give me something to drink."

Réné filled a glass with water and with trembling hand gave it to Charles, who swallowed it at a draught.

" Now," said he, taking a pen and dipping it into the ink, " write in this book."

" What must I write ? "

" What I am going to dictate to you :

" *' This book on hawking was given by me to the queen mother, Catharine de Médicis.'* " ·

Réné took the pen and wrote.

" Now sign your name."

The Florentine obeyed.

" You promised to save my life."

"I will keep my promise."

"But," said Réné, "the queen mother?"

"Oh!" said Charles, "I have nothing to do with her; if you are attacked defend yourself."

"Sire, may I leave France, where I feel that my life is in danger?"

"I will reply to that in a fortnight."

"But, in the meantime" —

Charles frowned and placed his finger on his livid lips.

"You need not be afraid of me, sire."

And happy to have escaped so easily the Florentine bowed and withdrew.

Behind him the nurse appeared at the door of her room.

"What is the matter, my Charlot?" said she.

"Nurse, I have been walking in the dew, and have taken cold."

"You are very pale, Charlot."

"It is because I am so weak. Give me your arm, nurse, as far as my bed."

The nurse hastily came forward.

Charles leaned on her and reached his room.

"Now," said Charles, "I will put myself to bed."

"If Maître Ambroise Paré comes?"

"Tell him that I am better and that I do not need him."

"But, meanwhile, what will you take?"

"Oh! a very simple medicine," said Charles, "the whites of eggs beaten in milk. By the way, nurse," he continued, "my poor Actéon is dead. To-morrow morning he must be buried in a corner of the garden of the Louvre. He was one of my best friends. I will have a tomb made for him — if I have time."

CHAPTER LIV.

THE FOREST OF VINCENNES.

ACCORDING to the order given by Charles IX., Henry was conducted that same evening to Vincennes. Such was the name given at that time to the famous castle of which to-day only a fragment remains, colossal enough, however, to give an idea of its past grandeur.

The trip was made in a litter, on either side of which walked four guards.

Monsieur de Nancey, bearing the order which was to open to Henry the door of the protecting abode, walked first.

At the postern of the prison they stopped. Monsieur de Nancey dismounted from his horse, opened the gate, which was closed with a padlock, and respectfully asked the king to follow.

Henry obeyed without uttering a word. Any dwelling seemed to him safer than the Louvre, and ten doors closed on him were at the same time ten doors shut between him and Catharine de Médicis.

The royal prisoner crossed the drawbridge between two soldiers, passed through the three doors on the ground floor and the three at the foot of the staircase; then, still preceded by Monsieur de Nancey, he ascended one flight. Arrived there, the captain of the guards, seeing that the king was about to mount another flight, said to him:

" My lord, you are to stop here."

" Ah!" said Henry, pausing, "it seems that I am given the honors of the first floor."

" Sire," replied Monsieur de Nancey, "you are treated like a crowned head."

" The devil! the devil!" said Henry to himself, "two or three floors more would in no way have humiliated me. I shall be too comfortable here; I suspect something."

" Will your majesty follow me?" asked Monsieur de Nancey.

" *Ventre saint gris!* " said the King of Navarre, "you know very well, monsieur, that it is not a question of what I will or will not do, but of what my brother Charles orders. Did he command that I should follow you?"

" Yes, sire."

" Then I will do so, monsieur."

They reached a sort of corridor at the end of which they came to a good-sized room, with dark and gloomy looking walls. Henry gazed around him with a glance not wholly free from anxiety.

" Where are we?" he asked.

" In the chamber of torture, my lord."

" Ah!" replied the king, looking at it more closely.

There was something of everything in this chamber — pitchers and wooden horses for the torture by water; wedges and mallets for the torture of the boot; besides stone benches nearly all around the room for the wretches who awaited the torture. Above these benches, at the seats themselves, and at their feet, were iron rings fastened into the walls, without other symmetry than that of the torturing art. But their proximity to the seats sufficiently indicated that they were there in order to await the limbs of those who were to occupy them.

Henry walked on without a word, but not a single detail of all the hideous apparatus which, so to speak, had stamped the history of suffering on the walls escaped him.

The king was so taken up with the objects about him that he forgot to look where he was going, and came to a sudden standstill.

"Ah!" said he, "what is that?"

And he pointed to a kind of ditch dug in the damp pavement which formed the floor.

"That is the gutter, sire."

"Does it rain here, then?"

"Yes, sire, blood."

"Ah!" said Henry, "very good. Shall we not soon reach my apartment?"

"Yes, my lord, here it is," said a figure in the dark, which, as it drew nearer, became clearer and more distinguishable.

Henry thought he recognized the voice, and advanced towards the figure.

"So it is you, Beaulieu," said he. "What the devil are you doing here?"

"Sire, I have just received my appointment as governor of the fortress of Vincennes."

"Well, my dear friend, your initiation does you honor. A king for a prisoner is not bad."

"Pardon me, sire," said Beaulieu, "but I have already had two gentlemen."

"Who are they? But, pardon me, perhaps I am indiscreet. If so, assume that I have said nothing."

"My lord, I have not been ordered to keep it secret. They are Monsieur de la Mole and Monsieur de Coconnas."

"Ah! that is true. I saw them arrested. Poor gentlemen, and how do they bear this misfortune?"

"Differently. One is gay, the other sad; one sings, the other groans."

"Which one groans?"

"Monsieur de la Mole, sire."

"Faith," said Henry, "I can understand more easily the one who groans than the one who sings. After what I have seen the prison is not a very lively place. On what floor are they?"

"High up; on the fourth."

Henry heaved a sigh. It was there that he wished to be.

"Come, Monsieur de Beaulieu," said he, "be good enough to show me my room. I am in haste to see it, as I am greatly fatigued from the journey we have just made."

"This is it, my lord," said Beaulieu, pointing to an open door.

"Number two," said Henry; "why not number one?"

"Because that is reserved, my lord."

"Ah! it seems, then, that you expect a prisoner of higher rank than I."

"I did not say, my lord, that it was a prisoner."

"Who is it, then?"

"I beg my lord not to insist, for by refusing to answer I should fail in the obedience due him."

"Ah! that is another thing," said Henry.

And he became more pensive than before. Number one perplexed him, apparently. The governor was assiduous in his attentions. With a thousand apologies he installed Henry in his apartment, made every excuse for the comforts he might lack, stationed two soldiers at the door, and withdrew.

"Now," said the governor, addressing the turnkey, "let us go to the others."

The turnkey walked ahead. They took the same road by which they had come, passed through the chamber of torture, crossed the corridor, and reached the stairway. Then, still following his guide, Monsieur de Beaulieu ascended three flights. On reaching the fourth floor the turnkey opened successively three doors, each ornamented with two locks and three enormous bolts. He had scarcely touched the third door before they heard a joyous voice exclaiming:

"By Heaven! open; if only to give us some air. Your stove is so warm that I am stifled here."

And Coconnas, whom the reader has no doubt already recognized from his favorite exclamation, bounded from where he stood to the door.

"One instant, my gentleman," said the turnkey, "I have not come to let you out, but to let myself in, and the governor is with me."

"The governor!" said Coconnas, "what does he want?"

"To pay you a visit."

"He does me great honor," said Coconnas; "and he is welcome."

Monsieur de Beaulieu entered and at once dispelled the cordial smile of Coconnas by one of those icy looks which belong to governors of fortresses, to jailers, and to hangmen.

"Have you any money, monsieur?" he asked of the prisoner.

"I?" said Coconnas; "not a crown."

"Jewels?"

"I have a ring."

"Will you allow me to search you?"

"By Heaven!" cried Coconnas, reddening with anger, "you take much on yourself, being in prison, and having me there also."

"We must suffer everything for the service of the King."

"So," said the Piedmontese, "those good fellows who rob on the Pont Neuf are like you, then, in the service of the King. By Heavens! I was very unjust, monsieur, for until now I have taken them for thieves."

"Good evening, monsieur," said Beaulieu. "Jailer, lock the door."

The governor went away, taking with him the ring, which was a beautiful sapphire, given him by Madame de Nevers to remind him of the color of her eyes.

"Now for the other," he said as he went out.

They crossed an empty chamber, and the game of three doors, six locks, and nine bolts began anew.

The last door open, a sigh was the first sound that greeted the visitors.

The apartment was more gloomy looking than the one Monsieur de Beaulieu had just left. Four long narrow windows admitted a feeble light into this mournful abode. Before these, iron bars were crossed in such a way that the eye of the prisoner was arrested by a dark line and prevented from catching even a glimpse of the sky. From each corner of the room pointed arches met in the middle of the ceiling, where they spread out in Gothic fashion.

La Mole was seated in a corner, and, in spite of the entrance of the visitors, appeared to have heard nothing.

The governor paused on the threshold and looked for an instant at the prisoner, who sat motionless, his head in his hands.

"Good evening, Monsieur de la Mole," said Beaulieu.

The young man slowly raised his head.

"Good evening, monsieur," said he.

"Monsieur," continued the governor, "I have come to search you."

"That is useless," said La Mole. "I will give you all I have."

"What have you?"

"About three hundred crowns, these jewels, and rings."

"Give them to me, monsieur," said the governor.

"Here they are."

La Mole turned out his pockets, took the rings from his finger, and the clasp from his hat.

"Have you nothing more?"

"Not that I know of."

"And that silk cord around your neck, what may that be?" asked the governor.

"Monsieur, that is not a jewel, but a relic."

"Give it to me."

"What! you demand it?"

"I am ordered to leave you only your clothes, and a relic is not an article of clothing."

La Mole made a gesture of anger, which, in the midst of the dignified and pained calm which distinguished him, seemed to impress the men accustomed to stormy emotions.

But he immediately recovered his self-possession.

"Very well, monsieur," said he, "you shall see what you ask for."

Then, turning as if to approach the light, he unfastened the pretended relic, which was none other than a medallion containing a portrait, which he drew out and raised to his lips. Having kissed it several times, he suddenly pretended to drop it as by accident, and placing the heel of his boot on it he crushed it into a thousand pieces.

"Monsieur!" said the governor.

And he stooped down to see if he could not save the unknown object which La Mole wished to hide from him; but the miniature was literally ground to powder.

"The King wished for this jewel," said La Mole, "but he

had no right to the portrait it contained. Now, here is the medallion; you may take it."

"Monsieur," said Beaulieu, "I shall complain of you to the King."

And without taking leave of his prisoner by a single word he went out, so angry that without waiting to preside over the task, he left to the turnkey the care of closing the doors.

The jailer turned to leave, but seeing that Monsieur de Beaulieu had already started down the stairs:

"Faith! monsieur," said he, turning back, "I did well to ask you to give me the hundred crowns at once for which I am to allow you to speak to your companion; for had you not done so the governor would have taken them from you with the three hundred others, and my conscience would not have allowed me to do anything for you; but as I was paid in advance, I promised that you should see your friend. So come. An honest man keeps his word. Only, if it is possible, for your sake as much as for mine, do not talk politics."

La Mole left his apartment and found himself face to face with Coconnas, who was walking up and down the flags of the intermediate room.

The two friends rushed into each other's arms.

The jailer pretended to wipe the corner of his eye, and then withdrew to watch that the prisoners were not surprised, or rather that he himself was not caught.

"Ah! here you are!" said Coconnas. "Well, has that dreadful governor paid his visit to you?"

"Yes, as he did to you, I presume?"

"Did he remove everything?"

"And from you, too?"

"Ah! I had not much; only a ring from Henriette, that was all."

"And money?"

"I gave all I had to the good jailer, so that he would arrange this interview for us."

"Ah!" said La Mole, "it seems that he had something from both of us."

"Did you pay him too?"

"I gave him a hundred crowns."

"So much the better."

"One can do everything with money, and I trust that we shall not lack for it."

" Do you know what has happened to us ? "

" Perfectly ; we have been betrayed."

" By that scoundrelly Duc d'Alençon. I should have been right to twist his neck."

" Do you think our position serious ? "

" I fear so."

" Then there is likelihood of the torture ? "

"I will not hide from you the fact that I have already thought of it."

" What should you do in that case ? "

" And you ? "

" I should be silent," replied La Mole, with a feverish flush.

" Silent ? " cried Coconnas.

" Yes, if I had the strength."

" Well," said Coconnas, " if they insult me in any such way I promise you I will tell them a few things."

" What things ? " asked La Mole, quickly.

" Oh, be easy — things which will prevent Monsieur d'Alençon from sleeping for some time."

La Mole was about to reply when the jailer, who no doubt had heard some noise, appeared, and pushing each prisoner into his respective cell, locked the doors again.

CHAPTER LV.

THE FIGURE OF WAX.

FOR a week Charles was confined to his bed by a slow fever, interrupted by violent attacks which resembled epileptic fits. During these attacks he uttered shrieks which the guards, watching in his chamber, heard with terror, and the echoes of which reached to the farthest corner of the old Louvre, aroused so often by many a dreadful sound. Then, when these attacks passed, Charles, completely exhausted, sank back with closed eyes into the arms of his nurse.

To say that, each in his way, without communicating the feeling to the other, for mother and son sought to avoid rather than to see each other, to say that Catharine de Médicis and the Duc d'Alençon revolved sinister thoughts in the depths

of their hearts would be to say that in that nest of vipers
moved a hideous swarm.

Henry was shut up in his chamber in the prison; and at his
own request no one had been allowed to see him, not even
Marguerite. In the eyes of every one his imprisonment was
an open disgrace. Catharine and D'Alençon, thinking him
lost, breathed once more, and Henry ate and drank more
calmly, hoping that he was forgotten.

At court no one suspected the cause of the King's illness.
Maître Ambroise Paré and Mazille, his colleague, thought it
was inflammation of the bowels, and had prescribed a regimen
which aided the special drink given by Réné. Charles received
this, his only nourishment, three times a day from the hands
of his nurse.

La Mole and Coconnas were at Vincennes in closest con-
finement. Marguerite and Madame de Nevers had made a
dozen attempts to reach them, or at least to send them a note,
but without success. One morning Charles felt somewhat
better, and wished the court to assemble. This was the usual
custom in the morning, although for some time no levee had
taken place. The doors were accordingly thrown open, and it
was easy to see, from his pale cheeks, yellow forehead, and
the feverish light in his deep-sunken eyes, which were surrounded by dark circles, what frightful ravages the unknown
disease had made on the young monarch.

The royal chamber was soon filled with curious and interested courtiers. Catharine, D'Alençon, and Marguerite had
been informed that the King was to hold an audience. Therefore all three entered, at short intervals, one by one; Catharine
calm, D'Alençon smiling, Marguerite dejected. Catharine
seated herself by the side of the bed without noticing the look
that Charles gave her as he saw her approach.

Monsieur d'Alençon stood at the foot.

Marguerite leaned against a table, and seeing the pale brow,
the worn features, and deep-sunken eyes of her brother, could
not repress a sigh and a tear.

Charles, whom nothing escaped, saw the tear and heard the
sigh, and with his head made a slight motion to Marguerite.

This sign, slight as it was, lighted the face of the poor
Queen of Navarre, to whom Henry had not had time or perhaps had not wished to say anything.

She feared for her husband, she trembled for her lover.

For herself she had no fear; she knew La Mole well, and felt she could rely on him.

"Well, my dear son," said Catharine, "how do you feel?"

"Better, mother, better."

"What do your physicians say?"

"My physicians? They are clever doctors, mother," said Charles, bursting into a laugh. "I take great pleasure, I admit, in hearing them discuss my malady. Nurse, give me something to drink."

The nurse brought Charles a cup of his usual beverage.

"What do they order you to take, my son?"

"Oh! madame, who knows anything about their preparations?" said the King, hastily swallowing the drink.

"What my brother needs," said François, "is to rise and get out into the open air; hunting, of which he is so fond, would do him a great deal of good."

"Yes," said Charles, with a smile, the meaning of which it was impossible for the duke to understand, "and yet the last hunt did me great harm."

Charles uttered these words in such a strange way that the conversation, in which the others present had not taken part, stopped. Then the King gave a slight nod of his head. The courtiers understood that the audience was over, and withdrew one after another.

D'Alençon started to approach his brother, but some secret feeling stopped him. He bowed and went out.

Marguerite seized the wasted hand her brother held out to her, pressed it, and kissed it. Then she, in turn, withdrew.

"Dear Margot!" murmured Charles.

Catharine alone remained, keeping her place at the side of the bed. Finding himself alone with her, Charles recoiled as if from a serpent.

Instructed by the words of Réné, perhaps still better by silence and meditation, Charles no longer had even the happiness of doubt.

He knew perfectly to whom and to what to attribute his approaching death.

So, when Catharine drew near to the bed and extended to him a hand as cold as his glance, the King shuddered in fear.

"You have remained, madame?" said he.

"Yes, my son," replied Catharine, "I must speak to you on important matters."

"Speak, madame," said Charles, again recoiling.

"Sire!" said the queen, "you said just now that your physicians were great doctors!"

"And I say so again, madame."

"Yet what have they done during your illness?"

"Nothing, it is true — but if you had heard what they said — really, madame, one might afford to be ill if only to listen to their learned discussions."

"Well, my son, do you want me to tell you something?"

"What is it, mother?"

"I suspect that all these clever doctors know nothing whatever about your malady."

"Indeed, madame!"

"They may, perhaps, see a result, but they are ignorant of the cause."

"That is possible," said Charles, not understanding what his mother was aiming at.

"So that they treat the symptoms and not the ill itself."

"On my soul!" said Charles, astonished, "I believe you are right, mother."

"Well, my son," said Catharine, "as it is good neither for my happiness nor the welfare of the kingdom for you to be ill so long, and as your mind might end by becoming affected, I assembled the most skilful doctors."

"In the science of medicine, madame?"

"No, in a more profound science : that which helps not only the body but the mind as well."

"Ah! a beautiful science, madame," said Charles, "and one which the doctors are right in not teaching to crowned heads! Have your researches had any result?" he continued.

"Yes."

"What was it?"

"That which I hoped for; I bring to your Majesty that which will cure not only your body but your mind."

Charles shuddered. He thought that finding that he was still living his mother had resolved to finish knowingly that which she had begun unconsciously.

"Where is this remedy?" said he, rising on his elbow and looking at his mother.

"In the disease itself," replied Catharine.

"Then where is that?"

"Listen to me, my son," said Catharine; "have you not

sometimes heard it said that there are secret enemies who in their revenge assassinate their victim from a distance ? "

" By steel or poison ? " asked Charles, without once turning his eyes from the impassible face of his mother.

"No, by a surer and much more terrible means," said Catharine.

" Explain yourself."

" My son," asked the Florentine, " do you believe in charms and magic ? "

Charles repressed a smile of scorn and incredulity.

" Fully," said he.

" Well," said Catharine, quickly, " from magic comes all your suffering. An enemy of your Majesty who would not have dared to attack you openly has conspired in secret. He has directed against your Majesty a conspiracy much more terrible in that he has no accomplices, and the mysterious threads of which cannot be traced."

" Faith, no ! " said Charles, aghast at such cunning.

" Think well, my son," said Catharine, " and recall to mind certain plans for flight which would have assured impunity to the murderer."

" To the murderer ! " cried Charles. " To the murderer, you say ? Has there been an attempt to kill me, mother ? "

Catharine's changing eye rolled hypocritically under its wrinkled lid.

" Yes, my son ; you doubt it, perhaps, but I know it for a certainty."

" I never doubt what you tell me, mother," replied the King, bitterly. " How was the attempt made ? I am anxious to know."

" By magic."

" Explain yourself, madame," said Charles, recalled by his loathing to his rôle of observer.

" If the conspirator I mean, and one whom at heart your Majesty already suspects, had succeeded in his plans, no one would have fathomed the cause of your Majesty's sufferings. Fortunately, however, sire, your brother watched over you."

" Which brother ? "

" D'Alençon."

" Ah ! yes, that is true ; I always forget that I have a brother," murmured Charles, laughing bitterly ; " so you say, madame " —

" That fortunately he revealed the conspiracy. But while he, inexperienced child that he is, sought only the traces of an ordinary plot, the proofs of a young man's escapade, I sought for proofs of a much more important deed; for I understand the reach of the guilty one's mind."

" Ah! mother, one would say you were speaking of the King of Navarre," said Charles, anxious to see how far this Florentine dissimulation would go.

Catharine hypocritically dropped her eyes.

"I have had him arrested and taken to Vincennes for his escapade," continued the King; "is he more guilty than I suspected, then ? "

" Do you feel the fever that consumes you ? " asked Catharine.

" Yes, certainly, madame," said Charles, frowning.

" Do you feel the fire that burns you internally ? "

" Yes, madame," replied Charles, his brow darkening more and more.

" And the sharp pains in your head, which shoot from your eyes to your brain like so many arrows ? "

" Yes, madame. I feel all that. You describe my trouble perfectly ! "

"Well! the explanation is very simple," said the Florentine. "See."

And she drew from under her cloak an object which she gave to the King.

It was a figure of yellow wax, about six inches high, clothed in a robe covered with golden stars also of wax, like the figure ; and over this a royal mantle of the same material.

" Well," asked Charles, " what is this little statue ? "

" See what it has on its head," said Catharine.

" A crown," replied Charles.

" And in the heart ? "

" A needle."

" Well, sire, do you recognize yourself ? "

" Myself ? "

" Yes, you, with your crown and mantle ? "

" Who made this figure ? " asked Charles, whom this farce was beginning to weary ; " the King of Navarre, no doubt ? "

" No, sire."

" No ? then I do not understand you."

"I say *no*," replied Catharine, " because you asked the

question literally. I should have said *yes* had you put it differently."

Charles made no answer. He was striving to penetrate all the thoughts of that shadowy mind, which constantly closed before him just as he thought himself ready to read it.

" Sire," continued Catharine, " this statue was found by the Attorney-General Laguesle, in the apartment of the man who on the day you last went hawking led a horse for the King of Navarre."

" Monsieur de la Mole ? "

" Yes, and, if you please, look again at the needle in the heart, and see what letter is written on the label attached to it."

" I see an ' M,' " said Charles.

" That means *mort*, death; it is the magic formula, sire. The maker thus wrote his vow on the very wound he gave. Had he wished to make a pretence at killing, as did the Duc de Bretagne for King Charles VI., he would have driven the needle into the head and put an ' F ' instead of an ' M.' "

" So," said Charles IX., " according to your idea, the person who seeks to end my days is Monsieur de la Mole ? "

" Yes, he is the dagger ; but behind the dagger is the hand that directs it."

" This then is the sole cause of my illness? the day the charm is destroyed the malady will cease?   But how go to work ? " asked Charles, " you must know, mother; but I, unlike you, who have spent your whole life studying them, know nothing about charms and spells."

" The death of the conspirator destroys the charm, that is all.   The day the charm is destroyed your illness will cease," said Catharine.

" Indeed ! " said Charles, with an air of surprise.

" Did you not know that ? "

" Why ! I am no sorcerer," said the King.

" Well, now," said Catharine, " your Majesty is convinced, are you not ? "

" Certainly."

" Conviction has dispelled anxiety ? "

" Completely."

" You do not say so out of complaisance ? "

" No, mother ! I say it from the bottom of my heart."

Catharine's face broke into smiles.

" Thank God ! " she exclaimed, as if she believed in God.

" Yes, thank God ! " repeated Charles, ironically; " I know now, as you do, to whom to attribute my present condition, and consequently whom to punish."

" And you will punish "—

" Monsieur de la Mole; did you not say that he was the guilty party ? "

" I said that he was the instrument."

" Well," said Charles, " Monsieur de la Mole first; he is the most important. All these attacks on me might arouse dangerous suspicions. It is imperative that there be some light thrown on the matter and from this light the truth may be discovered."

" So Monsieur de la Mole "—

" Suits me admirably as the guilty one; therefore I accept him. We will begin with him; and if he has an accomplice, he shall speak."

" Yes," murmured Catharine, " and if he does not, we will make him. We have infallible means for that."

Then rising:

" Will you permit the trial to begin, sire ? "

" I desire it, madame," replied Charles, " and the sooner the better."

Catharine pressed the hand of her son without comprehending the nervous grasp with which he returned it, and left the apartment without hearing the sardonic laugh of the King, or the terrible oath which followed the laugh.

Charles wondered if it were not dangerous to let this woman go thus, for in a few hours she would have done so much that there would be no way of stopping it.

As he watched the curtain fall after Catharine, he heard a light rustle behind him, and turning he perceived Marguerite, who raised the drapery before the corridor leading to his nurse's rooms.

Marguerite's pallor, her haggard eyes and oppressed breathing betrayed the most violent emotion.

" Oh, sire ! sire ! " she exclaimed, rushing to her brother's bedside; " you know that she lies."

" She ? Who ? " asked Charles.

" Listen, Charles, it is a terrible thing to accuse one's mother; but I suspected that she remained with you to persecute them again. But, on my life, on yours, on our souls, I tell you what she says is false ! "

" To persecute them ! Whom is she persecuting ? "

Both had instinctively lowered their voices ; it seemed as if they themselves feared even to hear them.

" Henry, in the first place; your Henriot, who loves you, who is more devoted to you than any one else."

" You think so, Margot ? " said Charles.

" Oh! sire, I am sure of it."

" Well, so am I," said Charles.

" Then if you are sure of it, brother," said Marguerite, surprised, " why did you have him arrested and taken to Vincennes ? "

" Because he asked me to do so."

" He asked you, sire ? "

" Yes, Henriot has singular ideas. Perhaps he is wrong, perhaps right; at any rate, one of his ideas was that he would be safer in disgrace than in favor, away from me at Vincennes instead of near me in the Louvre."

" Ah ! I see," said Marguerite, " and is he safe there ? "

" As safe as a man can be whose head Beaulieu answers for with his own."

" Oh! thank you, brother ! so much for Henry.   But " —

" But what ? "

" There is another, sire, in whom perhaps I am wrong to be interested, but " —

" Who is it ? "

" Sire, spare me. I would scarcely dare name him to my brother, much less to my King."

" Monsieur de la Mole, is it not ? " said Charles.

" Alas ! " said Marguerite, " you tried to kill him once, sire, and he escaped from your royal vengeance only by a miracle."

" He was guilty of only one crime then, Marguerite; now he has committed two."

" Sire, he is not guilty of the second."

" But," said Charles, " did you not hear what our good mother said, my poor Margot ? "

" Oh, I have already told you, Charles," said Marguerite, lowering her voice, " that what she said was false."

" You do not know perhaps that a waxen figure has been found in Monsieur de la Mole's rooms ? "

" Yes, yes, brother, I know it."

" That this figure is pierced to the heart by a needle, and that it bears a tag with an ' M ' on it ? "

" I know that, too."

" And that over the shoulders of the figure is a royal mantle, and that on its head is a royal crown ? "

" I know all that."

" Well! what have you to say to it ? "

" This : that the figure with a royal cloak and a crown on its head is that of a woman, and not that of a man."

" Bah ! " said Charles, " and the needle in its heart ? "

" Was a charm to make himself beloved by this woman, and not a charm to kill a man."

" But the letter ' M ' ? "

" It does not mean *mort*, as the queen mother said."

" What does it mean, then ? " asked Charles.

" It means — it means the name of the woman whom Monsieur de la Mole loves."

" And what is the name of this woman ? "

" *Marguerite*, brother ! " cried the Queen of Navarre, falling on her knees before the King's bed, taking his hand between both of hers, and pressing her face to it, bathed in tears.

" Hush, sister ! " said Charles, casting a sharp glance about him beneath his frowning brow. " For just as you overheard a moment ago, we may now be overheard again."

" What does it matter ? " exclaimed Marguerite, raising her head, " if the whole world were present to hear me, I would declare before it that it is infamous to abuse the love of a gentleman by staining his reputation with a suspicion of murder."

" Margot, suppose I were to tell you that I know as well as you do who it is and who it is not ? "

" Brother ! "

" Suppose I were to tell you that Monsieur de la Mole is innocent ? "

" You know this ? "

" If I were to tell you that I know the real author of the crime ? "

" The real author ! " cried Marguerite; " has there been a crime committed, then ? "

" Yes; intentionally or unintentionally there has been a crime committed."

" On you ? "

" Yes."

" Impossible ! "

" Impossible ?   Look at me, Margot."

The young woman looked at her brother and trembled, seeing him so pale.

" Margot, I have not three months to live ! " said Charles.

" You, brother ! you, Charles ! " she cried.

" Margot, I am poisoned."

Marguerite screamed.

" Hush," said Charles.   " It must be thought that I am dying by magic."

" Do you know who is guilty ? "

" Yes."

" You said it was not La Mole ? "

" No, it is not he."

" Nor Henry either, surely — great God ! could it be "—

" Who ? "

" My brother — D'Alençon ? " murmured Marguerite.

" Perhaps."

" Or — or "— Marguerite lowered her voice as if frightened at what she was going to say, " or — our mother ? "

Charles was silent.

Marguerite looked at him, and read all that she asked in his eyes.   Then still on her knees she half fell over against a chair.

" Oh ! my God ! my God ! " she whispered, " that is impossible."

" Impossible ? " said Charles, with a strident laugh, " it is a pity Réné is not here to tell you the story."

" Réné ? "

" Yes ; he would tell you that a woman to whom he dares refuse nothing asked him for a book on hunting which was in his library ; that a subtle poison was poured on every page of this book ; that the poison intended for some one, I know not for whom, fell by a turn of chance, or by a punishment of Heaven, on another.   But in the absence of Réné if you wish to see the book it is there in my closet, and written in the Florentine's handwriting you will see that this volume, which still contains the death of many among its pages, was given by him to his fellow countrywoman."

" Hush, Charles, hush ! " said Marguerite.

" Now you see that it must be supposed that I die of magic."

" But it is monstrous, monstrous !   Pity ! Pity ! you know he is innocent."

" Yes, I know it, but he must be thought guilty. Let your lover die ; it is very little to do in order to save the honor of the house of France ; I myself shall die that the secret may die with me."

Marguerite bent her head, realizing that nothing could be obtained from the King towards saving La Mole, and withdrew weeping, having no hope except in her own resources.

Meantime Catharine, as Charles had divined, had lost not a minute, but had written to the Attorney-General Laguesle a letter, every word of which has been preserved by history and which throws a lurid light upon the drama :

" Monsieur le Procureur : I have this evening been informed beyond a doubt that La Mole has committed sacrilege. Many evil things such as books and papers have been found in his apartments in Paris. I beg you to summon the chief president, and to inform him as early as possible of the affair of the waxen figure meant for the King, and which was pierced to the heart.

" *CATHARINE.*" [1]

CHAPTER LVI.

THE INVISIBLE BUCKLERS.

THE day after that on which Catharine had written this letter the governor entered Coconnas's cell with an imposing retinue consisting of two halberdiers and four men in black gowns.

Coconnas was asked to descend to a room in which the Attorney Laguesle and two judges waited to question him according to Catharine's instructions.

During the week he had spent in prison Coconnas had reflected a great deal. Besides that, he and La Mole were together for a few minutes each day, through the kindness of their jailer, who, without saying anything to them, had arranged this surprise, which in all probability they did not owe to his philosophy alone, — besides, we say, La Mole and he had agreed on the course they were to pursue, which was to persist in absolute denial ; and they were persuaded that with a little skill the affair would take a more favorable turn ; the charges

---

[1] Textual.

were no greater against them than against the others. Henry and Marguerite had made no attempt at flight; they could not therefore be compromised in an affair in which the chief ring-leaders were free. Coconnas did not know that Henry was in the prison, and the complaisance of the jailer told him that above his head hovered a certain protection which he called the *invisible bucklers*.

Up to then the examination had been confined to the intentions of the King of Navarre, his plans of flight, and the part the two friends had played in them. To all these questions Coconnas had constantly replied in a way more than vague and much more than adroit; he was ready still to reply in the same way, and had prepared in advance all his little repartees, when he suddenly found the object of the examination was altered. It turned upon one or more visits to Réné, one or more waxen figures made at the instigation of La Mole.

Prepared as he was, Coconnas believed that the accusation lost much of its intensity, since it was no longer a question of having betrayed a king but of having made a figure of a queen; and this figure not more than ten inches high at the most. He, therefore, replied brightly that neither he nor his friend had played with a doll for some time, and noticed with pleasure that several times his answers made the judges smile.

It had not yet been said in verse: "I have laughed, therefore am I disarmed," but it had been said a great deal in prose. And Coconnas thought that he had partly disarmed his judges because they had smiled.

His examination over, he went back to his cell, singing so merrily that La Mole, for whom he was making all the noise, drew from it the happiest auguries.

La Mole was brought down, and like Coconnas saw with astonishment that the accusation had abandoned its first ground and had entered a new field. He was questioned as to his visits to Réné. He replied that he had gone to the Florentine only once. Then, if he had not ordered a waxen figure. He replied that Réné had showed him such a figure ready made. He was then asked if this figure did not represent a man. He replied that it represented a woman. Then, if the object of the charm was not to cause the death of the man. He replied that the purpose of the charm was to cause himself to be beloved by the woman.

These questions were put in a hundred different forms, but

La Mole always replied in the same way. The judges looked at one another with a certain indecision, not knowing what to say or do before such simplicity, when a note brought to the Attorney-General solved the difficulty.

"*If the accused denies resort to the torture.*

"*C.*"

The attorney put the note into his pocket, smiled at La Mole, and politely dismissed him.

La Mole returned to his cell almost as reassured, if not as joyous, as Coconnas.

"I think everything is going well," said he.

An hour later he heard footsteps and saw a note slipped under his door, without seeing the hand that did it. He took it up, thinking that in all probability it came from the jailer?

Seeing it, a hope almost as acute as a disappointment sprang into his heart; he hoped it was from Marguerite, from whom he had had no news since he had been a prisoner.

He took it up with trembling hand, and almost died of joy as he looked at the handwriting.

"*Courage!*" said the note. "*I am watching over you.*"

"Ah! if she is watching," cried La Mole, covering with kisses the paper which had touched a hand so dear, "if she is watching, I am saved."

In order for La Mole to comprehend the note and rely with Coconnas on what the Piedmontese called his *invisible bucklers* it is necessary for us to conduct the reader to that small house, to that chamber in which the reminders of so many scenes of intoxicating happiness, so many half-evaporated perfumes, so many tender recollections, since become agonizing, were breaking the heart of a woman half reclining on velvet cushions.

"To be a queen, to be strong, young, rich, beautiful, and suffer what I suffer!" cried this woman; "oh! it is impossible!"

Then in her agitation she rose, paced up and down, stopped suddenly, pressed her burning forehead against the ice-cold marble, rose pale, her face covered with tears, wrung her hands, and crying aloud fell back again hopeless into a chair.

Suddenly the tapestry which separated the apartment of the Rue Cloche Percée from that in the Rue Tizon was raised, and the Duchesse de Nevers entered.

"Ah!" exclaimed Marguerite, "is it you? With what impatience I have waited for you! Well! What news?"

" Bad news, my poor friend. Catharine herself is hurrying on the trial, and at present is at Vincennes."

" And Réné ? "

" Is arrested."

" Before you were able to speak to him ? "

" Yes."

" And our prisoners ? "

" I have news of them."

" From the jailer ? "

" Yes."

" Well ? "

" Well! They see each other every day. The day before yesterday they were searched. La Mole broke your picture to atoms rather than give it up."

" Dear La Mole ! "

" Annibal laughed in the face of the inquisitors."

" Worthy Annibal! What then ? "

" This morning they were questioned as to the flight of the king, his projects of rebellion in Navarre, and they said nothing."

" Oh ! I knew they would keep silence; but silence will kill them as much as if they spoke."

" Yes, but we must save them."

" Have you thought over our plan ? "

" Since yesterday I have thought of nothing else."

" Well ? "

" I have just come to terms with Beaulieu. Ah! my dear queen, what a hard and greedy man! It will cost a man's life, and three hundred thousand crowns."

" You say he is hard and greedy — and yet he asks only the life of a man and three hundred thousand crowns. Why, that is nothing ! "

" Nothing! Three hundred thousand crowns! Why, all your jewels and all mine would not be enough."

" Oh ! that is nothing. The King of Navarre will pay something, the Duc d'Alençon will pay part, and my brother Charles will pay part, or if not" —

" See! what nonsense you talk. I have the money."

" You ? "

" Yes, I."

" How did you get it ? "

" Ah! that is telling ! "

"Is it a secret?"

"For every one except you."

"Oh, my God!" said Marguerite, smiling through her tears, "did you steal it?"

"You shall judge."

"Well, let me."

"Do you remember that horrible Nantouillet?"

"The rich man, the usurer?"

"If you please."

"Well?"

"Well! One day seeing a certain blonde lady, with greenish eyes, pass by, wearing three rubies, one over her forehead, the other two over her temples, an arrangement which was very becoming to her, this rich man, this usurer, cried out:

"'For three kisses in the place of those three rubies I will give you three diamonds worth one hundred thousand crowns apiece!'"

"Well, Henriette?"

"Well, my dear, the diamonds appeared and are sold."

"Oh, Henriette! Henriette!" cried Marguerite.

"Well!" exclaimed the duchess in a bold tone at once innocent and sublime, which sums up the age and the woman, "well, I love Annibal!"

"That is true," said Marguerite, smiling and blushing at the same time, "you love him a very great deal, too much, perhaps."

And yet she pressed her friend's hand.

"So," continued Henriette, "thanks to our three diamonds, the three hundred thousand crowns and the man are ready."

"The man? What man?"

"The man to be killed; you forget a man must be killed."

"Have you found the necessary man?"

"Yes."

"At the same price?" asked Marguerite, smiling.

"At the same price I could have found a thousand," replied Henriette, "no, no, for five hundred crowns."

"For five hundred crowns you have found a man who has consented to be killed?"

"What can you expect? It is necessary for us to live."

"My dear friend, I do not understand you. Come, explain. Enigmas require too much time to guess at such a moment as this."

" Well, listen; the jailer to whom the keeping of La Mole and Coconnas is entrusted is an old soldier who knows what a wound is. He would like to help save our friends, but he does not want to lose his place. A blow of a dagger skilfully aimed will end the affair. We will give him a reward and the kingdom, indemnification. In this way the brave man will receive money from both parties and will renew the fable of the pelican."

" But," said Marguerite, " a thrust of a dagger " —

" Do not worry; Annibal will give it."

" Well," said Marguerite, " he has given as many as three blows of his sword to La Mole, and La Mole is not dead; there is therefore every reason to hope."

" Wicked woman! You deserve to have me stop."

" Oh! no, no; on the contrary, tell me the rest, I beg you. How are we to save them; come!"

" Well, this is the plan. The chapel is the only place in the castle where women can enter who are not prisoners. We are to be hidden behind the altar. Under the altar cloth they will find two daggers. The door of the vestry-room will be opened beforehand. Coconnas will strike the jailer, who will fall and pretend to be dead; we appear; each of us throws a cloak over the shoulders of her friend; we run with them through the small doors of the vestry-room, and as we have the password we can leave without hindrance."

" And once out? "

" Two horses will be waiting at the door; the men will spring on them, leave France, and reach Lorraine, whence now and then they will return incognito."

" Oh! you restore me to life," said Marguerite. " So we shall save them? "

" I am almost sure of it."

" Soon ? "

" In three or four days. Beaulieu is to let us know."

" But if you were recognized in the vicinity of Vincennes that might upset our plan."

" How could any one recognize me? I go there as a nun, with a hood, thanks to which not even the tip of my nose is visible."

" We cannot take too many precautions."

" I know that well enough, by Heaven! as poor Annibal would say."

"Did you hear anything about the King of Navarre ? "

"I was careful to ask."

"Well ? "

"Well, he has never been so happy, apparently ; he laughs, sings, eats, drinks, and sleeps well, and asks only one thing, and that is to be well guarded."

"He is right. And my mother ? "

"I told you she is hurrying on the trial as fast as she can."

"Yes, but does she suspect anything about us ? "

"How could she ? Every one who has a secret is anxious to keep it. Ah ! I know that she told the judges in Paris to be in readiness."

"Let us act quickly, Henriette. If our poor prisoners change their abode, everything will have to be done over again."

"Do not worry. I am as anxious as you to see them free."

"Oh, yes, I know that, and thank you, thank you a hundred times for all you have done."

"Adieu, Marguerite. I am going into the country again."

"Are you sure of Beaulieu ? "

"I think so."

"Of the jailer ? "

"He has promised."

"Of the horses ? "

"They will be the best in the stables of the Duc de Nevers."

"I adore you, Henriette."

And Marguerite threw her arms about her friend's neck, after which the two women separated, promising to see each other again the next day, and every day, at the same place and hour.

These were the two charming and devoted creatures whom Coconnas, with so much reason, called his *invisible bucklers.*

CHAPTER LVII.

THE JUDGES.

"WELL, my brave friend," said Coconnas to La Mole, when the two were together after the examination, at which, for the first time, the subject of the waxen image had been discussed, " it seems to me that everything is going on finely, and that it will not be long before the judges will dismiss us.

And this diagnosis is entirely different from that of a dismissal by physicians. When the doctor gives up the patient it is because he cannot cure him, but when the judge gives up the accused it is because he has no further hope of having him beheaded."

" Yes," said La Mole; " and moreover, it seems to me, from the politeness and gentleness of the jailer and the looseness of the doors, that I recognize our kind friends ; but I do not recognize Monsieur de Beaulieu, at least from what I had been told of him."

" I recognize him," said Coconnas; " only it will cost dearly. But one is a princess, the other a queen; both are rich, and they will never have so good an opportunity to use their money. Now let us go over our lesson. We are to be taken to the chapel, and left there in charge of our turnkey ; we shall each find a dagger in the spot indicated. I am to make a hole in the body of our guide."

" Yes, but a slight one in the arm ; otherwise you will rob him of his five hundred crowns."

" Ah, no ; not in the arm, for in that case he would have to lose it, and it would be easy to see that it was given intentionally. No, it must be in his right side, gliding skilfully along his ribs; that would look natural, but in reality would be harmless."

" Well, aim for that, and then " —

" Then you will barricade the front door with benches while our two princesses rush from behind the altar, where they are to be hidden, and Henriette opens the vestry door. Ah, faith, how I love Henriette to-day ! She must have been faithless to me in some way for me to feel as I do."

" And then," said La Mole, with the trembling voice which falls from lips like music, " then we shall reach the forest. A kiss given to each of us will make us strong and happy. Can you not picture us, Annibal, bending over our swift horses, our hearts gently oppressed ? Oh, what a good thing is fear ! Fear in the open air when one has one's naked sword at one's side, when one cries ' hurra ' to the courser pricked by the spur, and which at each shout speeds the faster."

" Yes," said Coconnas, " but fear within four walls — what do you say to that, La Mole ? I can speak of it, for I have felt something of it. When Beaulieu, with his pale face, entered my cell for the first time, behind him in the darkness shone halberds, and I heard a sinister sound of iron striking against iron. I swear to you I immediately thought of the Duc d'Alençon, and I expected to see his ugly face between the two hateful heads of the halberdiers. I was mistaken, however, and this was my sole consolation. But that was not all; night came, and I dreamed."

"So," said La Mole, who had been following his happy train of thought without paying attention to his friend, "so they have foreseen everything, even the place in which we are to hide. We shall go to Lorraine, dear friend. In reality I should rather have had it Navarre, for there I should have been with her, but Navarre is too far; Nancey would be better; besides, once there, we should be only eighty leagues from Paris. Have you any feeling of regret, Annibal, at leaving this place?"

"Ah, no! the idea! Although I confess I am leaving everything that belongs to me."

"Well, could we manage to take the worthy jailer with us instead of"—

"He would not go," said Coconnas, "he would lose too much. Think of it! five hundred crowns from us, a reward from the government; promotion, perhaps; how happy will be that fellow's life when I shall have killed him! But what is the matter?"

"Nothing! An idea came to me."

"It is not a funny one, apparently, for you are frightfully pale."

"I was wondering why they should take us to the chapel."

"Why," said Coconnas, "to receive the sacrament. This is the time for it, I think."

"But," said La Mole, "they take only those condemned to death or the torture to the chapel."

"Oh!" said Coconnas, becoming somewhat pale in turn, "this deserves our attention. Let us question the good man whom I am to split open. Here, turnkey!"

"Did monsieur call?" asked the jailer, who had been keeping watch at the top of the stairs.

"Yes; come here."

"Well?"

"It has been arranged that we are to escape from the chapel, has it not?"

"Hush!" said the turnkey, looking round him in terror.

"Do not worry; no one can hear us."

"Yes, monsieur; it is from the chapel."

"They are to take us to the chapel, then?"

"Yes; that is the custom."

"The custom?"

"Yes; it is customary to allow every one condemned to death to pass the night in the chapel."

Coconnas and La Mole shuddered and glanced at each other.

"You think we are condemned to death, then?"

"Certainly. You, too, must think so."

"Why should we think so?" asked La Mole.

"Certainly; otherwise you would not have arranged everything for your escape."

"Do you know, there is reason in what he says!" said Coconnas to La Mole.

"Yes; and what I know besides is that we are playing a close game, apparently."

"But do you think I am risking nothing?" said the turnkey. "If in a moment of excitement monsieur should make a mistake" —

"Well! by Heaven! I wish I were in your place," said Coconnas, slowly, "and had to deal with no hand but this; with no sword except the one which is to graze you."

"Condemned to death!" murmured La Mole, "why, that is impossible!"

"Impossible!" said the turnkey, naïvely, "and why?"

"Hush!" said Coconnas, "I think some one is opening the lower door."

"To your cells, gentlemen, to your cells!" cried the jailer, hurriedly.

"When do you think the trial will take place?" asked La Mole.

"To-morrow, or later. But be easy; those who must be informed shall be."

"Then let us embrace each other and bid farewell to these walls."

The two friends rushed into each other's arms and then returned to their cells, La Mole sighing, Coconnas singing.

Nothing new happened until seven o'clock. Night fell dark and rainy over the prison of Vincennes, a perfect night for flight. The evening meal was brought to Coconnas, who ate with his usual appetite, thinking of the pleasure he would feel in being soaked in the rain which was pattering against the walls, and already preparing himself to fall asleep to the dull, monotonous murmur of the wind, when suddenly it seemed to him that this wind, to which he occasionally listened with a feeling of melancholy never before experienced by him until he came to prison, whistled more strangely than usual under the doors, and that the stove roared with a louder noise than common. This had happened every time one of the cells above or opposite him was opened. It was by this noise that Annibal always knew the jailer was coming from La Mole's cell.

But this time it was in vain that Coconnas remained with eye and ear alert.

The moments passed ; no one came.

" This is strange," said Coconnas, " La Mole's door has been opened and not mine. Could La Mole have called ? Can he be ill ? What does it mean ? "

With a prisoner everything is a cause for suspicion and anxiety, as everything is a cause for joy and hope.

Half an hour passed, then an hour, then an hour and a half.

Coconnas was beginning to grow sleepy from anger when the grating of the lock made him spring to his feet.

" Oh ! " said he, " has the time come for us to leave and are they going to take us to the chapel without condemning us ? By Heaven, what joy it would be to escape on such a night! It is as dark as an oven ! I hope the horses are not blind."

He was about to ask some jocular question of the turnkey when he saw the latter put his finger to his lips and roll his eyes significantly. Behind the jailer Coconnas heard sounds and perceived shadows.

Suddenly in the midst of the darkness he distinguished two helmets, on which the smoking candle threw a yellow light.

" Oh ! " said he in a low voice, " what is this sinister procession ? What is going to happen ? "

The jailer replied by a sigh which greatly resembled a groan.

" By Heaven ! " murmured Coconnas ; " what a wretched existence ! always on the ragged edge ; never on firm land ; either we paddle in a hundred feet of water or we hover above the clouds ; never a happy medium. Well, where are we going ? "

" Follow the halberdiers, monsieur," repeated the same voice.

He had to obey. Coconnas left his room, and perceived the

dark man whose voice had been so disagreeable. He was a clerk, small and hunchbacked, who no doubt had put on the gown in order to hide his bandy legs, as well as his back. He slowly descended the winding stairs. At the first landing the guards paused.

"That is a good deal to go down," murmured Coconnas, "but not enough."

The door opened. The prisoner had the eye of a lynx and the scent of a bloodhound. He scented the judges and saw in the shadow the silhouette of a man with bare arms; the latter sight made the perspiration mount to his brow. Nevertheless, he assumed his most smiling manner, and entered the room with his head tipped to one side, and his hand on his hip, after the most approved manner of the times.

A curtain was raised, and Coconnas perceived the judges and the clerks.

A few feet away La Mole was seated on a bench.

Coconnas was led to the front of the tribunal. Arrived there, he stopped, nodded and smiled to La Mole, and then waited.

"What is your name, monsieur?" inquired the president.

"Marcus Annibal de Coconnas," replied the gentleman with perfect ease. "Count de Montpantier, Chenaux, and other places; but they are known, I presume."

"Where were you born?"

"At Saint Colomban, near Suza."

"How old are you?"

"Twenty-seven years and three months."

"Good!" said the president.

"This pleases him, apparently," said Coconnas.

"Now," said the president after a moment's silence which gave the clerk time to write down the answers of the accused; "what was your reason for leaving the service of Monsieur d'Alençon?"

"To rejoin my friend Monsieur de la Mole, who had already left the duke three days before."

"What were you doing the day of the hunt, when you were arrested?"

"Why," said Coconnas, "I was hunting."

"The King was also present at that hunt, and was there seized with the first attack of the malady from which he is at present suffering."

"I was not near the King, and I can say nothing about this. I was even ignorant of the fact that he had been ill."

The judges looked at one another with a smile of incredulity.

"Ah! you were ignorant of his Majesty's illness, were you?" said the president.

"Yes, monsieur, and I am sorry to hear of it. Although the King of France is not my king, I have a great deal of sympathy for him."

"Indeed!"

"On my honor! It is different so far as his brother the Duc d'Alençon is concerned. The latter I confess" —

"We have nothing to do with the Duc d'Alençon, monsieur; this concerns his Majesty."

"Well, I have already told you that I am his very humble servant," said Coconnas, turning about in an adorably impudent fashion.

"If as you pretend, monsieur, you are really his servant, will you tell us what you know of a certain waxen figure?"

"Ah, good! we have come back to the figure, have we?"

"Yes, monsieur; does this displease you?"

"On the contrary, I prefer it; go ahead."

"Why was this statue found in Monsieur de la Mole's apartments?"

"At Monsieur de la Mole's? At Réné's, you mean?"

"You acknowledge that it exists, then, do you?"

"Why, if you will show it to me."

"Here it is. Is this the one you know?"

"It is."

"Clerk," said the president, "write down that the accused recognizes the image as the one seen at Monsieur de la Mole's."

"No, no!" said Coconnas, "do not let us misunderstand each other — as the one seen at Réné's."

"At Réné's; very good! On what day?"

"The only day La Mole and myself were at Réné's."

"You admit, then, that you were at Réné's with Monsieur de la Mole?"

"Why, did I ever deny it?"

"Clerk, write down that the accused admits having gone to Réné's to work conjurations."

"Stop there, Monsieur le Président. Moderate your enthusiasm, I beg you. I did not say that at all."

" You deny having been at Réné's to work conjurations ? "

" I deny it. The magic took place by accident. It was unpremeditated."

" But it took place ? "

" I cannot deny that something resembling a charm did take place."

" Clerk, write down that the accused admits that he obtained at Réné's a charm against the life of the King."

" What! against the King's life ? That is an infamous lie! There was no charm obtained against the life of the King."

" You see, gentlemen ! " said La Mole.

" Silence ! " said the president; then turning to the clerk : " Against the life of the King," he continued. " Have you that ? "

" Why, no, no ! " cried Coconnas. " Besides, the figure is not that of a man, but of a woman."

" What did I tell you, gentlemen ? " said La Mole.

" Monsieur de la Mole," said the president, " answer when you are questioned, but do not interrupt the examination of others."

" So you say that it is a woman ? "

" Certainly I say so."

" In that case, why did it have a crown and a cloak ? "

" By Heaven ! " said Coconnas, " that is simple enough, because it was " —

La Mole rose and put his finger on his lips.

" That is so," said Coconnas, " what was I going to say that could possibly concern these gentlemen ? "

" You persist in stating that the figure is that of a woman ? "

" Yes ; certainly I persist."

" And you refuse to say what woman ? "

" A woman of my country," said La Mole, " whom I loved and by whom I wished to be loved in return."

" We are not asking you, Monsieur de la Mole," said the president; " keep silent, therefore, or you shall be gagged."

" Gagged ! " exclaimed Coconnas; " what do you mean, monsieur of the black robe ? My friend gagged ? A gentleman ! the idea ! "

" Bring in Réné," said the Attorney-General Laguesle.

" Yes; bring in Réné," said Coconnas; " we shall see who is right here, we two or you three."

Réné entered, pale, aged, and almost unrecognizable to the two friends, bowed under the weight of the crime he was about to commit much more than because of those he had already committed.

"Maître Réné," said the judge, "do you recognize the two accused persons here present?"

"Yes, monsieur," replied Réné, in a voice which betrayed his emotion.

"From having seen them where?"

"In several places; and especially at my house."

"How many times did they go to your house?"

"Once only."

As Réné spoke the face of Coconnas expanded; La Mole's, on the contrary, looked as though he had a presentiment of evil.

"For what purpose were they at your house?"

Réné seemed to hesitate a moment.

"To order me to make a waxen figure," said he.

"Pardon me, Maître Réné," said Coconnas, "you are making a slight mistake."

"Silence!" said the president; then turning to Réné, "was this figure to be that of a man or a woman?"

"A man," replied Réné.

Coconnas sprang up as if he had received an electric shock.

"A man!" he exclaimed.

"A man," repeated Réné, but in so low a tone that the president scarcely heard him.

"Why did this figure of a man have on a mantle and a crown?"

"Because it represented a king."

"Infamous liar!" cried Coconnas, infuriated.

"Keep still, Coconnas, keep still," interrupted La Mole, "let the man speak; every one has a right to sell his own soul."

"But not the bodies of others, by Heaven!"

"And what was the meaning of the needle in the heart of the figure, with the letter 'M' on a small banner?"

"The needle was emblematical of the sword or the dagger; the letter 'M' stands for *mort*."

Coconnas sprang forward as though to strangle Réné, but four guards restrained him.

"That will do," said the Attorney Laguesle, "the court is

sufficiently informed. Take the prisoners to the waiting-room."

"But," exclaimed Coconnas, "it is impossible to hear one's self accused of such things without protesting."

"Protest, monsieur, no one will hinder you. Guards, did you hear?"

The guards seized the two prisoners and led them out, La Mole by one door, Coconnas by another.

Then the attorney signed to the man whom Coconnas had perceived in the shadow, and said to him:

"Do not go away, my good fellow, you shall have work this evening."

"Which shall I begin with, monsieur?" asked the man, respectfully holding his cap in his hand.

"With that one," said the president, pointing to La Mole, who could still be seen disappearing in the distance between the two guards. Then approaching Réné, who stood trembling, expecting to be led back to the cell in which he had been confined:

"You have spoken well, monsieur," said he to him, "you need not worry. Both the King and the queen shall know that it is to you they are indebted for the truth of this affair."

But instead of giving him strength, this promise seemed to terrify Réné, whose only answer was a deep sigh.

CHAPTER LVIII.

THE TORTURE OF THE BOOT.

IT was only when he had been led away to his new cell and the door was locked on him that Coconnas, left alone, and no longer sustained by the discussion with the judges and his anger at Réné, fell into a train of mournful reflections.

"It seems to me," thought he, "that matters are turning against us, and that it is about time to go to the chapel. I suspect we are to be condemned to death. It looks so. I especially fear being condemned to death by sentences pronounced behind closed doors, in a fortified castle, before faces as ugly as those about me. They really wish to cut off our heads. Well! well! I repeat what I said just now, it is time to go to chapel."

These words, uttered in a low tone, were followed by a silence, which in turn was broken by a cry, shrill, piercing, lugubrious, unlike anything human. It seemed to penetrate the thick walls, and vibrate against the iron bars.

In spite of himself Coconnas shivered; and yet he was so brave that his courage was like that of wild beasts. He stood still, doubting that the cry was human, and taking it for the sound of the wind in the trees or for one of the many night noises which seem to rise or descend from the two unknown worlds between which floats our globe. Then he heard it again, shriller, more prolonged, more piercing than before, and this time not only did Coconnas distinguish the agony of the human tone in it, but he thought it sounded like La Mole's.

As he realized this the Piedmontese forgot that he was confined behind two doors, three gates, and a wall twelve feet thick. He hurled his entire weight against the sides of the cell as though to push them out and rush to the aid of the victim, crying, "Are they killing some one here?" But he unexpectedly encountered the wall and the shock hurled him back against a stone bench on which he sank down.

Then there was silence.

"Oh, they have killed him!" he murmured; "it is abominable! And one is without arms, here, and cannot defend one's self!"

He groped about.

"Ah! this iron chain!" he cried, "I will take it and woe to him who comes near me!"

Coconnas rose, seized the iron chain, and with a pull shook it so violently that it was clear that with two such efforts he would wrench it away.

But suddenly the door opened and the light from a couple of torches fell into the cell.

"Come, monsieur," said the same voice which had sounded so disagreeable to him, and which this time, in making itself heard three floors below, did not seem to him to have acquired any new charm.

"Come, monsieur, the court is awaiting you."

"Good," said Coconnas, dropping his ring, "I am to hear my sentence, am I not?"

"Yes, monsieur."

"Oh! I breathe again; let us go," said he.

He followed the usher, who preceded him with measured tread, holding his black rod.

In spite of the satisfaction he had felt at first, as he walked along Coconnas glanced anxiously about him.

"Oh!" he murmured, "I do not perceive my good jailer. I confess I miss him."

They entered the hall the judges had just left, in which a man was standing alone, whom Coconnas recognized as the Attorney-General. In the course of the examination the latter had spoken several times, always with an animosity easy to understand.

He was the one whom Catharine, both by letter and in person, had specially charged with the trial.

At the farther end of this room, the corners of which were lost in darkness behind a partly raised curtain, Coconnas saw such dreadful sights that he felt his limbs give away, and cried out: "Oh, my God!"

It was not without cause that the cry had been uttered. The sight was indeed terrible. The portion of the room hidden during the trial by the curtain, which was now drawn back, looked like the entrance to hell.

A wooden horse was there, to which were attached ropes, pulleys, and other accessories of torture. Further on glowed a brazier, which threw its lurid glare on the surrounding objects, and which added to the terror of the spectacle. Against one of the pillars which supported the ceiling stood a man motionless as a statue, holding a rope in his hand. He looked as though made of the stone of the column against which he leaned. To the walls above the stone benches, between iron links, chains were suspended and blades glittered.

"Oh!" murmured Coconnas, "the chamber of horrors is all ready, apparently waiting only for the patient! What can it mean?"

"On your knees, Marc Annibal Coconnas," said a voice which caused that gentleman to raise his head. "On your knees to hear the sentence just pronounced on you!"

This was an invitation against which the whole soul of Annibal instinctively rebelled.

But as he was about to refuse two men placed their hands on his shoulders so unexpectedly and so suddenly that his knees bent under him on the pavement. The voice continued ·

"Sentence of the court sitting in the prison of Vincennes on Marc Annibal de Coconnas, accused and convicted of high treason, of an attempt to poison, of sacrilege and magic against the person of the King, of a conspiracy against the kingdom, and of having by his pernicious counsels driven a prince of the blood to rebellion."

At each charge Coconnas had shaken his head, keeping time like a fractious child. The judge continued :

"In consequence of which, the aforesaid Marc Annibal de Coconnas shall be taken from prison to the Place Saint Jean en Grève to be there beheaded; his property shall be confiscated; his woods cut down to the height of six feet; his castles destroyed, and a post planted there with a copper plate bearing an inscription of his crime and punishment."

"As for my head," said Coconnas, "I know you will cut that off, for it is in France, and in great jeopardy; but as for my woods and castles, I defy all the saws and axes of this most Christian kingdom to harm them."

"Silence!" said the judge; and he continued :

"Furthermore, the aforesaid Coconnas " —

"What!" interrupted Coconnas, "is something more to be done to me after my head is cut off? Oh! that seems to me very hard!"

"No, monsieur," said the judge, "*before.*"

And he resumed :

"Furthermore, the aforesaid Coconnas before the execution of his sentence shall undergo the severest torture, consisting of ten wedges " —

Coconnas sprang up, flashing a burning glance at the judge.

"And for what?" he cried, finding no other words but these simple ones to express the thousand thoughts that surged through his mind.

In reality this was complete ruin to Coconnas' hopes. He would not be taken to the chapel until after the torture, from which many frequently died. The braver and stronger the victim, the more likely he was to die, for it was considered an act of cowardice to confess; and so long as the prisoner refused to confess the torture was continued, and not only continued, but increased.

The judge did not reply to Coconnas; the rest of the sentence answered for him. He continued :

"In order to compel the aforesaid Coconnas to confess in

regard to his accomplices, and the details of the plan and conspiracy."

" By Heaven!" cried Coconnas; "this is what I call infamous; more than infamous — cowardly!"

Accustomed to the anger of his victims, which suffering always changed to tears, the impassible judge merely made a sign.

Coconnas was seized by the feet and the shoulders, overpowered, laid on his back, and bound to the rack before he was able even to see those who did the act.

" Wretches!" shouted he, in a paroxysm of fury, straining the bed and the cords so that the tormentors themselves drew back. "Wretches! torture me, twist me, break me to pieces, but you shall know nothing, I swear! Ah! you think, do you, that it is with pieces of wood and steel that a gentleman of my name is made to speak? Go ahead! I defy you!"

"Prepare to write, clerk," said the judge.

" Yes, prepare," shouted Coconnas; "and if you write everything I am going to tell you you infamous hangmen, you will be kept busy. Write! write!"

" Have you anything you wish to confess?" asked the judge in his calm voice.

"Nothing; not a word! Go to the devil!"

" You had better reflect, monsieur. Come, executioner, adjust the boot."

At these words the man, who until then had stood motionless, the ropes in his hand, stepped forward from the pillar and slowly approached Coconnas, who turned and made a grimace at him.

It was Maître Caboche, the executioner of the provostship of Paris.

A look of sad surprise showed itself on the face of Coconnas, who, instead of crying out and growing agitated, lay without moving, unable to take his eyes from the face of the forgotten friend who appeared at that moment.

Without moving a muscle of his face, without showing that he had ever seen Coconnas anywhere except on the rack, Caboche placed two planks between the limbs of the victim, two others outside of his limbs, and bound them securely together by means of the rope he held in his hand.

This was the arrangement called the "boot."

For ordinary torture six wedges were inserted between the two planks, which, on being forced apart, crushed the flesh.

For severe torture ten wedges were inserted, and then the planks not only broke the flesh but the bones.

The preliminaries over, Maître Caboche slipped the end of the wedge between the two planks, then, mallet in hand, bent on one knee and looked at the judge.

"Do you wish to speak?" said the latter.

"No," resolutely answered Coconnas, although he felt the perspiration rise to his brow and his hair begin to stand on end.

"Proceed, then," said the judge. "Insert the first wedge."

Caboche raised his arm, with its heavy mallet, and struck the wedge a tremendous blow, which gave forth a dull sound. The rack shook.

Coconnas did not utter a single word at the first wedge, which usually caused the most resolute to groan. Moreover, the only expression on his face was that of indescribable astonishment. He watched Caboche in amazement, who, with arm raised, half turned towards the judge, stood ready to repeat the blow.

"What was your idea in hiding in the forest?" asked the judge.

"To sit down in the shade," replied Coconnas.

"Proceed," said the judge.

Caboche gave a second blow which resounded like the first.

Coconnas did not move a muscle; he continued to watch the executioner with the same expression.

The judge frowned.

"He is a hard Christian," he murmured; "has the wedge entered?"

Caboche bent down to look, and in doing so said to Coconnas:

"Cry out, you poor fellow!"

Then rising:

"Up to the head, monsieur," said he.

"Second wedge," said the judge, coldly.

The words of Caboche explained all to Coconnas. The worthy executioner had rendered his friend the greatest service in his power: he was sparing him not only pain, but more, the shame of confession, by driving in wedges of leather, the upper part of which was covered with wood, instead of oak wedges. In this way he was leaving him all his strength to face the scaffold.

"Ah! kind, kind Caboche," murmured Coconnas, "fear nothing; I will cry out since you ask me to, and if you are not satisfied it will be because you are hard to please."

Meanwhile Caboche had introduced between the planks the end of a wedge larger than the first.

"Strike," cried the judge.

At this word Caboche struck as if with a single blow he would demolish the entire prison of Vincennes.

"Ah! ah! Stop! stop!" cried Coconnas; "a thousand devils! you are breaking my bones! Take care!"

"Ah!" said the judge, smiling, "the second seems to take effect; that surprises me."

Coconnas panted like a pair of bellows.

"What were you doing in the forest?" asked the judge.

"By Heaven! I have already told you. I was enjoying the fresh air."

"Proceed," said the judge.

"Confess," whispered Caboche.

"What?"

"Anything you wish, but something."

And he dealt a second blow no less light than the former.

Coconnas thought he would strangle himself in his efforts to cry out.

"Oh! oh!" said he; "what is it you want to know, monsieur? By whose order I was in the forest?"

"Yes."

"I was there by order of Monsieur d'Alençon."

"Write," said the judge.

"If I committed a crime in setting a trap for the King of Navarre," continued Coconnas, "I was only an instrument, monsieur, and I was obeying my master."

The clerk began to write.

"Oh! you denounced me, pale-face!" murmured the victim; "but just wait!"

And he related the visit of François to the King of Navarre, the interviews between De Mouy and Monsieur d'Alençon, the story of the red cloak, all as though he were just remembering them between the blows of the hammer.

At length he had given such precise, terrible, uncontestable evidence against D'Alençon, making it seem as though it was extorted from him only by the pain, — he grimaced, roared, and yelled so naturally, and in so many different tones of voice, — that the judge himself became terrified at having to record details so compromising to a son of France.

"Well!" said Caboche to himself, "here is a gentleman who does not need to say things twice, and who gives full measure of work to the clerk. Great God! what if, instead of leather, the wedges had been of wood!"

Coconnas was excused from the last wedge; but he had had nine others, which were enough to have crushed his limbs completely.

The judge reminded the victim of the mercy allowed him on account of his confession, and withdrew.

The prisoner was alone with Caboche.

"Well," asked the latter, "how are you?"

"Ah! my friend! my kind friend, my dear Caboche!" exclaimed Coconnas. "You may be sure I shall be grateful all my life for what you have done for me."

"The deuce! but you are right, monsieur, for if they knew what I have done it would be I who would have to take your place on the rack, and they would not treat me as I have treated you."

"But how did the idea come to you?"

"Well," said Caboche, wrapping the limbs of Coconnas in bloody bands of linen; "I knew you had been arrested, and that your trial was going on. I knew that Queen Catharine was anxious for your death. I guessed that they would put you to the torture and consequently took my precautions."

"At the risk of what might have happened?"

"Monsieur," said Caboche, "you are the only gentleman who ever gave me his hand, and we all have memories and hearts, even though we are hangmen, and perhaps for that very reason. You will see to-morrow how well I will do my work."

"To-morrow?" said Coconnas.

"Yes."

"What work?"

Caboche looked at Coconnas in amazement.

"What work? Have you forgotten the sentence?"

"Ah! yes, of course! the sentence!" said Coconnas; "I had forgotten it."

The fact is that Coconnas had not really forgotten it, but he had not been thinking of it.

What he was thinking of was the chapel, the knife hidden under the altar cloth, of Henriette and the queen, of the vestry door, and the two horses waiting on the edge of the forest; he was thinking of liberty, of the ride in the open air, of safety beyond the boundaries of France.

"Now," said Caboche, "you must be taken skilfully from the rack to the litter. Do not forget that for every one, even the guards, your limbs are broken, and that at every jar you must give a cry."

"Ah! ah!" cried Coconnas, as the two assistants advanced.

"Come! come! Courage," said Caboche, "if you cry out already, what will you do in a little while?"

"My dear Caboche," said Coconnas, "do not have me touched, I beg, by your estimable acolytes; perhaps their hands are not as light as yours."

"Place the litter near the racks," said Caboche.

The attendants obeyed. Maître Caboche raised Coconnas in his arms as if he were a child and laid him in the litter, but in spite of every care Coconnas uttered loud shrieks.

The jailer appeared with a lantern.

"To the chapel," said he.

The bearers started after Coconnas had given Caboche a second grasp of the hand. The first had been of too much use to the Piedmontese for him not to repeat it.

CHAPTER LIX.

THE CHAPEL.

IN profound silence the mournful procession crossed the two drawbridges of the fortress and the courtyard which leads to the chapel, through the windows of which a pale light colored the white faces of the red-robed priests.

Coconnas eagerly breathed the night air, although it was heavy with rain. He looked at the profound darkness and rejoiced that everything seemed propitious for the flight of himself and his companion. It required all his will-power, all his prudence, all his self-control to keep from springing from the litter when on entering the chapel he perceived near the choir, three feet from the altar, a figure wrapped in a great white cloak.

It was La Mole.

The two soldiers who accompanied the litter stopped outside of the door.

"Since they have done us the final favor of once more leaving us together," said Coconnas in a drawling voice, "take me to my friend."

The bearers had had no different order, and made no objection to assenting to Coconnas's demand.

La Mole was gloomy and pale; his head rested against the marble wall; his black hair, bathed with profuse perspiration, gave to his face the dull pallor of ivory, and seemed still to stand on end.

At a sign from the turnkey the two attendants went to find the priest for whom Coconnas had asked.

This was the signal agreed on.

Coconnas followed them with anxious eyes; but he was not the only one whose glance was riveted on them.

Scarcely had they disappeared when two women rushed from behind the altar and hurried to the choir with cries of joy, rousing the air like a warm and restless breeze which precedes a storm.

Marguerite rushed towards La Mole, and caught him in her arms.

La Mole uttered a piercing shriek, like one of the cries Coconnas had heard in his dungeon and which had so terrified him.

"My God! What is the matter, La Mole?" cried Marguerite, springing back in fright.

La Mole uttered a deep moan and raised his hands to his eyes as though to hide Marguerite from his sight.

The queen was more terrified at the silence and this gesture than she had been at the shriek.

"Oh!" she exclaimed, "what is the matter? You are covered with blood."

Coconnas, who had rushed to the altar for the dagger, and who was already holding Henriette in his arms, now came back.

"Rise," said Marguerite, "rise, I beg you! You see the time has come."

A hopelessly sad smile passed over the white lips of La Mole, who seemed almost unequal to the effort.

"Beloved queen!" said the young man, "you counted without Catharine, and consequently without a crime. I underwent the torture, my bones are broken, my whole body is nothing but a wound, and the effort I make now to press my lips to your forehead causes me pain worse than death."

Pale and trembling, La Mole touched his lips to the queen's brow.

"The rack!" cried Coconnas, "I, too, suffered it, but did not the executioner do for you what he did for me?"

Coconnas related everything.

"Ah!" said La Mole, "I see; you gave him your hand the day of our visit; I forgot that all men are brothers, and was proud. God has punished me for it!"

La Mole clasped his hands.

Coconnas and the women exchanged a glance of indescribable terror.

"Come," said the jailer, who until then had stood at the door to keep watch, and had now returned, "do not waste time, dear Monsieur de Coconnas; give me my thrust of the dagger, and do it in a way worthy of a gentleman, for they are coming."

Marguerite knelt down before La Mole, as if she were one of the marble figures on a tomb, near the image of the one buried in it.

"Come, my friend," said Coconnas, "I am strong, I will carry you, I will put you on your horse, or even hold you in front of me, if you cannot sit in the saddle; but let us start. You hear what this good man says; it is a question of life and death."

La Mole made a superhuman struggle, a final effort.

"Yes," said he, "it is a question of life or death."

And he strove to rise.

Annibal took him by the arm and raised him. During the process La Mole uttered dull moans, but when Coconnas let go of him to attend to the turnkey, and when he was supported only by the two women his legs gave way, and in spite of the effort of Marguerite, who was wildly sobbing, he fell back in a heap, and a piercing shriek which he could not restrain echoed pitifully throughout the vaults of the chapel, which vibrated long after.

"You see," said La Mole, painfully, "you see, my queen! Leave me; give me one last kiss and go. I did not confess, Marguerite, and our secret is hidden in our love and will die with me. Good-by, my queen, my queen."

Marguerite, herself almost lifeless, clasped the dear head in her arms, and pressed on it a kiss which was almost holy.

"You Annibal," said La Mole, "who have been spared these agonies, who are still young and able to live, flee, flee; give me the supreme consolation, my dear friend, of knowing you have escaped."

"Time flies," said the jailer; "make haste."

Henriette gently strove to lead Annibal to the door. Marguerite on her knees before La Mole, sobbing, and with dishevelled hair, looked like a Magdalene.

"Flee, Annibal," said La Mole, "flee; do not give our enemies the joyful spectacle of the death of two innocent men."

Coconnas quietly disengaged himself from Henriette, who was leading him to the door, and with a gesture so solemn that it seemed majestic said:

"Madame, first give the five hundred crowns we promised to this man."

"Here they are," said Henriette.

Then turning to La Mole, and shaking his head sadly:

"As for you, La Mole, you do me wrong to think for an instant that I could leave you. Have I not sworn to live and die with you? But you are suffering so, my poor friend, that I forgive you."

And seating himself resolutely beside his friend Coconnas leaned forward and kissed his forehead.

Then gently, as gently as a mother would do to her child, he drew the dear head towards him, until it rested on his breast.

Marguerite was numb. She had picked up the dagger which Coconnas had just let fall.

"Oh, my queen," said La Mole, extending his arms to her, and understanding her thought, "my beloved queen, do not forget that I die in order to destroy the slightest suspicion of our love!"

"But what can I do for you, then," cried Marguerite, in despair, "if I cannot die with you?"

"You can make death sweet to me," replied La Mole; "you can come to me with smiling lips."

Marguerite advanced and clasped her hands as if asking him to speak.

"Do you remember that evening, Marguerite, when in exchange for the life I then offered you, and which to-day I lay down for you, you made me a sacred promise."

Marguerite gave a start.

"Ah! you do remember," said La Mole, "for you shudder."

"Yes, yes, I remember, and on my soul, Hyacinthe, I will keep that promise."

Marguerite raised her hand towards the altar, as if calling God a second time to witness her oath.

La Mole's face lighted up as if the vaulted roof of the chapel had opened and a heavenly ray had fallen on him.

"They are coming!" said the jailer.

Marguerite uttered a cry, and rushed to La Mole, but the fear of increasing his agony made her pause trembling before him.

Henriette pressed her lips to Coconnas's brow, and said to him:

"My Annibal, I understand, and I am proud of you. I well know that your heroism makes you die, and for that heroism I love you. Before God I will always love you more than all else, and what Marguerite has sworn to do for La Mole, although I know not what it is, I swear I will do for you also."

And she held out her hand to Marguerite.

"Ah! thank you," said Coconnas; "that is the way to speak."

"Before you leave me, my queen," said La Mole, "one last favor. Give me some last souvenir, that I may kiss it as I mount the scaffold."

"Ah! yes, yes," cried Marguerite; "here!"

And she unfastened from her neck a small gold reliquary suspended from a chain of the same metal.

"Here," said she, "is a holy relic which I have worn from childhood. My mother put it around my neck when I was very little and she still loved me. It was given me by my uncle, Pope Clement and has never left me. Take it! take it!"

La Mole took it, and kissed it passionately.

"They are at the door," said the jailer; "flee, ladies, flee!"

The two women rushed behind the altar and disappeared.

At the same moment the priest entered.

CHAPTER LX.

THE PLACE SAINT JEAN EN GRÈVE.

IT was seven o'clock in the morning, and a noisy crowd was waiting in the squares, the streets, and on the quays. At six o'clock a tumbril, the same in which after their duel the two friends had been conveyed half dead to the Louvre, had started from Vincennes and slowly crossed the Rue Saint Antoine. Along its route the spectators, so huddled together that they crushed one another, seemed like statues with fixed eyes and open mouths.

This day there was to be a heartrending spectacle offered by the queen mother to the people of Paris.

On some straw in the tumbril, we have mentioned, which was making its way through the streets, were two young men, bareheaded, and entirely clothed in black, leaning against each other. Coconnas supported on his knees La Mole, whose head hung over the sides of the tumbril, and whose eyes wandered vaguely here and there.

The crowd, eager to see even the bottom of the vehicle, crowded forward, lifted itself up, stood on tiptoe, mounted posts, clung to the angles of the walls, and appeared satisfied only when it had succeeded in seeing every detail of the two bodies which were going from the torture to death.

It had been rumored that La Mole was dying without having confessed one of the charges imputed to him; while, on the contrary, Coconnas, it was asserted, could not endure the torture, and had revealed everything.

So there were cries on all sides:

"See the red-haired one! It was he who confessed! It was he who told everything! He is a coward, and is the cause of the other's death! The other is a brave fellow, and confessed nothing."

The two young men heard perfectly, the one the praises, the other the reproaches, which accompanied their funeral march; and while La Mole pressed the hands of his friend a sublime expression of scorn lighted up the face of the Piedmontese, who from the foul tumbril gazed upon the stupid mob as if he were looking down from a triumphal car.

Misfortune had done its heavenly work, and had ennobled

the face of Coconnas, as death was about to render divine his soul.

"Are we nearly there?" asked La Mole. "I can stand no more, my friend. I feel as if I were going to faint."

"Wait! wait! La Mole, we are passing by the Rue Tizon and the Rue Cloche Percée; look! look!"

"Oh! raise me, raise me, that I may once more gaze on that happy abode."

Coconnas raised his hand and touched the shoulder of the executioner, who sat at the front of the tumbril driving.

"Maître," said he, "do us the kindness to stop a moment opposite the Rue Tizon."

Caboche nodded in assent, and drew rein at the place indicated.

Aided by Coconnas, La Mole raised himself with an effort, and with eyes blinded by tears gazed at the small house, silent and mute, deserted as a tomb. A groan burst from him, and in a low voice he murmured:

"Adieu, adieu, youth, love, life!"

And his head fell forward on his breast.

"Courage," said Coconnas; "we may perhaps find all this above."

"Do you think so?" murmured La Mole.

"I think so, because the priest said so; and above all, because I hope so. But do not faint, my friend, or these staring wretches will laugh at us."

Caboche heard the last words and whipping his horse with one hand he extended the other, unseen by any one, to Coconnas. It contained a small sponge saturated with a powerful stimulant, and La Mole, after smelling it and rubbing his forehead with it, felt himself revived and reanimated.

"Ah!" said La Mole, "I am better," and he kissed the reliquary, which he wore around his neck.

As they turned a corner of the quay and reached the small edifice built by Henry II. they saw the scaffold rising bare and bloody on its platform above the heads of the crowd.

"Dear friend," said La Mole, "I wish I might be the first to die."

Coconnas again touched the hangman's shoulder.

"What is it, my gentleman?" said the latter, turning around.

"My good fellow," said Coconnas, "you will do what you can for me, will you not? You said you would."

" Yes, and I repeat it."

" My friend has suffered more than I and consequently has less strength " —

" Well ? "

" Well, he says that it would cause him too much pain to see me die first. Besides, if I were to die before him he would have no one to support him on the scaffold."

" Very well," said Caboche, wiping away a tear with the back of his hand; " be easy, it shall be as you wish." ·

" And with one blow, eh ? " said the Piedmontese in a low tone.

" With one blow."

" That is well. If you have to make up for it, make up on me."

The tumbril stopped. They had arrived. Coconnas put on his hat.

A murmur like that of the waves at sea reached the ears of La Mole. He strove to rise, but strength failed him. Caboche and Coconnas supported him under the arms.

The place was paved with heads; the steps of the Hôtel de Ville seemed an amphitheatre peopled with spectators. Each window was filled with animated faces, the eyes of which seemed on fire.

When they saw the handsome young man, no longer able to support himself on his bruised legs, make a last effort to reach the scaffold, a great shout rose like a cry of universal desolation. Men groaned and women uttered plaintive shrieks.

" He was one of the greatest courtiers ! " said the men; " and he should not have to die at Saint Jean en Grève, but at the Pré aux Clercs."

" How handsome he is ! How pale ! " said the women; " he is the one who would not confess."

" Dearest friend," said La Mole, " I cannot stand. Carry me ! "

" Wait," said Coconnas.

He signed to the executioner, who stepped aside; then, stooping, he lifted La Mole in his arms as if he were a child, and without faltering carried his burden up the steps of the scaffold, where he put him down, amid the frantic shouting and applause of the multitude. Coconnas raised his hat and bowed. Then he threw the hat on the scaffold beside him.

"Look round," said La Mole, "do you not see them some. where?"

Coconnas slowly glanced around the place, and, having reached a certain point, without removing his eyes from it he laid his hand on his friend's shoulder.

"Look," said he, "look at the window of that small tower!"

With his other hand he pointed out to La Mole the little building which still stands at the corner of the Rue de la Vannerie and the Rue Mouton, — a reminder of past ages.

Somewhat back from the window two women dressed in black were leaning against each other.

"Ah!" said La Mole, "I feared only one thing, and that was to die without seeing her again. I have seen her; now I can go."

And with his eyes riveted on the small window he raised the reliquary to his lips and covered it with kisses.

Coconnas saluted the two women with as much grace as if he were in a drawing-room. In response to this they waved their handkerchiefs bathed in tears.

Caboche now touched Coconnas on the shoulder, and looked at him significantly.

"Yes, yes," said the Piedmontese. Then turning to La Mole:

"Embrace me," said he, "and die like a man. This will not be hard for you, my friend; you are so brave!"

"Ah!" said La Mole, "there will be no merit in my dying bravely, suffering as I do."

The priest approached and held the crucifix before La Mole, who smiled and pointed to the reliquary in his hand.

"Never mind," said the priest, "ask strength from Him who suffered what you are about to suffer."

La Mole kissed the feet of the Christ.

"Commend me to the prayers of the nuns of the Avens Sainte Vierge."

"Make haste, La Mole," said Coconnas, "you cause me such suffering that I feel myself growing weak."

"I am ready," said La Mole.

"Can you keep your head steady?" inquired Caboche, holding his sword behind La Mole, who was on his knees.

"I hope so," said the latter.

"Then all will go well."

"But," said La Mole, "you will not forget what I asked of you? This reliquary will open the doors to you."

"Be easy. Now try to keep your head straight."

La Mole raised his head and turned his eyes towards the little tower.

"Adieu, Marguerite," said he; "bless" —

He never finished. With one blow of his sword, as swift as a stroke of lightning, Caboche severed the head, which rolled to the feet of Coconnas.

The body fell back gently as if going to rest.

A great cry rose from thousands of voices, and, among them, it seemed to Coconnas that he heard a shriek more piercing than all the rest.

"Thank you, my good friend," said Coconnas; and a third time he extended his hand to the hangman.

"My son," said the priest, "have you nothing to confess to God?"

"Faith no, father," said the Piedmontese; "all that I had to say I said to you yesterday."

Then turning to Caboche:

"Now, executioner, my last friend, one more favor!"

Before kneeling down he turned on the crowd a glance so calm and serene that a murmur of admiration rose, which soothed his ear and flattered his pride. Then, raising the head of his friend and pressing a kiss on the purple lips, he gave a last look toward the little tower, and kneeling down, still holding the well-loved head in his hand, he said:

"Now!"

Scarcely had he uttered the word before Caboche had cut off his head.

This done, the poor hangman began to tremble.

"It was time it was over," said he. "Poor fellow!"

And with difficulty he drew from the clinched fingers of La Mole the reliquary of gold. Then he threw his cloak over the sad remains which the tumbril was to convey to his own abode.

The spectacle over, the crowd dispersed.

CHAPTER LXI.

THE HEADSMAN'S TOWER.

NIGHT descended over the city, which still trembled at the remembrance of the execution, the details of which passed from mouth to mouth, saddening the happy supper hour in every home. In contrast to the city, which was silent and mournful, the Louvre was noisy, joyous, and illuminated. There was a grand fête at the palace, a fête ordered by Charles IX., a fête he had planned for that evening at the very time that he had ordered the execution for the morning.

The previous evening the Queen of Navarre had received word to be present, and, in the hope that La Mole and Coconnas would have escaped during the night, since every measure had been taken for their safety, she had promised her brother to comply with his wishes.

But when she had lost all hope, after the scene in the chapel, after, out of a last feeling of piety for that love, the greatest and the deepest she had ever known, she had been present at the execution, she resolved that neither prayers nor threats should force her to attend a joyous festival at the Louvre the same day on which she had witnessed so terrible a scene at the Grève.

That day King Charles had given another proof of the will power which no one perhaps carried as far as he. In bed for a fortnight, weak as a dying man, pale as a corpse, yet he rose about five o'clock and donned his most beautiful clothes, although during his toilet he fainted three times.

At eight o'clock he asked what had become of his sister, and inquired if any one had seen her and what she was doing. No one could tell him, for the queen had gone to her apartments about eleven o'clock and had absolutely refused admittance to every one.

But there was no refusal for Charles. Leaning on the arm of Monsieur de Nancey, he went to the queen's rooms and entered unannounced by the secret corridor.

Although he had expected a melancholy sight, and had prepared himself for it in advance, that which he saw was even more distressing than he had anticipated.

Marguerite, half dead, was lying on a divan, her head buried in the cushions, neither weeping nor praying, but moaning like one in great agony; and this she had been doing ever since her return from the Grève. At the other end of the chamber Henriette de Nevers, that daring woman, lay stretched on the carpet unconscious. On coming back from the Grève her strength, like Marguerite's, had given out, and poor Gillonne was going from one to the other, not daring to offer a word of consolation.

In the crises which follow great catastrophes one hugs one's grief like a treasure, and any one who attempts to divert us, ever so slightly, is looked on as an enemy. Charles IX. closed the door, and leaving Nancey in the corridor entered, pale and trembling.

Neither of the women had seen him. Gillonne alone, who was trying to revive Henriette, rose on one knee, and looked in a startled way at the King.

The latter made a sign with his hand, whereupon the girl rose, courtesied, and withdrew.

Charles then approached Marguerite, looked at her a moment in silence, and in a tone of which his harsh voice was supposed to be incapable, said:

"Margot! my sister!"

The young woman started and sat up.

"Your Majesty!" said she.

"Come, sister, courage."

Marguerite raised her eyes to Heaven.

"Yes," said Charles, "but listen to me."

The Queen of Navarre made a sign of assent.

"You promised me to come to the ball," said Charles.

"I!" exclaimed Marguerite.

"Yes, and after your promise you are expected; so that if you do not come every one will wonder why."

"Excuse me, brother," said Marguerite, "you see that I am suffering greatly."

"Exert yourself."

For an instant Marguerite seemed to try to summon her courage, then suddenly she gave way and fell back among the cushions.

"No, no, I cannot go," said she.

Charles took her hand and seating himself on the divan said:

"You have just lost a friend, I know, Margot; but look at me. Have I not lost all my friends, even my mother? You can always weep when you wish to; but I, at the moment of my greatest sorrows, am always forced to smile. You suffer; but look at me! I am dying. Come, Margot, courage! I ask it of you, sister, in the name of our honor! We bear like a cross of agony the reputation of our house; let us bear it, sister, as the Saviour bore his cross to Calvary; and if on the way we stagger, as he did, let us like him rise brave and resigned."

"Oh, my God! my God!" cried Marguerite.

"Yes," said Charles, answering her thought; "the sacrifice is severe, sister, but each one has his own burden, some of honor, others of life. Do you suppose that with my twenty-five years, and the most beautiful throne in the world, I do not regret dying? Look at me! My eyes, my complexion, my lips are those of a dying man, it is true; but my smile, does not my smile imply that I still hope? and in a week, a month at the most, you will be weeping for me, sister, as you now weep for him who died to-day."

"Brother!" exclaimed Marguerite, throwing her arms about Charles's neck.

"So dress yourself, dear Marguerite," said the King, "hide your pallor and come to the ball. I have given orders for new jewels to be brought to you, and ornaments worthy of your beauty."

"Oh! what are diamonds and dresses to me now?" said Marguerite.

"Life is long, Marguerite," said Charles, smiling, "at least for you."

The pages withdrew; Gillonne alone remained.

"Prepare everything that is necessary for me, Gillonne," said Marguerite.

"Sister, remember one thing: sometimes it is by stifling or rather by dissimulating our suffering that we show most honor to the dead."

"Well, sire," said Marguerite, shuddering, "I will go to the ball."

A tear, which soon dried on his parched eyelid, moistened Charles's eye.

He leaned over his sister, kissed her forehead, paused an instant before Henriette, who had neither seen nor heard him, and murmured:

"Poor woman!"

Then he went out silently.

Soon after several pages entered, bringing boxes and jewel-caskets.

Marguerite made a sign for them to set everything down.

Gillonne looked at her mistress in astonishment.

" Yes," said Marguerite, in a tone the bitterness of which it is impossible to describe; yes, I will dress and go to the ball; I am expected. Make haste; the day will then be complete. A fête on the Grève in the morning, a fête in the Louvre in the evening."

" And the duchess ? " said Gillonne.

" She is quite happy. She may remain here; she can weep; she can suffer at her ease. She is not the daughter of a king, the wife of a king, the sister of a king. She is not a queen. Help me to dress, Gillonne."

The young girl obeyed. The jewels were magnificent, the dress gorgeous. Marguerite had never been so beautiful.

She looked at herself in a mirror.

" My brother is right," said she; " a human being is indeed a miserable creature."

At that moment Gillonne returned.

" Madame," said she, " a man is asking for you."

" For me ? "

" Yes."

" Who is he ? "

" I do not know, but he is terrible to look at; the very sight of him makes me shudder."

" Go and ask him his name," said Marguerite, turning pale.

Gillonne withdrew, and returned in a few moments.

" He will not give his name, madame, but he begged me to give you this."

Gillonne handed to Marguerite the reliquary she had given to La Mole the previous evening.

" Oh! bring him in, bring him in ! " said the queen quickly, growing paler and more numb than before.

A heavy step shook the floor. The echo, indignant, no doubt, at having to repeat such a sound, moaned along the wainscoting. A man stood on the threshold.

" You are " — said the queen.

" He whom you met one day near Montfaucon, madame, and who in his tumbril brought back two wounded gentlemen to the Louvre."

"Yes, yes, I know you. You are Maître Caboche."

"Executioner of the provostship of Paris, madame."

These were the only words Henriette had heard for an hour. She raised her pale face from her hands and looked at the man with her sapphire eyes, from which a double flame seemed to dart.

"And you come" — said Marguerite, trembling.

"To remind you of your promise to the younger of the two gentlemen, who charged me to give you this reliquary. You remember the promise, madame ? "

"Yes, yes," exclaimed the queen, "and never has a noble soul had more satisfaction than his shall have; but where is " —

"At my house with the body."

"At your house ? Why did you not bring it ? "

"I might have been stopped at the gate of the Louvre, and compelled to raise my cloak. What would they have said if they had seen a head under it ? "

"That is right; keep it. I will come for it to-morrow."

"To-morrow, madame," said Caboche, " may perhaps be too late."

"How so ? "

"Because the queen mother wanted the heads of the first victims executed by me to be kept for her magical experiments."

"Oh! What profanation! The heads of our well-beloved ! Henriette," cried Marguerite, turning to her friend, who had risen as if a spring had placed her on her feet, " Henriette, my angel, do you hear what this man says ? "

"Yes ; what must we do ? "

"Go with him."

Then uttering a cry of pain by which great sufferers return to life:

"Ah! I was so happy," said Henriette ; "I was almost dead."

Meanwhile Marguerite had thrown a velvet cloak over her bare shoulders.

"Come," said she, " we will go and see them once more."

Telling Gillonne to have all the doors closed, the queen gave orders for a litter to be brought to the private entrance, and taking Henriette by the arm, she descended by the secret corridor, signing to Caboche to follow.

At the lower door was the litter; at the gate Caboche's

attendant waited with a lantern. Marguerite's porters were
trusty men, deaf and dumb, more to be depended on than if
they had been beasts of burden.

They walked for about ten minutes, preceded by Caboche
and his servant, carrying the lantern. Then they stopped.
The hangman opened the door, while his man went ahead.

Marguerite stepped from the litter and helped out the
Duchesse de Nevers. In the deep grief which bound them
together it was the nervous organism which was the stronger.

The headsman's tower rose before them like a dark, vague
giant, giving out a lurid gleam from two narrow upper windows.

The attendant reappeared at the door.

" You can enter, ladies," said Caboche; " every one is
asleep in the tower."

At the same moment the light from above was extinguished.

The two women, holding to each other, passed through the
small gothic door, and reached a dark hall with damp and
uneven pavement. At the end of a winding corridor they perceived a light and guided by the gruesome master of the
place they set out towards it. The door closed behind them.

Caboche, a wax torch in hand, admitted them into a lower
room filled with smoke. In the centre was a table containing
the remains of a supper for three. These three were probably
the hangman, his wife, and his chief assistant. In a conspicuous place on the wall a parchment was nailed, sealed with
the seal of the King. It was the hangman's license. In a
corner was a long-handled sword. This was the flaming
sword of justice.

Here and there were various rough drawings representing
martyrs undergoing the torture.

At the door Caboche made a low bow.

" Your majesty will excuse me," said he, " if I ventured to
enter the Louvre and bring you here. But it was the last
wish of the gentleman, so that I felt I " —

" You did well, Maître," said Marguerite, " and here is a
reward for you."

Caboche looked sadly at the large purse which Marguerite
laid on the table.

" Gold ! " said he ; " always gold ! Alas ! madame, if I only
could buy back for gold the blood I was forced to spill to-
day ! "

"Maître," said Marguerite, looking around with a sad hesitation, "Maître, do we have to go to some other room? I do not see" —

"No, madame, they are here; but it is a sad sight, and one which I could have spared you by wrapping up in my cloak that for which you have come."

Marguerite and Henriette looked at each other.

"No," said the queen, who had read in her friend's eye the same thought as in her own; "no, show us the way and we will follow."

Caboche took the torch and opened an oaken door at the top of a short stairway, which led to an underground chamber. At that instant a current of air blew some sparks from the torch and brought to the princesses an ill-smelling odor of dampness and blood. Henriette, white as an alabaster statue, leaned on the arm of her less agitated friend; but at the first step she swayed.

"I can never do it," said she.

"When one loves truly, Henriette," replied the queen, "one loves beyond death."

It was a sight both horrible and touching presented by the two women, glowing with youth, beauty, and jewels, as they bent their heads beneath the foul, chalky ceiling, the weaker leaning on the stronger, the stronger clinging to the arm of the hangman.

They reached the final step. On the floor of the cellar lay two human forms covered with a wide cloth of black serge.

Caboche raised a corner of it, and, lowering the torch:

"See, madame," said he.

In their black clothes lay the two young men, side by side, in the strange symmetry of death. Their heads had been placed close to their bodies, from which they seemed to be separated only by a bright red circle about the neck. Death had not disunited their hands, for either from chance or the kind care of the hangman the right hand of La Mole rested in Coconnas's left hand.

There was a look of love under the lids of La Mole, and a smile of scorn under those of Coconnas.

Marguerite knelt down by the side of her lover, and with hands that sparkled with gems gently raised the head she had so greatly love.

The Duchesse de Nevers leaned against the wall, unable to

MARGUERITE IN THE HEADSMAN'S TOWER.

remove her eyes from that pale face on which so often she had gazed for pleasure and for love.

"La Mole! Dear La Mole!" murmured Marguerite.

"Annibal! Annibal!" cried the duchess, "so beautiful! so proud! so brave! Never again will you answer me!"

And her eyes filled with tears.

This woman, so scornful, so intrepid, so insolent in happiness; this woman who carried scepticism as far as absolute doubt, passion to the point of cruelty; this woman had never thought of death.

Marguerite was the first to move.

She put into a bag, embroidered with pearls and perfumed with finest essences, the head of La Mole, more beautiful than ever as it rested against the velvet and the gold, and the beauty of which was to be preserved by a special preparation, used at that time in the embalming of royal personages.

Henriette then drew near and wrapped the head of Coconnas in a fold of her cloak.

And both women, bending beneath their grief more than beneath their burdens, ascended the stairs with a last look at the remains which they left to the mercy of the hangman in that sombre abode of ordinary criminals.

"Do not fear, madame," said Caboche, who understood their look, "the gentlemen, I promise you, shall be buried in holy ground."

"And you will have masses said for them with this," said Henriette, taking from her neck a magnificent necklace of rubies, and handing it to the hangman.

They returned to the Louvre by the same road by which they had gone. At the gate the queen gave her name; at the foot of her private stairway she descended and, returning to her rooms, laid her sad burden in the closet adjoining her sleeping-room, destined from that moment to become an oratory. Then, leaving Henriette in her room, paler and more beautiful than ever, she entered the great ballroom, the same room in which, two years and a half ago, the first chapter of our history opened.

All eyes were turned on her, but she bore the general gaze with a proud and almost joyous air.

She had religiously carried out the last wish of her friend.

Seeing her, Charles pushed tremblingly through the gilded crowd around her.

" Sister," said he, aloud, " I thank you."

Then in a low tone :

"Take care ! " said he, " you have a spot of blood on your arm."

" Ah ! what difference does that make, sire," said Marguerite, " since I have a smile on my lips ? "

CHAPTER LXII.

THE SWEAT OF BLOOD.

A few days after the terrible scene we have just described, that is, on the 30th of May, 1574, while the court was at Vincennes, suddenly a great commotion was heard in the chamber of the King. The latter had been taken ill in the midst of the ball he had given the day of the execution of the two young men, and had been ordered by his physicians into the pure air of the country.

It was eight o'clock in the morning. A small group of courtiers were talking excitedly in the antechamber, when suddenly a cry was heard, and Charles's nurse appeared at the door, her eyes filled with tears, calling frantically :

"Help ! Help ! "

" Is his Majesty worse ? " asked the Captain de Nancey, whom, as we know, the King had relieved from all duty to Queen Catharine in order to attach him to himself.

" Oh ! Blood ! Blood ! " cried the nurse. " The doctors ! call the doctors ! "

Mozille and Ambroise Paré in turn attended the august patient, and the latter, seeing the King fall asleep, had taken advantage of the fact to withdraw for a few moments. Meanwhile a great perspiration had broken out all over the King ; and as Charles suffered from a relaxation of the capillary vessels, which caused a hæmorrhage of the skin, the bloody sweat had alarmed the nurse, unaccustomed to this strange phenomenon, who, being a Protestant, kept repeating that it was a judgment for the blood of the Huguenots shed in the massacre of Saint Bartholomew.

The courtiers went in all directions in search of the doctor, who could not be far away, and whom they could not fail to meet. The antechamber, therefore, became deserted, every one being anxious to show his zeal in bringing the much-needed physician.

Just then a door opened and Catharine appeared. She passed hurriedly through the antechamber and hastily entered the apartment of her son.

Charles was stretched on his bed, his eyes closed, his breast heaving; from his body oozed a crimson sweat. His hand hung over the bed, and from the end of each finger dropped a ruby liquid. It was a horrible sight.

At the sound of his mother's steps, as if he knew she was there, Charles sat up.

"Pardon, madame," said he, looking at her, "but I desire to die in peace."

"To die, my son?" said Catharine. "This is only a passing attack of your wretched trouble. Would you have us despair in this way?"

"I tell you, madame, I feel that my soul is about to pass away. I tell you, madame, that death is near me, by Heaven! I feel what I feel, and I know what I am talking about!"

"Sire," said the queen, "your imagination is your most serious trouble. Since the well-merited punishment of those two sorcerers, those assassins, La Mole and Coconnas, your physical suffering should have diminished. The mental trouble alone continues, and if I could talk with you for just ten minutes I could prove to you" —

"Nurse," said Charles, "watch at the door that no one may enter. Queen Catharine de Médicis wishes to speak with her well-loved son Charles IX."

The nurse withdrew.

"Well," continued Charles, "this interview will have to take place some day or other, and better to-day than to-morrow. Besides, to-morrow may be too late. But a third person must be present."

"Why?"

"Because I tell you I am dying," repeated Charles with frightful seriousness; "because at any moment death may enter this chamber, as you have done, pale, silent, and unannounced. It is, therefore, time. Last night I settled my personal affairs; this morning I will arrange those of the kingdom."

" What person do you desire to see ? " asked Catharine.

" My brother, madame. Have him summoned."

" Sire," said the queen, " I see with pleasure that the prejudices dictated by hatred rather than pain are leaving your mind, as they soon will fade from your heart. Nurse ! " cried Catharine, " nurse ! "

The woman, who was keeping watch outside, opened the door.

" Nurse," said Catharine, " by order of my son, when Monsieur de Nancey returns say to him to summon the Duc d'Alençon."

Charles made a sign which detained the woman.

" I said my brother, madame," said Charles.

Catharine's eyes dilated like those of a tigress about to show her anger. But Charles raised his hand imperatively.

" I wish to speak to my brother Henry," said he. " Henry alone is my brother; not he who is king yonder, but he who is a prisoner here. Henry shall know my last wishes."

" And do you think," exclaimed the Florentine, with unusual boldness in the face of the dread will of her son, her hatred for the Béarnais being strong enough to make her forget her customary dissimulation, — " do you think that if, as you say, you are near the tomb, I will yield to any one, especially a stranger, my right to be present at your last hour ; my right as queen and mother ? "

" Madame," said Charles, " I am still King ; and I still command. I tell you that I desire to speak to my brother Henry and yet you do not summon my captain of the guard. A thousand devils ! I warn you, madame, I still have strength enough to go for him myself."

The King made a movement as if to rise from the bed, which brought to light his body, bloody like Christ's after the flogging.

" Sire," cried Catharine, holding him back, " you wrong us all. You forget the insults given to our family, you repudiate our blood. A son of France alone should kneel before the death-bed of a King of France. As to me, my place is marked out; it is here by the laws of nature as well as the laws of royalty. Therefore I shall remain."

" And by what right do you remain, madame ? " demanded Charles IX.

" Because I am your mother."

"You are no more my mother, madame, than is the Duc d'Alençon my brother."

"You are mad, monsieur," said Catharine; "since when is she who gives birth to a child no longer his mother?"

"From the moment, madame, when the unnatural mother takes away that which she gives," replied Charles, wiping away a bloody sweat from his lips.

"What do you mean, Charles? I do not understand you," murmured Catharine, gazing at her son, her eyes dilated with astonishment.

"But you will, madame."

Charles searched under his pillow and drew out a small silver key.

"Take this, madame, and open my travelling-box. It contains certain papers which will speak for me."

Charles pointed to a magnificent carved box, closed with a silver lock, like the key, which occupied the most conspicuous place in the room.

Catharine, dominated by the look and manner of Charles, obeyed, advanced slowly to the box, and opened it. But no sooner had she looked into it than she suddenly sprang back as if she had seen some sleeping reptile inside it.

"Well," said Charles, who had not taken his eyes from his mother, "what is there in the box to startle you, madame?"

"Nothing," said Catharine.

"Then put in your hand, madame, and take out a book that is there; there is one, is there not?" added Charles, with a pale smile, more terrible in him than a threat in another.

"Yes," faltered Catharine.

"A book on hunting?"

"Yes."

"Take it out and bring it to me."

In spite of her assurance Catharine turned pale, and trembled in every limb, as she extended her hand towards the box.

"Fatality!" she murmured, raising the book.

"Very good," said Charles, "now listen; this book on hunting — I loved the chase madly, above everything else — I read this book too eagerly, do you understand, madame?"

Catharine gave a dull moan.

"It was a weakness," continued Charles; "burn it, madame. The weakness of kings and queens must not be known!"

Catharine stepped to the glowing hearth, and dropped the book into the flames.

Then, standing motionless and silent, she watched with haggard eye the bluish light which rose from the poisoned leaves.

As the book burned a strong odor of arsenic spread through the room. Soon the volume was entirely destroyed.

" And now, madame," said Charles, with irresistible majesty, " call my brother."

Catharine, overcome, crushed under a multiple emotion which her profound wisdom could not analyze, and which her almost superhuman strength could not combat, took a step forward as if to speak.

The mother grew remorseful; the queen was afraid; the poisoner felt a return of hatred.

The latter sentiment dominated.

" Curse him!" she cried, rushing from the room, "he triumphs, he gains his end; curse him! curse him!"

" You understand, my brother, my brother Henry," cried Charles, calling after his mother; "my brother Henry, with whom I wish to speak instantly regarding the regency of the kingdom!"

Almost at the same instant Maître Ambroise Paré entered through the door opposite the one by which the queen had just left, and, pausing on the threshold, noticed the peculiar odor in the room.

" Who has been burning arsenic here?" said he.

" I," replied Charles.

CHAPTER LXIII.

THE DONJON OF THE PRISON OF VINCENNES.

HENRY OF NAVARRE was strolling dreamily along the terrace of the prison. He knew the court was at the château, not a hundred feet away, and through the walls it seemed as if his piercing eye could picture Charles as he lay dying.

The weather was perfect. A broad band of sunlight lay on the distant fields, bathing in liquid gold the tops of the forest trees, proud of the richness of their first foliage. The very stones of the prison itself, gray as they were, seemed impregnated with the gentle light of heaven, and some flowers, lured by the breath of the east wind, had pushed through the crevices of the wall, and were raising their disks of red and yellow velvet to the kisses of the warm air.

But Henry's eyes were fixed neither on the verdant plains nor on the gilded tree tops. His glance went beyond, and was fixed, full of ambition, on the capital of France, destined one day to become the capital of the world.

"Paris," murmured the King of Navarre, "there is Paris; that is, joy, triumph, glory, power, and happiness. Paris, in which is the Louvre, and the Louvre, in which is the throne; and only one thing separates me from this Paris, for which I so long, and that something the stones at my feet, which shut me in with my enemy!"

As he glanced from Paris to Vincennes, he perceived on his left, in a valley, partly hidden by flowering almond-trees, a man, whose cuirass sparkled in the sunlight at its owner's slightest movement.

This man rode a fiery steed and led another which seemed no less impatient.

The King of Navarre fixed his eyes on this cavalier and saw him draw his sword from his sheath, place his handkerchief on the point, and wave it like a signal.

At the same instant the signal was repeated from the opposite hill, then all around the château a belt of handkerchiefs seemed to flutter.

It was De Mouy and his Huguenots, who, knowing the King was dying, and fearing that some attempt might be made on Henry's life, had gathered together, ready to defend or attack.

Henry, with his eyes still on the horseman he had seen first, bent over the balustrade, and shading his eyes with his hand to keep out the dazzling rays of the sun, recognized the young Huguenot.

"De Mouy!" he exclaimed, as though the latter could hear him.

And in his joy at seeing himself surrounded by friends, the king raised his hat and waved his scarf.

All the white banners were again set in motion with an energy which proved the joy of their owners.

"Alas! they are waiting for me," said Henry, "and I cannot join them. Why did I not do so when I could? Now it is too late!"

He made a despairing gesture, to which De Mouy returned a sign which meant, "I will wait."

Just then Henry heard steps on the stone stairs. He hastily withdrew. The Huguenots understood the cause of his sudden disappearance, and their swords were returned to their sheaths and their handkerchiefs disappeared.

Henry saw on the stairs a woman whose quick breathing showed that she had come in haste.

He recognized, not without the secret dread he always felt on seeing her, Catharine de Médicis.

Behind her were two guards who stopped at the head of the stairs.

"Oh!" thought Henry, "it must be something new and important that makes the queen mother come to seek me on the balcony of the prison of Vincennes.

Catharine seated herself on a stone bench against the battlement to recover her breath.

Henry approached her, and with his most gracious smile:

"Are you seeking me, my good mother?"

"Yes, monsieur," replied Catharine, "I wish to give you a final proof of my attachment. The King is dying and wishes to see you."

"Me!" said Henry, with a start of joy.

"Yes. He has been told, I am sure, that not only do you covet the throne of Navarre but that of France as well."

"Oh!" exclaimed Henry.

"It is not true, I know, but he believes it, and no doubt the object of the interview he wishes with you is to lay a snare for you."

"For me?"

"Yes. Before dying Charles wants to know what there is to hope or fear from you. And on your answer to his offer, mark you, will depend his final commands, that is, your life or death."

"But what will he offer me?"

"How do I know? Impossibilities, probably."

"But have you no idea?"

"No; but suppose for instance" —

Catharine paused.

"What."

"Suppose he credited you with these ambitious aims of yours he has heard about; suppose he should wish to hear these aims from your own lips; suppose he should tempt you as once they used to tempt the guilty in order to provoke a confession without torture; suppose," continued Catharine, looking fixedly at Henry, "he were to offer you a kingdom, the regency!"

A thrill of indescribable joy pervaded Henry's weary heart, but he guessed the snare and his strong and supple soul rebounded.

"Me?" said he; "the snare would be too palpable; offer me the regency when there is you yourself and my brother D'Alençon?"

Catharine compressed her lips to conceal her satisfaction.

"Then," said she, quickly, "you would refuse it?"

"The King is dead," thought Henry, "and she is laying a trap for me."

Aloud, he said:

"I must first hear what the King of France has to say; for from your own words, madame, all this is mere supposition."

"Doubtless," said Catharine; "but you can tell me your intentions."

"Why!" said Henry, innocently, "having no pretensions, I have no intentions."

"That is no answer," said Catharine, feeling that time was flying, and giving way to her anger; "you can give some answer."

"I cannot answer suppositions, madame; a positive resolution is so difficult and so grave a thing to assume that I must wait for facts."

"Listen, monsieur," said Catharine; "there is no time to lose, and we are wasting it in vain discussion, in toying with words. Let us play our rôle of king and queen. If you accept the regency you are a dead man."

"The King lives," thought Henry.

Then aloud:

"Madame," said he, firmly, "God holds the lives of men and of kings in his hands. He will inspire me. Let his Majesty be informed that I am ready to see him."

"Reflect, monsieur."

"During the two years in which I have been persecuted, during the month I have been a prisoner," replied Henry, bravely, "I have had time to reflect, madame, and I have reflected. Have the goodness, therefore, to go to the King before

me, and to tell him that I am following you. These two
guards," added Henry, pointing to the soldiers, " will see that
I do not escape. Moreover, that is not my intention."

There was such firmness in Henry's tone that Catharine
saw that all her attempts, under whatever disguise, would not
succeed. Therefore she hastily descended.

As soon as she had disappeared Henry went to the parapet
and made a sign to De Mouy, which meant: " Draw near and
be ready in case of necessity."

De Mouy, who had dismounted, sprang into the saddle,
and still leading the second horse galloped to within musket-
shot of the prison.

Henry thanked him by a gesture, and descended.

On the first landing he found the two soldiers who were
waiting for him.

A double troop of Swiss and light-horse guarded the
entrance to the court, and to enter or leave the château it was
necessary to traverse a double line of halberds.

Catharine had stopped and was waiting for him.

She signed to the two soldiers to go on, and laying her
hand on Henry's arm, said :

" This court has two gates. At one, behind the apartments of the King, if you refuse the regency, a good horse and
freedom await you. At the other, through which you have just
passed, if you listen to the voice of ambition — What do you
say ? "

" I say that if the King makes me regent, madame, I, and
not you, shall give orders to the soldiers. I say that if I leave
the castle at night, all these pikes, halberds, and muskets shall
be lowered before me."

" Madman ! " murmured Catharine, exasperated, " believe me,
and do not play this terrible game of life and death with me."

" Why not ? " said Henry, looking closely at Catharine ;
" why not with you as well as with another, since up to this
time I have won ? "

" Go to the King's apartments, monsieur, since you are
unwilling to believe or listen to anything," said Catharine,
pointing to the stairway with one hand, and with the other
toying with one of the two poisoned daggers she always wore
in the black shagreen case, which has become historical.

" Pass before me, madame," said Henry; " so long as I am
not regent, the honor of precedence belongs to you."

Catharine, thwarted in all her plans, did not attempt to struggle, but ascended the stairs ahead of the King of Navarre.

CHAPTER LXIV.

THE REGENCY.

THE King, beginning to grow impatient, had summoned Monsieur de Nancey to his room, and had just given him orders to go in search of Henry, when the latter appeared.

On seeing his brother-in-law at the door Charles uttered a cry of joy, but Henry stood motionless, as startled as if he had come face to face with a corpse.

The two physicians who were at the bedside and the priest who had been with Charles withdrew.

Charles was not loved, and yet many were weeping in the antechambers. At the death of kings, good or bad, there are always persons who lose something and who fear they will not find it again under the successor.

The mourning, the sobbing, the words of Catharine, the sinister and majestic surroundings of the last moments of a king, the sight of the King himself, suffering from a malady common enough afterwards, but which, at that time, was new to science, produced on Henry's mind, which was still youthful and consequently still susceptible, such a terrible impression that in spite of his determination not to cause Charles fresh anxiety as to his condition, he could not as we have said repress the feeling of terror which came to his face on perceiving the dying man dripping with blood.

Charles smiled sadly. Nothing of those around them escapes the dying.

" Come, Henriot," said he, extending his hand with a gentleness of voice Henry had never before noticed in him. " Come in; I have been very unhappy at not seeing you for so long. I have tormented you greatly during my life, my poor friend, and sometimes, believe me, I have reproached myself for it. Sometimes I have taken the hands of those who tormented you, it is true, but a king cannot control circumstances, and besides my mother Catharine, my brothers D'Anjou and D'Alençon, I had to consider during my lifetime something else which was troublesome and which ceases the moment I draw near to death — state policy."

"Sire," murmured Henry, "I remember only the love I have always had for my brother, the respect I have always felt for my King."

"Yes, yes, you are right," said Charles, "and I am grateful to you for saying this, Henriot, for truly you have suffered a great deal under my reign without counting the fact that it was during my reign that your poor mother died. But you must have seen that I was often driven? Sometimes I have resisted, but oftener I have yielded from very fatigue. But, as you said, let us not talk of the past. Now it is the present which concerns me; it is the future which frightens me."

And the poor King hid his livid face in his emaciated hands.

After a moment's silence he shook his head as if to drive away all gloomy thoughts, thus causing a shower of blood to fall about him.

"We must save the state," he continued in a low tone, leaning towards Henry. "We must prevent its falling into the hands of fanatics or women."

As we have just said, Charles uttered these words in a low tone, yet Henry thought he heard behind the headboard something like a dull exclamation of anger. Perhaps some opening made in the wall at the instigation of Charles himself permitted Catharine to hear this final conversation.

"Of women?" said the King of Navarre to provoke an explanation.

"Yes, Henry," said Charles, "my mother wishes the regency until my brother returns from Poland. But mind what I tell you, he will not come back."

"Why not?" cried Henry, whose heart gave a joyful leap.

"No, he cannot return," continued Charles, "because his subjects will not let him leave."

"But," said Henry, "do you not suppose, brother, that the queen mother has already written to him?"

"Yes, but Nancey stopped the courier at Château Thierry, and brought me the letter, in which she said I was to die. I wrote to Varsovia myself, my letter reached there, I am sure, and my brother will be watched. So, in all probability, Henry, the throne will be vacant."

A second sound louder than the first was heard in the alcove.

"She is surely there," thought Henry, "and is listening."

Charles heard nothing.

"Now," he continued, "I am dying without male heir." Then he stopped. A sweet thought seemed to light up his face, and, laying his hand on the King of Navarre's shoulder:

"Alas!" said he, "do you remember, Henriot, the poor little boy I showed you one evening sleeping in his silken cradle, watched over by an angel? Alas! Henriot, they will kill him!"

"Oh, sire!" cried Henry, whose eyes filled with tears, "I swear to you that I will watch over him all the days and nights of my life. Command me, my King."

"Thanks, Henriot, thanks!" said Charles, with a show of feeling unusual in him, but which the situation had roused, "I accept your promise. Do not make him a king, — fortunately he was not born for a throne, — but make him happy. I have left him an independent fortune. Let him inherit his mother's nobility, that of the heart. Perhaps it would be better for him if he were to enter the church. He would inspire less fear. Oh! it seems to me that I should die, if not happy, at least calm, if I had the kisses of the child and the sweet face of its mother to console me."

"Sire, could you not send for them?"

"Ah, poor wretches! They would never be allowed to leave the Louvre! Such is the condition of kings, Henriot. They can neither live nor die as they please. But since you promise I am more resigned."

Henry reflected.

"Yes, no doubt, my King. I have promised, but can I keep my word?"

"What do you mean?"

"Shall I not be persecuted, and threatened like him, even more than him? For I am a man, and he is only a child."

"You are mistaken," said Charles; "after my death you shall be great and powerful. Here is what will make you so."

And the King drew a parchment from under the pillow.

"See!" said he.

Henry glanced over the document sealed with the royal seal.

"The regency for me, sire!" said he, growing pale with joy.

"Yes, for you, until the return of the Duc d'Anjou, and as in all probability the duke will never return it is not the regency only but the throne that this gives you."

"The throne!" murmured Henry.

"Yes," said Charles, "you alone are worthy of it; you alone are capable of governing these debauched gallants, and these bold women who live by blood and tears. My brother D'Alençon is a traitor, and would deceive every one. Leave him in the prison in which I have placed him. My mother will try to kill you, therefore banish her. My brother D'Anjou in three or four months, perhaps in a year, will leave Varsovia and will come to dispute the throne with you. Answer him by a bull from the pope. I have already arranged that matter through my ambassador, the Duc de Nevers, and you will receive the document before long."

"Oh, my King!"

"You have but one thing to fear, Henry, — civil war; but by remaining converted you will avoid this, for the Huguenots are strong only when you put yourself at their head, and Monsieur de Condé is nothing when opposed to you. France is a country of plains, Henry, and consequently a Catholic country. The King of France ought to be the king of the Catholics and not the king of the Huguenots, for the King of France ought to be the king of the majority. It is said I feel remorse for the massacre of Saint Bartholomew; doubts, yes; remorse, no. It is said I am bleeding the blood of those Huguenots from every pore. I know what is flowing from me. It is arsenic and not blood."

"What do you mean, sire?"

"Nothing. If my death must be avenged, Henriot, it must be avenged by God alone. Let us speak now of the future. I leave you a faithful parliament and a trusty army. Lean on them and they will protect you against your only enemies — my mother and the Duc d'Alençon."

Just then the sound of arms and military commands were heard in the vestibule.

"I am dead!" murmured Henry.

"You fear? You hesitate?" said Charles, anxiously.

"I! sire," replied Henry; "no, I do not fear, nor do I hesitate. I accept."

Charles pressed Henry's hand. At that moment the nurse approached with a drink she had been preparing in the adjoining room, not knowing that the fate of France was being decided three feet from her.

"Call my mother, nurse, and have Monsieur d'Alençon also summoned."

CHAPTER LXV.

THE KING IS DEAD! LONG LIVE THE KING!

A FEW moments later Catharine and the Duc d'Alençon, pale
with fright and trembling with rage, entered Charles's room.
As Henry had conjectured, Catharine had overheard everything and in a few words had told all to François.

Henry was standing at the head of Charles's bed.

The King spoke his wishes:

" Madame," said he to his mother, " had I a son, you would
be regent, or in default of you it would be the King of Poland;
or in default of him it would be my brother François; but I have
no son, and after me the throne belongs to my brother the
Duc d'Anjou, who is absent. As some day he will claim this
throne I do not wish him to find in his place a man who by
almost equal rights might dispute it with him, and who consequently might expose the kingdom to civil war. This is why
I do not appoint you regent, madame, for you would have to
choose between your two sons, which would be painful for a
mother. This is why I do not choose my brother François, for
he might say to his elder brother, ' You had a throne, why did
you leave it?' No, I have chosen as regent one who can
take the crown on trust, and who will keep it in his hand and
not on his head. Salute this regent, madame; salute him,
brother; it is the King of Navarre!"

And with a gesture of supreme authority the King himself
saluted Henry.

Catharine and D'Alençon made a gesture between a nervous
shudder and a salute.

" Here, my Lord Regent," said Charles to the King of Navarre, "here is the parchment which, until the return of the
King of Poland, gives you the command of the armies, the keys
of the treasury, and the royal power and authority."

Catharine devoured Henry with her eyes; François swayed
so that he could scarcely stand; but this weakness of the
one and strength of the other, instead of encouraging Henry,
showed him the danger which threatened him.

Nevertheless he made a violent effort and overcoming his
fears took the parchment from the hands of the King,

raised himself to his full height, and gave Catharine and François a look which meant:

"Take care! I am your master."

"No," said she, "never; never shall my race bow to a foreign one; never shall a Bourbon reign in France while a Valois remains!"

"Mother," cried Charles IX., sitting up among the crimson sheets of his bed, more frightful looking than ever, "take care, I am still King. Not for long, I well know; but it does not take long to give an order; it does not take long to punish murderers and poisoners."

"Well! give the order, if you dare, and I will give mine! Come, François, come!"

And the queen left the room rapidly, followed by the Duc d'Alençon.

"Nancey!" cried Charles; "Nancey! come here! I order you, Nancey, to arrest my mother, and my brother, arrest"—

A stream of blood choked his utterance, just as the captain of the guards opened the door, and, almost suffocated, the King fell back on his bed. Nancey had heard only his name; the orders which followed, and which had been uttered in a less audible tone, were lost in space.

"Guard the door," said Henry, "and let no one enter."

Nancey bowed and withdrew.

Henry looked at the almost lifeless body, which already would have seemed like that of a corpse had not a light breath stirred the fringe of foam on the lips.

Henry looked for several moments, then, speaking to himself:

"The final moment has come!" said he; "shall I reign? shall I live?"

Just then the tapestry of the alcove was raised, a pale face appeared behind it, and a voice vibrated through the silence of death which reigned throughout the royal chamber.

"Live!" said this voice.

"Réné!" cried Henry.

"Yes, sire."

"Your prediction was false, then; I shall not be king?"

"You shall be, sire; but the time has not yet come."

"How do you know? Speak, that I may know if I may believe you."

"Listen."

"Well?"

"Stoop down."

Henry leaned over Charles. Réné did the same. They were separated by the width of the bed alone, and even this distance was lessened by their positions. Between them, silent and motionless, lay the dying King.

"Listen," said Réné; "placed here by the queen mother to ruin you, I prefer to serve you, for I have faith in your horoscope. By serving you I shall profit both in body and soul."

"Did the queen mother command you to say this also?" asked Henry, full of doubt and pain.

"No," said Réné; "but I will tell you a secret."

He leaned still further over.

Henry did likewise, so that their heads almost touched.

This interview between two men bending over the body of a dying king was so sombre that the hair of the superstitious Florentine rose on end, and Henry's face became covered with perspiration.

"Listen," continued Réné, "I will tell you a secret known only to me. I will reveal it to you if you will swear over this dying man to forgive me for the death of your mother."

"I have already promised you this," said Henry, with darkening brow.

"You promised, but you did not swear," said Réné, drawing back.

"I swear it," said Henry, raising his right hand over the head of the King.

"Well, sire," said the Florentine, hastily, "the King of Poland will soon arrive!"

"No," said Henry, "the messenger was stopped by King Charles."

"King Charles intercepted only the one on the road to Château Thierry. But the queen mother wisely sent couriers by three different routes."

"Oh! I am lost!" exclaimed Henry.

"A messenger arrived this morning from Varsovia. The king left after him without any one's thinking of opposing him, for at Varsovia the illness of the King of France was not yet known. This courier only preceded Henry of Anjou by a few hours."

"Oh! had I but eight days!" cried Henry.

"Yes, but you have not eight hours.   Did you hear the noise of arms ? "

" Yes."

" They are making ready to kill you.   They will seek you even here in the apartment of the King."

" The King is not yet dead."

Réné looked closely at Charles.

" He will be in ten minutes ; you have ten minutes to live, therefore ; perhaps less."

" What shall I do ? "

" Flee instantly, without delaying a minute, a second."

" But how ?   If they are waiting in the antechamber they will kill me as I go out."

" Listen !   I will risk everything for you.   Never forget this."

" Fear not."

" Follow me by the secret corridor.   I will lead you to the postern.   Then, to gain time, I will tell the queen mother that you are coming down ; you will be seen to have discovered this secret passage, and to have profited by it to escape.   Flee !   Flee ! "

" Nurse ! " murmured Charles, " nurse ! "

Henry took from the bed Charles's sword, of no further use to the dying King, put the parchment which made him regent in his breast, kissed Charles's brow for the last time, and turning away hurried through the door, which closed behind him.

" Nurse ! " cried the King, in a stronger voice, " nurse ! "

The woman ran to him.

" What is it, Charlot ? " she asked.

" Nurse," said the King, his eye dilated by the terrible fixity of death, " something must have happened while I slept.   I see a great light.   I see God, our Master, I see Jesus, and the Blessed Virgin Mary.   They are praying and interceding for me.   The all-powerful Lord pardons me — calls to me — My God !   my God !   In thy mercy, receive me !   My God !   forget that I have been King, for I come to you without sceptre or crown.   My God !   forget the crimes of the King, and remember only the suffering of the man.   My God, I come ! "

And Charles, who as he spoke had risen more and more as if to go to the One who was calling him, after uttering these words heaved a sigh and fell back still and cold in the arms of his nurse.

Meantime, while the soldiers, commanded by Catharine, were beginning to fill the main corridor in which they expected Henry to appear, the latter, guided by Réné, passed along the secret passage and reached the postern, sprang on the horse which was waiting for him, and galloped to the place where he knew he would find De Mouy.

Hearing the sound of the horse's hoofs, the galloping of which fell on the hard pavement, some sentinels turned and cried:

" He flees ! He flees ! "

" Who ? " cried the queen mother, stepping to a window.

" The King of Navarre ! " cried the sentinels.

" Fire on him ! Fire ! " cried Catharine.

The sentinels levelled their muskets, but Henry was already too far away.

" He flees ! " cried the queen mother; " then he is vanquished ! "

" He flees ! " murmured the Duc d'Alençon; " then I am king ! "

At that instant, while François and his mother were still before the window, the drawbridge thundered under horses' hoofs, and preceded by a clanking of arms and great noise a young man galloped up, his hat in his hand, shouting as he entered the court: " France ! " He was followed by four gentlemen, covered like himself with perspiration, dust, and foam.

" My son ! " exclaimed Catharine, extending both arms out of the window.

" Mother ! " replied the young man, springing from his steed.

" My brother D'Anjou ! " cried François, stepping back in amazement.

" Am I too late ? " asked Henry d'Anjou.

" No, just in time, and God must have guided you, for you could not have arrived at a better moment. Look and listen ! "

Monsieur de Nancey, captain of the guards, had come out upon the balcony from the chamber of the King.

All eyes were turned towards him.

Breaking a wand in two, with arms extended, he took a piece in either hand and cried three times:

" King Charles IX. is dead ! King Charles IX. is dead ! King Charles IX. is dead ! "

Then he dropped the pieces of the wand.

"Long live King Henry III.!" shouted Catharine, making the sign of the cross. "Long live King Henry III.!"

All took up the cry except Duc François.

"Ah, she has betrayed me!" murmured he, digging his nails into his breast.

"I have won," cried Catharine, "and that hateful Béarnais will not reign!"

CHAPTER LXVI.

EPILOGUE.

ONE year had elapsed since the death of Charles IX. and the accession of his successor to the throne.

King Henry III., happily reigning by the grace of God and his mother Catharine, was attending a fine procession given in honor of Notre Dame de Cléry.

He had gone on foot with the queen, his wife, and all the court.

King Henry III. could well afford this little pastime, for no serious business occupied him for the moment. The King of Navarre was in Navarre, where he had so long desired to be, and where he was said to be very much taken up with a beautiful girl of the blood of the Montmorencies whom he called La Fosseuse. Marguerite was with him, sad and gloomy, finding in the beautiful mountains not distraction but a softening of the two greatest griefs of life, — absence and death.

Paris was very quiet and the queen mother, really regent since her dear son Henry had been King, resided sometimes at the Louvre, sometimes at the Hôtel de Soissons, which occupied the site to-day covered by the Halle au Blé, of which nothing remains beyond the beautiful column which is still standing.

One evening when she was deeply engaged in studying the stars with Réné, of whose little act of treason she was still ignorant, and who had been reinstated in her favor after the false testimony he had so opportunely given at the trial of Coconnas and La Mole, she was informed that a man waited for her in her oratory with something to tell her of the greatest importance.

Hastily descending, the queen found the Sire de Maurevel.

"*He* is here!" cried the ancient captain of the guards, not giving Catharine time to address him, according to royal etiquette.

"What *he?*" demanded Catharine.

"Who but the King of Navarre, madame!"

"Here!" said Catharine, "here! He— Henry— And what has he come for, the madman?"

"If appearances are to be believed, he comes to see Madame de Sauve. That is all. If probabilities are to be considered, he comes to conspire against the King."

"How do you know he is here?"

"Yesterday I saw him enter a house, and an instant later Madame de Sauve joined him there."

"Are you sure it was he?"

"I waited until he came out, that is, part of the night. At three o'clock the two lovers appeared. The king led Madame de Sauve as far as the gate of the Louvre, where, thanks to the porter, who no doubt is in her pay, she was admitted without opposition, and the king returned, humming a tune, and with a step as free as if he were among his own mountains."

"Where did he go then?"

"To the Rue de l'Arbre Sec, Hôtel de la Belle Étoile, the same inn in which the two sorcerers used to lodge whom your majesty had executed a year ago."

"Why did you not come and tell me this at once?"

"Because I was not yet sure of my man."

"And now?"

"Now I am certain."

"Did you see him?"

"Yes. I hid in a wine merchant's opposite. I saw him enter the same building as on the previous night. Then as Madame de Sauve was late he imprudently put his face against the window pane on the first floor, and I had no further doubt. Besides, a few minutes later Madame de Sauve came and again joined him."

"Do you think that like last night they will remain until three o'clock in the morning?"

"It is probable."

"Where is the house?"

"Near the Croix des Petits Champs, close to Saint Honoré."

"Very good," said Catharine. "Does Monsieur de Sauve know your handwriting?"

" No."

" Sit down, then, and write."

Maurevel took a pen and obeyed.

" I am ready, madame," said he.

Catharine dictated :

" *While the Baron de Sauve is on service at the Louvre the baroness is with one of her friends, in a house near the Croix des Petit Champs, close to Saint Honoré.   The Baron de Sauve will know the house by a red cross on the wall.*"

" Well ? " said Maurevel.

" Make a copy of the letter," said Catharine.

Maurevel obeyed in silence.

" Now," said the queen, " have one of these letters taken by a clever man to the Baron de Sauve, and drop the other in the corridors of the Louvre."

" I do not understand," said Maurevel.

Catharine shrugged her shoulders.

" You do not understand that a husband who receives such a note will be angry ? "

" But the King of Navarre never used to be angry, madame."

" It is not always with a king as' with a simple courtier. Besides, if De Sauve is not angry you can be so for him."

" I ! "

" Yes.   You can take four men or six, if necessary, put on a mask, break down the door, as if you had been sent by the baron, surprise the lovers in the midst of their tête à tête, and strike your blow in the name of the King.   The next day the note dropped in the corridor of the Louvre, and picked up by some kind friend who already will have circulated the news, will prove that it was the husband who had avenged himself.   Only by chance, the gallant happened to be King of Navarre ; but who would have imagined that, when every one thought him at Pau."

Maurevel looked at Catharine in admiration, bowed, and withdrew.

As Maurevel left the Hôtel de Soissons Madame de Sauve entered the small house near the Croix des Petits Champs.

Henry was waiting for her at the half-open door.

As soon as he saw her on the stairs, he said :

" You have not been followed, have you ? "

" Why, no," said Charlotte, " at least, not so far as I know."

"I think I have been," said Henry, "not only to-night but last evening as well."

"Oh! my God!" said Charlotte, "you frighten me, sire! If this meeting between you and one of your old friends should bring any harm to you I should be inconsolable."

"Do not worry, my love," said the Béarnais, "we have three swordsmen watching in the darkness."

"Three are very few, sire."

"Three are enough when they are De Mouy, Saucourt, and Barthélemy."

"Is De Mouy in Paris with you?"

"Certainly."

"He dared to return to the capital? Has he, then, like you, some poor woman who is in love with him?"

"No, but he has an enemy whose death he has sworn to have. Nothing but hate, my dear, commits as many follies as love."

"Thank you, sire."

"Oh," said Henry, "I do not refer to our present follies. I mean those of the past and the future. But do not let us discuss this; we have no time to lose."

"You still plan to leave Paris?"

"To-night."

"Are your affairs which brought you back to Paris finished?"

"I came back only to see you."

"Gascon!"

"*Ventre saint gris!* My love, that is true; but let us put aside such thoughts. I have still two or three hours in which to be happy; then farewell forever."

"Ah! sire," said Madame de Sauve, "nothing is forever except my love."

Henry had just said that he had no time for discussion; therefore he did not discuss this point. He believed, or sceptic that he was, he pretended to believe.

As the King of Navarre had said, De Mouy and his two companions were hidden near by.

It was arranged that Henry should leave the small house at midnight instead of at three o'clock; that, as on the previous night, they would escort Madame de Sauve back to the Louvre, and from there they would go to the Rue de la Cerisaie, where Maurevel lived.

It was only during that day that De Mouy had been sure of

his enemy's whereabouts. The men had been on guard about an hour when they perceived a man, followed at a few feet by five others, who drew near to the door of the small house and tried several keys successively. De Mouy, concealed within the shelter of a neighboring door, made one bound from his hiding-place, and seized the man by the arm.

" One moment," said he; " you cannot enter there."

The man sprang back, and in doing so his hat fell off.

" De Mouy de Saint Phale ! " he cried.

"Maurevel!" thundered the Huguenot, raising his sword. " I sought you, and you have come to me. Thanks ! "

But his anger did not make him forget Henry, and turning to the window he whistled in the manner of the Béarnais shepherds.

" That will be enough," said he to Saucourt. " Now, then, murderer ! "

And he sprang towards Maurevel.

The latter had had time to draw a pistol from his belt.

" Ah! now," said the King's Slayer, aiming at the young man, " I think you are a dead man ! "

He fired. De Mouy jumped to one side and the ball passed by without touching him.

" It is my turn now ! " cried the young man.

And he dealt Maurevel such a violent thrust with his sword that, although the blade had to encounter his buff belt, the sharp point pierced this obstacle and sank into the flesh.

The assassin gave a terrible cry of pain; whereupon the soldiers with him, thinking he was killed, fled in alarm down the Rue Saint Honoré.

Maurevel was not brave. Seeing himself abandoned by his followers, and having to face an adversary like De Mouy, he strove to escape, and ran after the guard, shouting, " help ! help ! "

De Mouy, Saucourt, and Barthélemy, carried away by their ardor, pursued him. As they entered the Rue de Grenelle, which they had taken as a short cut, a window opened and a man sprang out from the first floor, landing on the ground lately wet by the rain.

It was Henry.

De Mouy's whistle had warned him of some danger and the pistol-shot had showed him that the danger was great, and had drawn him to the aid of his friends.

Energetic and vigorous, he dashed after them, sword in hand.

A cry guided him; it came from the Barrier des Sergents. It was Maurevel, who being hard pressed by De Mouy was calling a second time for help from his men who had run away.

Maurevel had to turn or be run through the back; he turned, therefore, and, meeting his enemy's steel, gave him back so skilful a thrust that the scarf of the latter was cut through. But De Mouy at once lunged. The sword again sank into the flesh it had already broken, and a second jet of blood spurted from a second wound.

"At him!" cried Henry, coming up. "Quick, quick, De Mouy!"

De Mouy needed no encouragement.

Again he charged at Maurevel; but the latter had not waited. Pressing his left hand over his wound, he again took to flight.

"Kill him! Quick! Kill him!" cried the king, "here are the soldiers, and the despair of cowards is of no moment to the brave."

Maurevel, who was well nigh exhausted, whose every breath caused a bloody perspiration, fell down; but almost immediately he rose again, and turning on one knee presented the point of his sword to De Mouy.

"Friends! Friends!" cried Maurevel. "There are only two. Fire at them! Fire!"

Saucourt and Barthélemy had gone in pursuit of the other soldiers, down the Rue des Poulies, and the king and De Mouy were alone with the four men.

"Fire!" cried Maurevel again, while one of the soldiers levelled his gun.

"Yes, but first," said De Mouy, "die, traitor, murderer, assassin!" and seizing Maurevel's sword with one hand, with the other he plunged his own up to its hilt into the breast of his enemy, with such force that he nailed him to the earth.

"Take care! Take care!" cried Henry.

De Mouy sprang back, leaving his sword in Maurevel's body, just as a soldier was in the act of firing at him.

Henry at once passed his sword through the body of the soldier, who gave a cry and fell by the side of Maurevel.

The two others took to flight.

"Come, De Mouy, come!" cried Henry, "let us not lose an instant: if we are recognized it will be all over with us."

"Wait, sire. Do you suppose I want to leave my sword in the body of this wretch?" and De Mouy approached Maurevel, who lay apparently without sign of life.

But just as he took hold of his sword, which was run through Maurevel's body, the latter raised himself, and with the gun the soldier had dropped fired directly at De Mouy's breast.

The young man fell without a cry. He was killed outright.

Henry rushed at Maurevel, but the latter had fallen again, and the king's sword pierced only a dead body.

It was necessary to flee. The noise had attracted a large number of persons; the night watch might arrive at any moment. Henry looked around to see if there was any face he knew, and gave a cry of delight on recognizing La Hurière.

As the scene had occurred at the foot of the Croix du Trahoir, that is, opposite the Rue de l'Arbre Sec, our old friend, whose naturally gloomy disposition had been still further saddened since the death of La Mole and Coconnas, his two favorite lodgers, had left his furnaces and his pans in the midst of his preparations for the King of Navarre's supper, and had run to the fight.

"My dear La Hurière, I commend De Mouy to your care, although I greatly fear nothing can be done for him. Take him to your inn, and if he still live, spare nothing. Here is my purse. As to the other, leave him in the gutter, that he may die like a dog."

"And yourself?" said La Hurière.

"I have a farewell to make. I must hasten, but in ten minutes I shall be with you. Have my horses ready."

Henry immediately set out towards the Croix des Petits Champs; but as he turned from the Rue de Grenelle he stopped in terror.

A large crowd was before the door.

"What is the matter?" asked Henry. "What is going on in the house?"

"Oh!" answered the man addressed, "a terrible affair, monsieur. A beautiful young woman has just been stabbed by her husband, to whom a note had been given informing him that his wife was here with her lover."

"And the husband?" cried Henry.

"Has escaped."

"And the wife?"

"She is in the house."

"Dead?"

"Not yet, but, thank God, there is scarcely any hope."

"Oh!" exclaimed Henry, "I am accursed indeed!" and he rushed into the house.

The room was full of people standing around a bed on which lay poor Charlotte, who had been stabbed twice.

Her husband, who had hidden his jealousy for two years, had seized this opportunity to avenge himself on her.

"Charlotte! Charlotte!" cried Henry, pushing through the crowd and falling on his knees before the bed.

Charlotte opened her beautiful eyes, already veiled by death. and uttered a cry which caused the blood to flow afresh from her two wounds. Making an effort to rise, she said:

"Oh! I well knew I could not die without seeing you again!"

And as if she had waited only for that moment to return to Henry the soul he had so loved, she pressed her lips to the King's forehead, again whispered for a last time, "I love you!" and fell back dead.

Henry could not remain longer without risking his own life. He drew his dagger, cut a lock of the beautiful blonde hair which he had so often loosened that he might admire its length, and went out sobbing, in the midst of the tears of all present, who did not doubt but that they were weeping for persons of high degree.

"Friend! mistress!" cried Henry in despair — "all forsake me, all leave me, all fail me at once!"

"Yes, sire," said a man in a low tone, who had left the group in front of the house, and who had followed Henry; "but you still have the throne!"

"Réné!" exclaimed Henry.

"Yes, sire, Réné, who is watching over you. That scoundrel Maurevel uttered your name as he died. It is known you are in Paris; the archers are hunting for you. Flee! Flee!"

"And you say that I shall be King, Réné? I, a fugitive?"

"Look, sire," said the Florentine, pointing to a brilliant star, which appeared from behind the folds of a black cloud, "it is not I who say so, but the star!"

Henry heaved a sigh, and disappeared in the darkness.

END.

CPSIA information can be obtained
at www.ICGtesting.com
Printed in the USA
LVHW081738240820
664076LV00006B/139